Java for C/C++ Programmers

Michael C. Daconta

WILEY COMPUTER PUBLISHING

John Wiley & Sons, Inc.
New York • Chichester • Brisbane • Toronto • Singapore

Publisher: Katherine Schowalter
Editor: Robert Elliott
Managing Editor: Frank Grazioli
Text Design & Composition: Publishers' Design and Production Services, Inc.

Designations used by companies to distinguish their products are often claimed as trademarks. In all instances where John Wiley & Sons, Inc. is aware of a claim, the product names appear in initial capital or all capital letters. Readers, however, should contact the appropriate companies for more complete information regarding trademarks and registration.

This text is printed on acid-free paper.

This publication is designed to provide accurate and authoritative information in regard to the subject matter covered. It is sold with the understanding that the publisher is not engaged in rendering legal, accounting, or other professional service. If legal advice or other expert assistance is required, the services of a competent professional person should be sought.

Library of Congress Cataloging-in-Publication Data:

ISBN 0 471-15324-9

Printed in the United States of America

10 9 8 7 6 5 4 3 2 1

Dedication and Acknowledgments

I have to admit that I enjoy writing the dedication to a book almost more than writing the book itself. Part of the reason is that the book is complete, which is a big weight off my shoulders. But seriously, I enjoy writing the dedication because I feel that it is one small way in which I can give a nod of both appreciation and admiration to the people who have helped me along the way.

First is family. I'd like to especially thank my wife Lynne who suffered through hardship as I locked myself away for three months. During this time, Lynne had our third child and only girl, Samantha Lynne Daconta. Samantha is so precious that no success compares to her smile. To my boys, CJ and Gregory. To my parents, Joseph Daconta and Josephine Worner. To my inlaws, Buddy and Shirley Belden. To my sister and her family, Rob and Lori Desmond and their children Bobby and Jimmy. Thank you all for supporting me through the years.

Second is the professionals who make book publishing a worthwhile endeavor. Special thanks go to Bob Elliott, my editor, for not only helping me decide to take up this challenge, but for his understanding and support for someone wired on Java. To Rich O'Hanley, my former editor, who is still a friend and source of wisdom and guidance. To Terry Canela, who patiently works with someone who loses the author guidelines every 6 months. To Micheline Frederick, who did an outstanding job producing my last book. To Katherine Schowalter, the publisher, who continues to support and have faith in my abilities. Thank you all for your hard work.

Third is my friends and co-workers at Mystech Associates, Inc. To the managers who back me every step of the way: Dave Young, Bob Cotter, Don Penzler, Harv Watson and Maria Shugars. Special thanks to Gerry McIntyre who has earned my respect as a great manager and person. To my development team: Ted Wagner, John LeCompte, and Cory Adams. To the Tacsim team: Rob Olson, Ken Wood, Pete Rontos, Laura Park, and Pete Phipps. Thank you all for being so enjoyable to work with. Special thanks go to Everett Nelson, who is one of the finest people I know.

Fourth are my online and internet friends. Thanks to all of the people in the Java-interest mailing list and comp.lang.java newsgroup for your enthusiasm and support. Special thanks go to Rick Dormer for reviewing chapters and Ari Weinstein for providing artwork.

Finally, I'd like to thank all the readers of my books who have emailed me or sent me letters. Your enthusiastic thanks, suggestions and encouragement make the long, lonely hours of a writer worth it. Thank you for your support.

To those not mentioned here, but who have also helped me in my pursuits—thank you.

Michael Daconta
Sierra Vista, AZ

Contents

Welcome to *Java for C/C++ Programmers*

Every technology goes through three stages: first, a crudely simple and quite unsatisfactory gadget; second, an enormously complicated group of gadgets designed to overcome the shortcomings of the original and achieving thereby somewhat satisfactory performance through extremely complex compromise; third, a final proper design therefrom.

—Robert A. Heinlein

In a move that's seen as a capitulation to emerging Internet software standards, Microsoft Corporation announced plans to license a new, universal programming language called Java.

—CNN correspondent Brian Nelson

Welcome to Java for C/C++ programmers! This book is designed to assist C and C++ programmers to leverage their existing knowledge of C or C++ to make an easy transition to the Java programming language. You will be surprised at just how familiar Java really is. In fact, you will be able to produce simple Java programs within one hour and more complex programs in a few days! In this introduction you will learn why Java is the best choice for programming both stand-alone applications and web applications (called applets). Then we will discuss the organization of this book and how its design will allow you to quickly gain proficiency in Java.

WHAT IS JAVA?

The first fundamental point to understand about Java is that it was born out of necessity. In 1991, a small team of Sun Microsystems programmers set out to develop a distributed system for the consumer electronics market. They started by using the most popular language of the day, a language that was both familiar and object-oriented: the C++ programming language. After trial and error, they realized that the inherent historical flaws and complexity in the evolution of C and C++ were holding them back. Their solution was to design a simple, more refined language that was not hindered by compatibility yet still remained familiar. That solution became Java.

The Java language and environment are best understood by the attributes they embody: familiar, simple, object-oriented, architecture-neutral, portable, interpreted, high-performance, threaded, robust, secure, and strategic. Let's examine these Java characteristics in detail.

- **Familiar.** This is the most important characteristic. Change is always difficult; however, small changes are much more readily accepted than large leaps. Java is derived from C and C++ and many of the keywords are identical to those in C and C++. Java code "looks like" C++ code. You will immediately recognize it and feel comfortable around it.
- **Simple.** This was one of Java's overriding design goals. Java is based on the so-called KISS principle—Keep it Small and Simple (or "Keep it Simple, Stupid!"). The Java development team removed many C and C++ language "features" that were either redundant, sources of numerous confusion, or sources of unreliable code. Examples of such reduction are: no pointers, no multiple inheritance, no operator overloading, and no need to explicitly free memory. This paring down to the essentials reduces the complexity of the language while increasing the reliability.
- **Object-oriented.** Unlike C++, Java is a true object-oriented language. This is one of the areas where Java needed to be free from the shackles of compatibility. Everything in Java is an object and a descendant from a root object. Also, Java is more than just a language—it is a whole environment complete with class hierarchies for networking, input/output, graphical user interface design, and numerous utilities.
- **Architecture-neutral, portable, and interpreted.** Java was designed to thrive in a heterogeneous, networked environment. Java applications will run on multiple hardware systems and

operating systems. Java runtime environments exist for Solaris, Windows NT, Windows 95, and the Mac OS. Ports are under way for AIX, HP-UX, IRIX, and LINUX. How does Java accomplish this? The answer is architecture-neutral byte-codes and the Java interpreter. The Java compiler translates Java code into an intermediate format called byte-codes. This format is very compact and can easily be transported efficiently to multiple hardware and software platforms. These byte-codes are then verified and then executed by the Java interpreter. The best way to think about the Java interpreter is as a virtual machine that represents a generic computer.

The portability of Java is one of its most exciting features. The ability to take a Java program written on a Solaris workstation and run it unmodified on a Macintosh or a Windows PC has enormous potential. This portability even extends to the graphical user interface, which has long been the bane of cross-platform development. As you will discover throughout this book the wealth of the Java environment (i.e., file I/O, system functionality, abstract window toolkit, networking classes, . . .), you will be excited at the potential of all that power being portable.

- **High-performance.** Although most interpreted languages are much slower than compiled languages, Java maintains a high-level of performance using many techniques. First, the Java language supports multi-threading at the language level which improves the interactivity and response of applications performing multiple, simultaneous tasks. See the discussion of threading below. Second, much effort and a special patented algorithm make the Java interpreter run faster than most other interpreters. Third, applications requiring even more speed have the option of rewriting computer-intensive portions of the code in a native language like C. Fourth, the java runtime environment will soon provide a "just-in-time" compiler that translates the architecture-neutral byte codes into machine code at run time.

- **Threaded.** Modern, networked applications are often required to perform multiple tasks simultaneously like scrolling a window while downloading a file and playing background music. Java has built-in support for threads via a Thread class that makes it simple to construct programs using these powerful techniques.

- **Robust and Secure.** Java is a robust language in its many safeguards to ensure reliable code. First, there is no Java preprocessor or operator overloading, which often lends itself to programmer error on large projects. In Java, the program will execute just as it is written without worry that a variable is #defined to mean something else. Second, Java has strict compile time and run time checking for the proper use of the type system. Third, Java programmers are free from the numerous memory bugs that haunt C and C++ programmers because Java is a garbage-collected[1] language. Java garbage collection frees the programmer from worrying about explicitly deallocating memory. Also, since there are no pointers in Java, array overruns and memory overwrites are impossible.

The portable nature of Java programs has opened an entire new area of development: applets in the World Wide Web. Until now, the World Wide Web was composed of client browsers automatically downloading static text and images from web servers across the globe. The portable nature of the Java byte codes, combined with the Hot Java and Netscape browsers, enables a new level of interactivity on the World Wide Web by allowing Java programs to be transported over the internet and executed on the client browser. The automatic downloading of programs across the unsecure internet made security a very high priority for the Java development team. That is why the Java interpreter and environment was designed with numerous security features built in. The first key security feature is that computer memory is not directly accessible by any Java program. Memory layout decisions for the program are postponed until runtime. Second, all byte-codes are verified for accuracy and tested for security violations. Third, the class loader always checks for local classes first and thereby protects against "class spoofing." Lastly, Java's network package allows the user to set the level of access (and therefore protection) for each system.

■ **Strategic.** It is my belief that Java represents a milestone in the evolution of programming languages. It is evolution without forced compatibility, which is true progress. It takes the best of what we know about object-oriented programming; it takes a bold step in putting reliability and robustness above "nifty features." Because of these reasons and all the characteristics listed above, Java will achieve phenomenal acceptance and growth. Part of this fantastic growth will be fueled by Java's role as the first and premier application language of the World Wide Web. But this will not be the only use for Java. Java will also soon become the premiere language for stand-alone applications. In essence, Java is the successor to C and C++.

---

[1]Garbage collection is a language technique that eliminates the need for memory management by periodically reclaiming unused memory.

ORGANIZATION OF THIS BOOK

This book is designed to teach the Java language and runtime environment to C and C++ programmers by revealing the language as an evolutionary step up from C and C++. This approach builds on your existing base of knowledge to rapidly have you coding non-trivial Java programs. Secondly, this book goes far beyond just teaching the Java language. We will cover all of Java: the language, class hierarchy, common algorithms implemented in Java, applet programming, and much more. The goal of this book is to be both a tutorial and reference guide—the book you turn to first and then repeatedly until the pages are dog-eared and smudged from use.

This book is divided into three parts: Part 1, Learning the Language, focuses on explaining and demonstrating all of the language features; how those features compare to C and C++; and what other object-oriented programming (OOP) languages influenced those features. Lastly, this part covers the Java equivalent of the C and C++ standard library, which is inseparable from any discussion of C and C++.

Part 2, Programming in Java and JavaScript, covers three exciting new areas of programming: the Java cross-platform graphical user interface called the abstract window toolkit (AWT), HotJava and Java applets, and the new cross-platform internet scripting language, JavaScript. After reading these chapters you will know why the entire internet is talking about Java and JavaScript!

The Appendixes provide clear and concise references on both the Java and JavaScript languages and the class application programmer interface (API) for all the Java packages.

The first part of the book is designed to be read sequentially; however, Part 2 and the appendixes can be read as the reader sees fit. The second part can also be read sequentially in a tutorial-like fashion, but some advanced readers may prefer to skip around. The appendixes are designed for rapid lookup of an item of interest.

WHY A POINTER EXPERT CHOSE TO PROGRAM IN JAVA

At first glance it seems strange for someone who has published two books on pointers and dynamic memory management to be writing about a language that has no pointers and is garbage-collected; however, it is precisely because I understand pointers and dynamic memory that I deliberately chose to program and teach the Java language. Pointers can be wonderfully elegant and expressive tools; however, that elegance has a very high price. In fact, the countless number of buggy C and C++ applications illustrates the fact that the price of those complex features is just too high.

The Java language sacrifices nothing. In these pages you will learn that the huge gains of this simple and robust object-oriented language and environment far outweigh the few features removed from C and C++. In fact, I will show you how to implement the same powerful techniques I highlighted in my first two books in the Java language.

INVITED COMMENTS

This book is written by a programmer for programmers. All comments, suggestions, and questions from the entire computing community are greatly appreciated. I can be reached electronically:

CompuServe: 71664,523

America Online: MikeDacon

Internet: daconta@primenet.com (or) MikeDacon@aol.com

Or you can write to:

Michael Daconta

c/o Robert Elliott

John Wiley & Sons, Inc.

605 Third Avenue

New York, NY 10158

PART 1

Learning the Language

CHAPTER 1

An Introduction to Java

Reality isn't static anymore. It's not a set of ideas you have to either fight or resign yourself to. It's made up, in part, of ideas that are expected to grow as you grow, and as we all grow, century after century.

—Robert M. Pirsig, *Zen and the Art of Motorcycle Maintenance*

> **OBJECTIVE**
>
> This chapter will give you a tutorial introduction to the Java language. This chapter is not meant to explain all of the concepts presented—that will be done in following chapters. Instead, this chapter gives you a "feel" for the language and its potential.

We will begin in the same manner as Kernighan and Ritchie in their landmark book, *The C Programming Language*. "The only way to learn a new programming language is by writing programs in it. The first program to write is the same for all languages: Print the words hello, world."[1] Source 1.1 lists the program.

---

[1]Brian W. Kernighan and Dennis Ritchie, *The C Programming Language*, (Englewood Cliffs, N.J.: Prentice Hall, 1988), p. 5.

SOURCE 1.1

```
class HelloWorld {
    public static void main(String args[])
    {
        System.out.println("Hello, World.\n");
    }
}
```

Let's dissect the program line by line and thereby slowly begin wading into this new language.

Line 1:   class HelloWorld {

This is a class declaration, which is an object-oriented construct. A class declaration defines a template for an object. By this, I mean that an object is an instantiated class or, in more C terms, a variable definition for a class. Java is a true object-oriented language so everything must be inside an object. In this simple program, we are just wrapping an object around the main function. C programmers should not be overly concerned about objects. In general they are just more powerful structures. Figure 1.1 shows the key characteristic of a class: the combining (also called encapsulation) of data and functions. We will go into classes in great detail in Chapter 2.

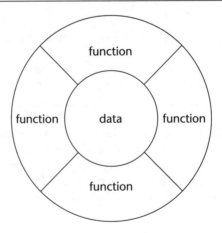

FIGURE 1.1   An object.

Line 2:   `public static void main(String args[])`

Line 2 is conceptually identical to the C/C++ main( ) function. The differences are the modifiers (public, static) and the String class array for the command line arguments. The public modifier is an access modifier that declares this function as unprotected and open to all other classes. The public modifier behaves the same as the C++ public modifier. The static modifier declares this function as being part of the entire class and not part of objects of the class. This is also a feature of C++. As you can see, the arguments to main are slightly different than in ANSI C; however, they are functionally equivalent. String is a class in Java that implements immutable (non-changing) strings. C programmers can think of a class as wrapping a whole slew of utility functions around a common data structure. This is the case with the String class. So, in Java the command line arguments come to us in an array of strings. We will discuss arrays in Java in the next chapter.

Line 3:   `{`

Line 3 is identical to the C/C++ braces to begin a block of code. This, of course, is familiar to both C and C++ programmers.

Line 4:   `System.out.println("Hello, World.\n");`

Line 4 is the Java equivalent of a printf( ). Remember, since Java is object oriented, every function must be part of an object (called an object's method). The function println( ) is a function (also called a method) of the out object, which is similar to stdout. The out object is a data member of the system object, thus the concatenation of System.out.println( ). The dot operator (.) separating elements in the class is familiar to C/C++ programmers because it is identical to how structure or class elements are accessed.

Now that we have typed the "Hello, World" program into a text file, let's review the process of compiling and running the program. You compile the program into architecture-neutral byte codes by using the Java compiler (named javac):

```
javac <filename>
```

which for the "Hello, World" program is:

```
javac hello.java
```

The Java compiler produces one file for every class. The compiler names the file <classname>.class. The file contains the byte-codes for that class. The Java interpreter (named java) executes the byte-codes. You run the interpreter on the class you just compiled like this:

```
java <classname>
```

which for the HelloWorld class is:

```
java HelloWorld
```

When this is typed, the console displays:

```
Hello, World.
```

Now let's move on to how familiar Java is to C/C++ programmers.

1.1   INSTANT RECOGNITION

One of the recurring themes you will see pop up in this book is that Java is "familiar" to C and C++ programmers. This will be even more apparent as we compare Java to ANSI C in the next chapter. For now, let's look at a simple program coded in both C and Java. Source 1.2 is a C implementation of that old high-school bus song, "99 Bottles of Beer on the Wall."

SOURCE 1.2

```c
/* 99 bottles of beer */
#include <stdio.h>
#include <stdlib.h>

void main(int argc, char *argv[])
{
    int i=0;

    for (i=99; i > 0; i--)
    {
        printf("%d bottles of beer on the wall,\n",i);
        printf("%d bottles of beer.\n",i);
        printf("If one of those bottles should happen to fall,\n");
        printf("%d bottles of beer on the wall.\n", i-1);
    }
}
```

The output of this program is:

```
99 bottles of beer on the wall,
99 bottles of beer.
If one of those bottles should happen to fall,
98 bottles of beer on the wall.
98 bottles of beer on the wall,
98 bottles of beer.
If one of those bottles should happen to fall,
97 bottles of beer on the wall.
...
If one of those bottles should happen to fall,
1 bottles of beer on the wall.
1 bottles of beer on the wall,
1 bottles of beer.
If one of those bottles should happen to fall,
0 bottles of beer on the wall.
```

Source 1.3 is the Java version of the same program. Although the program only has a few constructs like the main function, variable declaration, for loop and output, each one of those constructs are nearly identical in C and Java.

SOURCE 1.3

```
/* 99 bottles of beer */

class bottles {
    public static void main(String args[])
    {
            int i=0;

            for (i=99; i > 0; i--)
            {
                System.out.println(i + " bottles of beer on the wall,");
                System.out.println(i + " bottles of beer.");
                System.out.println("If one of the bottles should happen to fall,");
                System.out.println(i-1 + " bottles of beer on the wall.");
            }
        }
}
```

The only significant difference between the C and Java versions is the Java method used to output strings to the console. The Java function System.out.println( ) outputs a Java string to the console. Java strings are different from C strings as discussed in detail in Chapter 2. Let's briefly dissect one of the output statements:

```
System.out.println(i + " bottles of beer on the wall,");
```

There are two important points to note about the above statement:

1. The integer i is automatically converted to a string. Java has a built in toString( ) conversion function that gets called.
2. Java overloads the + operator to allow concatenation of Java strings.

The result of the above two actions is the creation of two strings and the concatenation of those two strings into a single Java string that is then output to the console.

C programmers will find it very straightforward to port their favorite utilities and programs to Java. Secondly, C and C++ programmers will find that their learning curve in this language is very short, on the order of a few days to begin programming non-trivial applications.

1.2   OBJECT-ORIENTED LANGUAGE

Java is a pure object-oriented language. This means that everything in a Java program is an object and everything is descended from a single object class. Let's now look at a program that implements and uses objects. As with my previous two books, the source code may be a little long, but I feel it is better to have meaningful examples that you can reuse in your code. Also, I always include a full running program and never just a "snippet of code." Our example program will be the start of a personal book inventory program. Like all object-oriented programs, the program is focused around a number of objects that communicate and perform actions. In our book inventory program we will have three objects: a book, a bookshelf, and a wrapper object for the main( ) function called bookMain. It is pretty clear that we are trying to model our program after real-world objects that you find in the home. This is the key power of object-oriented programs. Of course, you need to complete the analogy by making your object behave as closely as possible to the real-world object. Source 1.4 demonstrates my implementation of a book object. C++ programmers will be very familiar with the class construct, constructors, and method functions. C++ programmers will also note the lack of a destructor. This is a side effect of garbage collection, which we will discuss more in Chapter 2.

SOURCE 1.4

```java
// books.java
import java.lang.String;
import java.io.DataInputStream;
import java.lang.System;
import java.io.IOException;

class book {
        protected String title;
        protected String author;
        protected String publisher;
        book next;

        book()
        {
                title = author = publisher = " ";
                next = null;
        }

        book(book other)
        {
                title = other.title;
                author = other.author;
                publisher = other.publisher;
                next = null;
        }

        book(String aTitle, String anAuthor, String aPublisher)
        {
                title = aTitle;
                author = anAuthor;
                publisher = aPublisher;
                next = null;
        }

        void getBook()
        {
            try {
                DataInputStream dis = new DataInputStream(System.in);
                System.out.print("Enter title    : ");
                System.out.flush();
                title = dis.readLine();
```

```
              if (title.equals("done"))
                     return;
            System.out.print("Enter author   : ");
            System.out.flush();
            author = dis.readLine();
            System.out.print("Enter publisher: ");
            System.out.flush();
            publisher = dis.readLine();
            next = null;
      } catch (IOException ioe)
        {
            System.out.println(ioe.toString());
            System.out.println("Unable to get the book data.");
            return;
        }
   }


void showBook()
{
            System.out.println("Title    : " + title);
            System.out.println("Author   : " + author);
            System.out.println("Publisher: " + publisher);
}

// accessor
String getTitle() { return title; }
String getAuthor() { return author; }
String getPublisher() { return publisher; }

// mutator
void setTitle(String aTitle) { title = aTitle; }
void setAuthor(String anAuthor) { author = anAuthor; }
void setPublisher(String aPublisher) { publisher = aPublisher; }

}
```

The bookshelf class is an example of a container class. Source 1.5 contains the implementation of the bookshelf. This is actually a very important example in that it highlights a key difference between Java and C++. It demonstrates how Java can create self-referential data structures (linked lists, trees, etc.) without using pointers. This will be explained in detail in the section on pointers in the next chapter; however, for now suffice it to say that a non-instantiated object is a pointer to an object.

SOURCE 1.5

```
class Bookshelf {
      protected book first,last;
      protected long count;

      Bookshelf()
      {
            first = last = null;
            count = 0;
      }

      void add(book aBook)
      {
            if (first != null)
            {
                  last.next = new book(aBook);
                  last = last.next;
            }
            else
            {
                  first = new book(aBook);
                  last = first;
            }
            count++;
      }

      long size() { return count; }

      void print()
      {
            book curBook = first;
            int cnt=1;

            while (curBook != null)
            {
                  System.out.println("Book: " + cnt++);
                  curBook.showBook();
                  curBook = curBook.next;
            }
      }
}
```

The main( ) function is again wrapped in its own class. Source 1.6 is the implementation. The main function processes the input from the user and creates our linked list of books on our bookshelf. We then print the list and exit.

SOURCE 1.6

```
class bookMain {
        public static void main(String args[])
        {
                Bookshelf mybooks = new Bookshelf();
                boolean done = false;

                System.out.println("Enter your books.");
                System.out.println("Type 'done' when finished.");
                while (!done)
                {
                        book curBook = new book();
                        curBook.getBook();
                        if (!(curBook.getTitle()).equals("done"))
                        {
                                mybooks.add(curBook);
                        }
                        else
                                done = true;

                }

                // print the books in the shelf
                System.out.println("Number of books in bookshelf: " +
                                                mybooks.size());
                mybooks.print();
        }
}
```

Here is a run of the bookMain program:

```
Enter your books.
Type 'done' when finished.
Enter title    : Jonathan Livingston Seagull
Enter author   : Richard Bach
Enter publisher: Avon
```

```
Enter title    : The Grapes of Wrath
Enter author   : John Steinbeck
Enter publisher: Bantam
Enter title    : done
Number of books in bookshelf: 2
Book: 1
Title    : Jonathan Livingston Seagull
Author   : Richard Bach
Publisher: Avon
Book: 2
Title    : The Grapes of Wrath
Author   : John Steinbeck
Publisher: Bantam
```

We have already seen some of the built-in classes like System.out.println( ) in the above programs; however, there are hundreds of classes in the Java environment. The next program demonstrates some of them.

1.3   THE JAVA ENVIRONMENT

The current version of the Java environment includes hundreds of classes and methods in six major functional areas. All of these are covered in great detail in Chapter 4, The Java Standard Library:

- Language Support. A collection of classes and methods that support the robust language features in Java like strings, arrays, system-dependent functionality, threads, and exceptions.
- Utilities. A collection of classes to provide utility functions like random number generation, date and time functions, and storage classes like a Vector and Hashtable class. Source 1.7 demonstrates the use of the Vector class.
- Input/output. A collection of classes to get input from multiple sources and manipulate that input in numerous ways as well as output to multiple sources and in varying ways. The classes include filter classes, sequential and random access to files, and dozens of methods to read and write data of all types.
- Networking. A collection of classes to connect to other computers over either a local network or the internet. Classes include Socket, InternetAddress, and URL (Uniform Resource Locator) processing.
- Abstract Window Toolkit. A collection of classes that implements a platform-independent graphical user interface. Source 1.7 demonstrates the use of some of the AWT classes. Chapter 6 is dedicated entirely to the abstract window toolkit.

- Applet. A class that allows you to create a Java program that can be downloaded from a Web page and run on a client browser like HotJava or Netscape.

Source 1.7 is based on the same principles as the bookShelf class above with two important differences: first, we present a graphical user interface to input, display, and browse the books; second, instead of storing the books in a linked list, we store the books in a Vector. A Vector is a dynamic, growable array.

SOURCE 1.7

```
// gui classes
import java.awt.Frame;
import java.awt.TextField;
import java.awt.Panel;
import java.awt.Button;
import java.awt.GridLayout;
import java.awt.Event;
import java.awt.Color;
import java.awt.Label;

// our book class
import book;

// a utility class
import java.util.Vector;

class bookWindow extends Frame {
    TextField title;
    TextField author;
    TextField publisher;
    Vector theBooks;
    int currentIdx;

    bookWindow() {
        super("Book Shelf");

        // initialize the growable array
        theBooks = new Vector(3);
        currentIdx = 0;
```

```java
        Panel centerPanel = new Panel();
        centerPanel.setLayout(new GridLayout(0, 2));

        centerPanel.add(new Label("              Title"));
        centerPanel.add(title = new TextField(20));

        centerPanel.add(new Label("              Author"));
        centerPanel.add(author = new TextField(20));

        centerPanel.add(new Label("              Publisher"));
        centerPanel.add(publisher = new TextField(20));

        add("Center", centerPanel);

        Panel bottomPanel = new Panel();
        bottomPanel.add(new Button("store"));
        bottomPanel.add(new Button("clear"));
        bottomPanel.add(new Button("prev"));
        bottomPanel.add(new Button("next"));
        bottomPanel.add(new Button("exit"));
        add("South", bottomPanel);

        move(200, 100);
        pack();
        show();
}

public boolean handleEvent(Event evt) {
  if (evt.id == Event.ACTION_EVENT)
    {
        if ("store".equals(evt.arg))
        {
            book aBook = new book(title.getText(),
                                  author.getText(),
                                  publisher.getText());

            theBooks.addElement(aBook);
            currentIdx = theBooks.size();
            return true;
        }
        if ("clear".equals(evt.arg))
        {
```

```
                    title.setText("");
                    author.setText("");
                    publisher.setText("");
                    return true;
                }
            if ("prev".equals(evt.arg))
            {
                if (currentIdx > 0)
                {
                        book aBook = (book) theBooks.elementAt(--currentIdx);
                        title.setText(aBook.getTitle());
                        author.setText(aBook.getAuthor());
                        publisher.setText(aBook.getPublisher());
                }
            return true;
            }
            if ("next".equals(evt.arg))
            {
                if (currentIdx < (theBooks.size()-1))
                {
                        book aBook = (book) theBooks.elementAt(++currentIdx);
                        title.setText(aBook.getTitle());
                        author.setText(aBook.getAuthor());
                        publisher.setText(aBook.getPublisher());
                }
            return true;
            }
            if ("exit".equals(evt.arg))
            {
                System.exit(0);
            }
        }
    return true;
    }
}
class bookGUI {
    public static void main(String args[])
    {
        new bookWindow();
    }
}
```

A run of Source 1.7 produces the output shown in Figure 1.2.

The key points to note about Source 1.7 involve understanding the basics of the AWT classes and the Vector class. The purpose of the program is to display a window that lets you both enter and display records that are stored in the Vector class. Instead of giving a detailed explanation of the classes and all their methods (which is done in great detail later), let's walk through the required functionality and point out how it is implemented.

All functionality is from the graphical user interface, which is why the main function of Source 1.7 only contains the constructor for the bookWindow( ). The bookWindow class extends the Frame class (extends is the keyword for inheritance, which is discussed in detail in Chapter 3). The Frame class is a GUI component that implements a window with a border. A window is not only four corner points with a border. It is also a container that can hold other graphical user interface components (widgets to X-programmers). We therefore need to create the rest of our graphical components and add them to the frame with the add( ) method. You will notice that we also add something called a panel. Panels are used to group graphical components together. You use panels to break up your window into functional parts. Source 1.7 uses two panels, one to hold the record information and one to hold and lay out the buttons. The "center" panel uses a special layout called a grid layout. A grid layout allows you to create a matrix of rows and columns that form equal size cells in which to place a graphical component. We place the field label in one component (i.e., Title, Author, etc.) and a text field in the adjacent cell of our grid. A text field is a graphical component that implements an editable text string. Once we have added all the components, we can move the window to where we want and size it using either width and height or the pack( ) method, which sizes the window to the minimum size to display

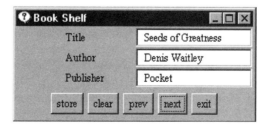

FIGURE 1.2   A bookshelf GUI.

all the components. Last, we call the show( ) method to display the window and all its components.

All graphical user interfaces are programmed with the event-driven programming model. This model structures a program as a series of event handlers that respond to events triggered by the user (i.e., mouse moves, button push, menu choice, etc.). In Java, your graphical user interface captures events from the system by overriding the handleEvent( ) method. The handleEvent( ) method is invoked whenever the user triggers an event and is passed an Event class that has the event just performed. AWT events fall into six categories: mouse, window, keyboard, component events (scrolling, list item selection, etc.), system events (window focus and file saves), and "action" events. Action events are both menu choices and button pushes. Our GUI is only concerned with button pushes. You can see how the name of the button is what is passed in the evt.arg field. All the main functionality of the program is driven by responding to the button pushes. The store button stores the current text in the textfields as a book record in the Vector. We use the Vector addElement( ) method to store a book class. That same record can be retrieved with the elementAt( ) method by providing the array index of the record. The clear button clears the text fields. The next and prev buttons display the next and previous book object stored in the vector respectively. The exit button exits the application (which also destroys the window).

As I demonstrated above, the Java environment provides a rich and robust programming environment that makes it a joy to program in. I think Arthur Van Hoff, one of the key members of the Java development team, describes this sentiment best in the way he signs off in his email: He always finishes with "Have Fun." We will!

CHAPTER 2

Comparing Java
to ANSI C

*When a feature that exists in both Java and ANSI C isn't fully
explained in this specification, the feature should be assumed to work
as it does in ANSI C.*

—*The Java Language Specification*

OBJECTIVE

This chapter will compare and contrast the Java language to
ANSI C. All major elements of ANSI C will be examined and all
differences will be highlighted.

Comparing Java to ANSI C is important because the constructs that
these languages share will make up the lion's share of your code. You
will learn that the keywords and operators that Java inherited from
ANSI C—particularly the data types, control flow constructs, and all
the operators—are the bulk of all your applications. The rest of a Java
application is the object-oriented constructs that we will discuss in the
next chapter; however, those familiar with object-oriented programming will agree that the OOP constructs are more about the framework and design of a program than the implementation. You can think
of the OOP constructs as the skeleton and ANSI C as the organs, mus-
cles, and tendons. So, let's examine those vital organs.

2.1   PROGRAM STRUCTURE

In its simplest form, a Java program contains classes with only one class implementing a main( ) method. Java classes may be in multiple files (also called compilation units). Each source code file ends with the ".java" suffix. Classes contain data members (data type declarations) and methods (functions that operate on the data members of a class). Class methods contain data type declarations and statements. Source 2.1 is the skeleton of a Java stand-alone program (the format of an applet is different and will be discussed in Chapter 6).

SOURCE 2.1

```
package mystech.util;      /* OPTIONAL - these classes may belong to a package */
import java.util.Vector;   /* OPTIONAL - import other classes for use in this class */
interface InputOutput {    /* OPTIONAL - an interface is a group of methods */
    void read();
    void write();
}


/* OPTIONAL - multiple classes per file */
class aClass {
}


class mainClass {
    public static void main(String args[])
    {
    }
}
```

At first glance, this program structure may not be familiar to a C programmer. This is because a Java program has an object-oriented structure that is more familiar to C++ programmers; however, I will explain these features from a C programmer's view point (in the next chapter we will examine them again from a C++ viewpoint). Let's discuss all the components of the above Java skeleton program.

- Package Statement. This declares the classes in this compilation unit to be part of a package called mystech.util. This means that all the classes in the file actually have the name mystech.util.<class-name>. The benefit of packages is that it allows the namespace of a program to be divided into functional components. This makes it easier to avoid name conflicts when importing third party classes. As stated in the comment, the package statement is optional because your classes do not have to be part of a package.

- Comments. Java uses the same comment syntax as ANSI C (/* */); however, Java also uses two additional syntaxes for comments:
  - // The C++ style comment for single-line comments.
  - /** */ This is a special comment form that can precede declarations and is used for auto-document generators.
- Import Statement. This is similar to the #include preprocessor statement in C. The purpose of this statement is to instruct the interpreter to load this class, which exists in another compilation unit. As we will discuss later on, this is the only similarity to the C preprocessor because there is no preprocessor in Java. This adheres to the Java design goal for simplicity. More on this later.
- Interface Statement. This is an object-oriented construct that we will discuss in Chapter 5.
- Class Declarations. You can declare multiple classes within a compilation unit. Classes are the primary and essential component of a Java program. Without at least one class you do not have a Java program. All the other constructs discussed so far are mere supporting characters to the class construct. Although I have shown above how it is possible to model your Java programs after C programs, I would not advise this. I believe that object-oriented programming is better than procedural programming and therefore it would behoove you to learn it. We will cover the primary OOP constructs in Java and how they compare to C++ in the next chapter.
- Main Method. Every Java stand-alone program requires a main function as its starting point. Although I say "main function," it is actually more technically correct to say main method. Java does not support separate functions, only class methods. The difference is that a method is a function bound to a class. This is yet another distinction where Java has taken the object-oriented path; however, in this chapter I will still often use the term function because it is more familiar to C programmers. The requirement for a main function is identical to C and C++ programs; however, the precise syntax of a Java main function is slightly different. The Java main function must have this format:

```
public static void main(String args)
{
    ...
}
```

This is the format the Java compiler looks for to denote the function to execute first and the function that should receive any command-line arguments from the operating system. When main( ) completes, the program terminates and control passes back to the operating system.

2.2   KEYWORDS AND OPERATORS

To me, the keywords and operators of a language give the computer language its "feel and expressiveness." In this, it is very obvious that Java has retained the feel and expressiveness of C. And this is a good thing. Programming in C, although procedural, has a very concise and quick feel to it. As a programmer's language, it has been honed to a fine edge. As we cover the keywords and operators of Java, you will appreciate the fact that Java retains the feel of a carefully crafted, concise, and quick programmer's language.

First let's examine the keywords common to both Java and C, depicted graphically in Figure 2.1.

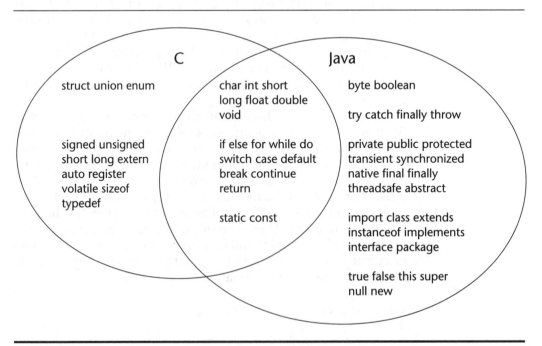

FIGURE 2.1   Common C and Java keywords.

The important item to note about the keywords common to both Java and C is that these are the keywords that make up the bulk of your programming. These keywords, combined with the operators (discussed next), make up the majority of statements that fill your functions. The framework may be object oriented but the implementation is very close to C. A detailed description of all the Java keywords can be found in the appendix. Now let's examine the operators in Java.

Operators are divided into several types: mathematical, relational, logical, and bitwise. In each category, Java supports all of the C operators in those categories. Here are the operators common to Java and C:

```
+   -   !   %   ^   &   *   |   ~   /   >   <
(  )   {  }   [  ]   ;   ?   :   ,   .   =
++   --   ==   <=   >=   !=   <<   >>
+=   -=   *=   /=   &=   |=
^=   %=   <<=   >>=   ||   &&
```

Source 2.2 is a simple program that demonstrates the use of some Java operators.

SOURCE 2.2

```java
import java.io.DataInputStream;
import java.lang.String;
import java.io.IOException;

class leapYear {
      public static void main(String args[])
      {
            DataInputStream dis = new DataInputStream(System.in);
            String Syear=null;
            System.out.print("Enter a year: ");
            System.out.flush();
            try {
              Syear = dis.readLine();
            } catch (IOException ioe)
              {
                    System.out.println(ioe.toString());
                    System.exit(1);
              }

            long year = Long.parseLong(Syear);
```

```
              System.out.println("year is " + year);
              if ( ((year % 4 == 0) && (year % 100 != 0))  ||
                   (year % 400 == 0) )
                      System.out.println(year + " is a leap year!");
              else
                      System.out.println(year + " is NOT a leap year.");
       }
}
```

Here is a run of Source 2.2.

```
Enter a year: 1992
year is 1992
1992 is a leap year!
```

Source 2.2 allows you to enter a year and then uses the Java mathematical and logical operators to determine if that year is a leap year. The key expression in the program is:

```
( ((year % 4 == 0) && (year % 100 != 0))  ||  (year % 400 == 0) )
```

which translates to: if the year is divisible by 4 AND if year is NOT divisible by 100 OR if year is divisible by 400 THEN it is a leap year. The modulus operator answers whether the number is evenly divisible by another number and the logical operators provide the boolean logic (AND, OR, etc.).

2.3   IDENTIFIERS

Identifiers are the programmer-defined names used to label variables, classes, functions (methods), packages, and interfaces in a program. Java identifiers follow the same rules as C with a few beneficial additions that you will appreciate. Source 2.3 both lists and demonstrates the rules associated with identifiers.

SOURCE 2.3

```
class IdentifierTst {
      public static void main(String args[])
      {
              // 1) C rule, names can be letters and digits, MUST
```

```
//    start with a letter.
int legal_name1;
// int 1_illegal;   // ILLEGAL

// 2) C rule, underscores count as a letter
int _123_name;

// 2a) Java addition to rule 2: dollar sign counts as a letter
int $123_name;

// 3) C rule, upper case and lower case are distinct
int Legal_name1;

// 4) Java allows identifiers greater than 32 characters
int The_number_of_dark_haired_children_in_family;


}
}
```

By far the most valuable Java improvement with identifiers is the ability to make identifiers as long as you wish. It is common knowledge that long, descriptive identifiers improve both code readability and maintenance.

2.4   LITERALS

Literals, also known as constants, are a sequence of characters, digits, or both that represent an integer, floating point number, boolean, character, or string. Java literals are identical to C literals with a few exceptions and a few additions. Source 2.4 demonstrates the Java literals as compared to C literals.

SOURCE 2.4

```
class LiteralTst {
    public static void main(String args[])
    {
        int myint = 123;         /* C-style int  literal      */
        long mylong = 123L;      /* C-style Long literal      */
        int hexnum = 0x1ac;      /* C-style Hexadecimal literal */
```

```
int octnum = 037;        /* C-style Octal literal      */
double mydouble = 3.12; /* C-style double literal     */

char mychar = 'c';       /* C-style character literal  */
char newline  = '\n';  /* C-style escape sequence    */
// char bell     = '\a'; - UNICODE conflict
char backspace = '\b';
char formfeed  = '\f';
char cr        = '\r';
char tab       = '\t';
// char vertTab  = '\v'; - UNICODE conflict
char backslash = '\\';
// char question  = '\?'; - UNICODE conflict
char snglequote= '\'';
char doubquote = '\"';
char Octal     = '\032';
char Unicodeltr= '\u0391'; /* Greek capital A
String myname = "Mike"; /* C-style string literal      */

/* Java-specific literals */
boolean done = false;
float javaFloat = 2e3f;
float javaFloat2 = 2E3f;
double javaDouble = 1e1;

    }
}
```

Literals are most often used for setting final variables (similar to constants) in Java. Now let's talk about another Java language feature that is identical to C: expressions.

2.5   EXPRESSIONS

An expression is any combination of operators, literals, and variables that can be evaluated to produce a value. An expression is recursive by definition, which means it may consist of subexpressions that may themselves have subexpressions, ad infinitum. Programming gains its power from the use of mathematics and logic and it cannot be emphasized enough that expressions are the primary tools to express them.

To its credit, Java has adopted C's powerful expression facilities in whole with only a few exceptions. The Java types are slightly different than C types in order to be platform-independent and international. Let's examine the Java basic data types.

byte A basic data type that represents a single byte as an 8-bit signed value. This is useful in moving C ASCII characters to Java UNICODE characters when implementing native methods. A native method is a C function linked to a Java program and called from a Java program.

boolean A basic data type that represents only two values: true or false. Both true and false are also keywords. The boolean data type only uses 1 bit of storage. The boolean type in Java eliminates the need for the common C and C++ practice of using #define to allow true and false to stand for 1 and 0 respectively.

char A basic data type used to declare character variables. A Java character is different than an ASCII character. Java uses the UNI-CODE character set, which is a 16-bit unsigned value. Java is very explicit about the size of all types. Since Java uses a "virtual machine" representation in the interpreter, the Java language specifies the exact size in bits for all basic types. This aids portability as there are no differences between sizes of the basic types on different platforms. This also makes the sizeof( ) macro obsolete.

double A basic data type used to declare double variables. A Java double is 64 bits and conforms to IEEE 754.

float A basic data type used to declare float variables. A Java float is 32 bits and conforms to the Institute of Electronic and Electrical Engineers Standard 754 (IEEE 754).

int A basic data type used to declare integer variables. A Java integer is a 32-bit signed value.

long A basic data type used to declare long integer variables. A Java long is a 64-bit signed value.

short A basic data type used to declare short integer variables. A Java short is a 16-bit signed value.

In addition to the new types, boolean and byte, you will notice that all Java types have fixed sizes. There is no ambiguity and all Java types are platform-independent. Java expressions combine the Java types with the Java operators in different ways, as demonstrated in Source 2.5.

SOURCE 2.5

```
class ExpressionTst {
      public static void main(String args[])
      {
            System.out.println("Arithmetic expressions");
            float fahr=60.0f, celsius =0;
            celsius = (5.0f/9.0f) * (fahr-32.0f);
            System.out.println("fahrenheit: " + fahr + " celsius: " +
                                celsius);
            System.out.println("");

            System.out.println("Relational and logical expressions");
            System.out.println(fahr > 20.0);
            /* System.out.println((fahr < 20.0) && (1));
               Legal in C but ILLEGAL in Java. */
            System.out.println(((fahr < 20.0) && (true)));
            System.out.println("");

            System.out.println("Casts and conversions in expressions");
            int age=10;
            float gpa = age;
            double salary=30000.3;
            System.out.println(gpa + salary);
            System.out.println((int)(gpa + salary));
            System.out.println("");

            System.out.println("Bitwise expressions");
            System.out.println(100 >> 1);  // division by 2
            System.out.println(age << 1);  // multiplication by 2
            int memoryBlock = (12 + 7) & ~7;
            System.out.println("12 rounded to a power of 8 is " +
                                memoryBlock);
            System.out.println("");

            System.out.println("Order of Evaluation in Expressions");
            int a = 5 & 1 + 2;
            System.out.println(a);
            a = (5 & 1) + 2;
            System.out.println(a);
      }
}
```

A run of Source 2.5 produces:

```
Arithmetic expressions
fahrenheit: 60 celsius: 15.5556

Relational and logical expressions
true
false

Casts and conversions in expressions
30010.3
30010

Bitwise expressions
50
20
12 rounded to a power of 8 is 16

Order of Evaluation in Expressions
1
3
```

You will happily discover that C expressions port very easily to Java. The next language element we will discuss is another cornerstone of programming: control flow.

2.6   CONTROL FLOW

Control flow constructs provide a language with the ability to perform branch selection via decision points and repetition also known as loops. The control flow constructs are the first items mastered in C and the most often used. Java adopted C's control flow constructs without any deviation or additions. Source 2.6 demonstrates the Java control flow constructs.

SOURCE 2.6

```
class ControlFlowTst {
    public static void main(String args[])
    {
        int a = 1, b = 2, c = 3;
```

```
System.out.print("The ");

if (a > 1)
        System.out.print("old ");
else
        System.out.print("young ");

System.out.print("man ");

switch (b) {
        case 1:
                System.out.print("is ");
                break;
        case 2:
                System.out.print("was ");
                break;
        case 3:
                System.out.print("can ");
                break;
        default:
                System.out.print("will ");
}

System.out.print("singing ");

for (int i=0; i < c; i++)
        System.out.print("FaLaLa, ");

System.out.println("and ");

while (c-- > 0)
        System.out.print("TaDeDa, ");

do {
        System.out.print("all ");
} while (c == 3);

System.out.println("the way home.");
    }
}
```

A run of Source 2.6 produces:

```
The young man was singing FaLaLa, FaLaLa, FaLaLa, and
TaDeDa, TaDeDa, TaDeDa, all the way home.
```

The break and continue keywords are not demonstrated above; however, Java also uses them exactly as C does with the added benefit that Java also allows multilevel break and continue to a label. Java did omit one control flow construct—the goto. I think Kernighan and Ritchie said it best: "Formally, the goto is never necessary, and in practice it is almost always easy to write code without it. We have not used goto in this book."[1]

2.7   ARRAYS AND STRINGS

The Java language treats arrays and strings as first-class objects that are no longer prone to the errors or confusion common to arrays and strings in C. Let's first examine arrays and then cover strings.

In C, an array is a group of contiguous, homogeneous data types that are accessed as offsets from a single name (which corresponds to an address). In C, there is no array bounds checking. In C, a pointer may be substituted for the array name to access array elements. The above attributes of an array have caused much confusion among programmers as well as being a source of numerous bugs. Java arrays are simpler than C arrays and protected from misuse. Java arrays are different from C arrays in three ways:

1. Just like all objects in Java, arrays are created by using the new operator. A side effect of this is that you do not enter a size of the array in the declaration. You enter the size in the new expression.

```
int intArray[] = new int[5];
```

2. As a first-class object, all arrays store the allocated size in a variable named length. You can access this at any time using:

```
int intArraySize = intArray.length;
```

3. Java arrays are protected from array overruns and underruns. An exception (the Java error-handling facility uses exceptions) is

---

[1]Brian W. Kernighan and Dennis M. Ritchie, *The C Programming Language*, p. 65.

thrown if you attempt to index an element beyond the end of an array or try to use a negative index.

Source 2.7 demonstrates the basics of declaring and allocating single and multidimensional arrays.

SOURCE 2.7

```
class ArrayBasics {
    public static void main(String args[])
    {
        /* 1) cannot put dimension in declaration */
        int myArray[];

        /* 2) must allocate storage with new. */
        myArray = new int[3];

        /* 3) You can get the size of the array */
        System.out.println("myArray size is : " + myArray.length);

        /* 4) for multi-dimensional arrays you allocate
            an array of arrays. */
        int multiArray[][];
        multiArray = new int[3][4];

        /* 5) with multi-dimensional arrays you do can
            allocate the size of each "row" later. */
        int dynamicMulti[][];
        dynamicMulti = new int[3][];

        dynamicMulti[0] = new int[5];
        dynamicMulti[1] = new int[10];
        dynamicMulti[2] = new int[20];

        /* 6) array overruns and underruns are impossible. */
    }
}
```

The dynamic allocation of Java arrays gives you the same flexibility as pointers without the risk. Accessing an element of an array is identical to indexing into the array in C. Also identical to C, Java arrays start at 0 and are contiguous in memory. Source 2.8 demonstrates array indexing and the Java runtime protection against array overruns.

SOURCE 2.8

```
class ArrayOverrun {
      public static void main(String args[])
      {
            int myArray[];

            myArray = new int[3];
            myArray[0] = 10;
            myArray[1] = 20;
            myArray[2] = 30;
            myArray[3] = 40; /* Oops! */
            myArray[-1] = 50; /* double Oops! */

      }

}
```

A run of Source 2.8 produces:

```
Exception in thread "main" java.lang.ArrayIndexOutOfBoundsException
        at ArrayOverrun.main(C:\hotjava\bin\ArrayOverrun.java:9)
```

Source 2.8 exits after the ArrayIndexOutOfBoundsException is thrown. Exceptions are a mechanism for error-handling; when used properly, they can significantly increase an application's robustness. The model is based on the idea that error conditions can be recognized by both the application and the system and an appropriate exception is thrown. In the next chapter we will discuss the exception model and exceptions in detail. The Java exception model is very similar to the C++ exception model.

Java single and multidimensional arrays can be initialized just as C arrays. Java arrays of objects (similar to arrays of structures) require an extra allocation step similar to the method used to allocate dynamic two-dimensional arrays (my two previous books cover allocation of dynamic two-dimensional arrays in detail). Source 2.9 demonstrates array initialization and arrays of objects.

SOURCE 2.9

```
class testObject {
        int anInt;
        String aString;

        testObject()
        {
                anInt = 0;
                aString = "";
        }

        testObject(int theInt, String theString)
        {
                anInt = theInt;
                aString = new String(theString);
        }

        void printObject()
        {
                System.out.println("anInt   : " + anInt);
                System.out.println("aString : " + aString);
        }
}

class arrayTest {
        public static void main(String args[])
        {
                int a[] = { 1, 2, 3 };
                int b[];
                int c[];

                b = a;
                c = new int[3];
                c = a;

                for (int i=0; i < b.length; i++)
                {
                        System.out.println("a[" + i +"] is " + a[i]);
                        System.out.println("b[" + i +"] is " + b[i]);
                        System.out.println("c[" + i +"] is " + c[i]);
                }
```

```
            testObject objArray[];
            testObject anObject;
            testObject realObject = new testObject(1,"Mike");

            objArray = new testObject[3];
            for (int i=0; i < objArray.length; i++)
                    objArray[i] = new testObject(i,"person"+i);

            anObject = realObject;

            for (int i=0; i < objArray.length; i++)
                    objArray[i].printObject();

            realObject.printObject();
            anObject.printObject();
        }
    }
```

Here is a run of this program.

```
a[0] is 1
b[0] is 1
c[0] is 1
a[1] is 2
b[1] is 2
c[1] is 2
a[2] is 3
b[2] is 3
c[2] is 3
anInt   : 0
aString : person0
anInt   : 1
aString : person1
anInt   : 2
aString : person2
anInt   : 1
aString : Mike
anInt   : 1
aString : Mike
```

Notice the assignments of one array object to another as in:

```
                    b = a;
```

This highlights the fact that Java arrays are implemented with pointers like this:

```
int a[];
```

is equivalent to

```
int *a;
```

This continues with two-dimensional arrays where

```
int a[][];
```

is equivalent to:

```
int **a;
```

You will notice that all Java objects are implemented via pointers (actually handles, but a handle is a pointer). This is also known as "using reference semantics." You were introduced to this with the linked list example in Chapter 1. We will cover this in greater detail in section 2.10.

Multidimensional arrays in Java are identical to C's multidimensional arrays. Java also uses "array of arrays" to implement multidimensional arrays. Source 2.10 is an example of using multidimensional arrays in Java.

SOURCE 2.10

```
/* this program will use Matrix rotation to demonstrate
   multi-dimensional arrays. */
import java.io.DataInputStream;
import java.lang.Integer;
import java.lang.Math;
import java.io.IOException;

class Rotate {
        public static void main(String args[])
        {
                /* enter number of coordinates to rotate. */
                DataInputStream dis = new DataInputStream(System.in);
```

```
System.out.print("Enter number of Coordinates: ");
System.out.flush();
String numStr = null;
try {
        numStr = dis.readLine();
} catch (IOException ioe)
  {
        System.out.println(ioe.toString());
        System.exit(1);
  }
int numCoords = Integer.parseInt(numStr);

/* create a matrix of 2-d coordinates. */
int coords[][] = new int[numCoords][2];

/* Fill the matrix */
for (int i=0; i < numCoords; i++)
{
    try {
        System.out.println("Coordinate #" + i);
        System.out.print("Enter x: ");
        System.out.flush();
        String xStr = dis.readLine();
        coords[i][0] = Integer.parseInt(xStr);

        System.out.print("Enter y: ");
        System.out.flush();
        String yStr = dis.readLine();
        coords[i][1] = Integer.parseInt(yStr);
    } catch (IOException ioe)
      {
        System.out.println(ioe.toString());
        System.exit(1);
      }
}

/* get the degree of Rotation */
System.out.print("Enter degree of rotation (1-360): ");
System.out.flush();
String degStr = null;
try {
        degStr = dis.readLine();
```

```
        } catch (IOException ioe)
          {
              System.out.println(ioe.toString());
              System.exit(1);
          }
        int degrees = Integer.parseInt(degStr);

        /* translate degrees to radians */
        double radians = ((double)degrees/180.0) * Math.PI;
        System.out.println(degrees + " degrees is " + radians +
                            " radians.");

        /* create rotation Matrix */
        double rotMatrix[][] = new double[numCoords][2];

        /* perform the rotation */
        for (int i=0; i < numCoords; i++)
        {
              /* new X */
              rotMatrix[i][0] = Math.cos(radians) -
                              coords[i][1] * Math.sin(radians);

              /* new Y */
              rotMatrix[i][1] = Math.cos(radians) +
                              coords[i][0] * Math.sin(radians);
        }

        /* print the Rotation matrix */
        for (int i=0; i < numCoords; i++)
        {
              System.out.println("Rotated Coordinate #" + i);
              System.out.println("x :" + rotMatrix[i][0]);
              System.out.println("y :" + rotMatrix[i][1]);
        }
    }
}
```

A run of Source 2.10 produces:

```
C:\hotjava\bin>java Rotate
Enter number of Coordinates: 7
Coordinate #0
```

```
Enter x: 2
Enter y: 5
Coordinate #1
Enter x: 4
Enter y: 7
Coordinate #2
Enter x: 2
Enter y: 9
Coordinate #3
Enter x: 7
Enter y: 9
Coordinate #4
Enter x: 7
Enter y: 4
Coordinate #5
Enter x: 5
Enter y: 6
Coordinate #6
Enter x: 3
Enter y: 4
Enter degree of rotation (1-360): 90
90 degrees is 1.5708 radians.
Rotated Coordinate #0
x :-5
y :2
Rotated Coordinate #1
x :-7
y :4
Rotated Coordinate #2
x :-9
y :2
Rotated Coordinate #3
x :-9
y :7
Rotated Coordinate #4
x :-4
y :7
Rotated Coordinate #5
x :-6
y :5
Rotated Coordinate #6
x :-4
y :3
```

A graphical representation of the rotation is depicted in Figure 2.2.

Just as arrays and strings are similar in C, Java arrays and strings are similar in how they differ from their C counterpart. In Java, strings are first-class objects and implemented using two classes: String and StringBuffer. The String class is used for immutable (nonchangeable) strings and the StringBuffer class is used for mutable (changeable) strings. We will first discuss strings and then string buffers.

In C, strings are simple NUL-terminated character arrays. There is a critical reliance on the ascii NUL character being there to terminate the string. In fact, in the standard header <string.h>, the majority of string manipulation functions depend on the NUL-terminator to complete processing. Due to C's lack of bounds-checking, the ability to overwrite the NUL terminator is a cause of numerous program bugs. This potential hazard is also magnified by the fact that string manipulation is the most common and pervasive part of most programs. Java strings fix the deficiencies of C strings to deliver safe, predictable, and reliable string manipulation. A Java string is an instantiated object of the String class. The String class provides numerous constructor and manipulator functions. Source 2.11 demonstrates both construction and manipulation of Java strings.

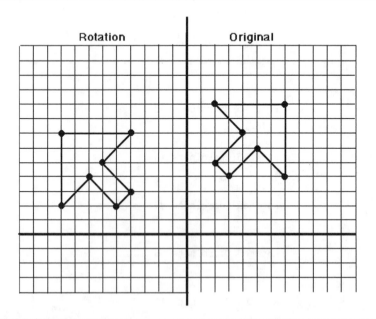

FIGURE 2.2   Martix rotations.

SOURCE 2.11

```
class StringBasics {
      public static void main(String args[])
      {
              /* 1) a String is NOT a character array. */
              // char charArray[] = "mike";   ILLEGAL
              char charArray[] = new char[4];
              charArray[0] = 'm';
              charArray[1] = 'i';
              charArray[2] = 'k';
              charArray[3] = 'e';
              // a Java character array is NOT NUL terminated. */
              System.out.println("charArray is " + charArray);
              System.out.println("length of charArray is " +
                                       charArray.length);


              /* 2) creating a String object. */
              String myName = new String("Michael");
              String sentence = new String("I live in a small town.");

              /* 3) get the string length. */
              System.out.println("Length of " + myName +
                              " is " + myName.length());

              /* 4) character access, char is UNICODE NOT ASCII! */
              for (int i=0; i < myName.length(); i++)
                      System.out.println("char #" + i +
                                      " is " + myName.charAt(i) +
                                      " which is " +
                      (new Character(myName.charAt(i))).toString());


              /* 5) String concatentation. */
              String fullName = myName + " Corey " + "Daconta";
              System.out.println("my fullName is " + fullName);

              /* 6) String comparison */
              if (myName.equals("Michael"))
                      System.out.println("My name is Michael.");
```

```
if ("Michael".equals(myName))
        System.out.println("... and Michael is my name.");

/* 7) String manipulation */
int idx = sentence.indexOf("small");

if (idx > 0)
{
        System.out.println("small starts at index: " + idx);
        String smallStr = sentence.substring(idx,"small".length());
        System.out.println("smallStr is " + smallStr);
}
    }
}
```

A run of Source 2.11 produces:

```
C:\hotjava\bin>java StringBasics
charArray is mike
length of charArray is 4
Length of Michael is 7
char #0 is 77 which is M
char #1 is 105 which is i
char #2 is 99 which is c
char #3 is 104 which is h
char #4 is 97 which is a
char #5 is 101 which is e
char #6 is 108 which is l
my fullName is Michael Corey Daconta
My name is Michael.
... and Michael is my name.
small starts at index: 12
smallStr is e in a
```

It is important to understand that the Java character set is UNI-CODE and not ascii. UNICODE is an international character set that encompasses all the characters in the majority of languages in the world. The implementation of a UNICODE character is a 16-bit unsigned value. To bridge the gap between 1-byte ascii strings and the UNICODE characters used in Java strings, the String class has the ability to be constructed from byte arrays.

Another Java string feature unfamiliar to C programmers is overloading the functionality of the + operator for the purpose of concatenating strings. You have already seen numerous examples of this in conjunction with the System.out.println( ) method. The last part of Source 2.11 demonstrates some of the string manipulation features. A more thorough introduction into the String class will be covered in Chapter 4, The Java Standard Library. Furthermore, a complete and detailed listing of the entire Java class hierarchy can be found in the appendix.

A Java StringBuffer is similar to a Java string in its bounds-checking; however, you have the ability to modify and extend a String-Buffer. You can also construct a StringBuffer from a Java string. Lastly, you can convert a StringBuffer back to a Java string by using the toString( ) method. Source 2.12 demonstrates the most common functions of a StringBuffer. Again, a complete listing of all the String-Buffer functionality can be found in the appendix.

SOURCE 2.12

```
class StringBufferBasics {
      public static void main(String args[])
      {
              /* 1) initialize */
              StringBuffer aSentence = new StringBuffer("Mary had a ");
              System.out.println("The sentence is " + aSentence);

              /* 2) modify chars */
              aSentence.setCharAt(5,'w');
              aSentence.setCharAt(7,'s');
              System.out.println("Modified sentence is " + aSentence);

              /* 3) append to end */
              aSentence.append("little girl.");
              System.out.println("Appended sentence is " + aSentence);

              /* 4) insert in middle */
              String aWord = new String(aSentence.toString());
              int idx = aWord.indexOf("little");

              if (idx > 0)
                      aSentence.insert(idx,"very ");
              System.out.println("Inserted sentence is " + aSentence);
      }
}
```

A run of Source 2.12 produces:

```
C:\hotjava\bin>java StringBufferBasics
The sentence is Mary had a
Modified sentence is Mary was a
Appended sentence is Mary was a little girl.
Inserted sentence is Mary was a very little girl.
```

Since arrays and strings are so common to programming, I provide one more example that combines the two concepts. Source 2.13 implements a simple CheckBook register. Remember that a class is similar to a structure. In fact, in Source 2.13 I make a class even more similar to a C structure by making the class data members have public access. This allows you to access the data members directly just as you would access structure data members (using the dot operator).

SOURCE 2.13

```
/* this program will demonstrate both Strings and Arrays */
import java.io.DataInputStream;
import java.lang.Integer;
import java.io.IOException;

class Check {
        public int number;
        public String to;
        public Float amount;
        public String memo;

        void enterCheck()
        {
           try {
                System.out.print("Check number: ");
                System.out.flush();
                String numStr = CheckBook.dis.readLine();
                number = Integer.parseInt(numStr);
                System.out.print("Check to: ");
                System.out.flush();
                to = CheckBook.dis.readLine();
                System.out.print("Check amount: ");
                System.out.flush();
```

```
            String amtStr = CheckBook.dis.readLine();
            amount = Float.valueOf(amtStr);
            System.out.print("Check memo: ");
            System.out.flush();
            memo = CheckBook.dis.readLine();
        } catch (IOException ioe)
          {
            System.out.println(ioe.toString());
            System.out.println("Unable to get Check data.");
            return;
          }
      }
}


class CheckBook {
      static DataInputStream dis = new DataInputStream(System.in);

      public static void main(String args[])
      {
            Check theCheckBook[];

            /* enter the checks */
            System.out.print("Enter number of checks used this month: ");
            System.out.flush();
            String numStr = null;
            try {
                  numStr = dis.readLine();
            } catch (IOException ioe)
              {
                  System.out.println(ioe.toString());
                  System.exit(1);
              }
            int numChecks = Integer.parseInt(numStr);

            theCheckBook = new Check[numChecks];

            for (int i=0; i < numChecks; i++)
            {
                  theCheckBook[i] = new Check();
                  theCheckBook[i].enterCheck();
            }
```

```
        /* print out check register.
          First print the header. */
        System.out.println("Check #\t          Payee          \t Amount \tMemo");
        System.out.println("--------------------------------------------");
        for (int i=0; i < numChecks; i++)
                System.out.println(theCheckBook[i].number + "\t" +
                    pad(theCheckBook[i].to,20,' ') + "\t" +
                    theCheckBook[i].amount + "\t" +
                    theCheckBook[i].memo);

        /* calculate total expenses */
        double total=0.0;
        for (int i=0; i < numChecks; i++)
        {
                total += theCheckBook[i].amount.doubleValue();
        }
        System.out.println("Total expenses for month: $" + total);
    }

static String pad(String inString, int desiredLength, char padChar)
{
        if (inString.length() >= desiredLength)
                return new String(inString);

        StringBuffer newStr = new StringBuffer(inString);
        for (int i=inString.length(); i < desiredLength; i++)
                newStr.append(padChar);

        return new String(newStr.toString());
    }
}
```

A run of Source 2.13 produces:

```
C:\hotjava\bin>java CheckBook
Enter number of checks used this month: 5
Check number: 101
Check to: Quality TV & Appliance
Check amount: 65.40
Check memo: TV Repair
Check number: 102
```

```
Check to: Smiths
Check amount: 99.45
Check memo: groceries
Check number: 103
Check to: Dr. Schaus
Check amount: 45.20
Check memo: office visit
Check number: 104
Check to: Livingstons Books
Check amount: 15.10
Check memo: Entertainment
Check number: 105
Check to: Southwest Gas
Check amount: 20.20
Check memo: gas bill
Check #        Payee            Amount         Memo
-----------------------------------------------------------
101     Quality TV & Appliance  65.4    TV Repair
102     Smiths                  99.45   groceries
103     Dr. Schaus              45.2    office visit
104     Livingstons Books       15.1    Entertainment
105     Southwest Gas           20.2    gas bill
Total expenses for month: $245.35
```

Another important point to note is the creation of the static utility function to pad the Java string to the proper length. You should notice that the function is not attached to any particular object through the use of the static keyword. We will cover this in more detail in the next section.

2.8   FUNCTIONS

Functions are the cornerstone of modular code and procedural programming and should not be underestimated in the age of object orientation. Functions are more than just a language feature, they are the implementation of a common-sense, problem-solving methodology. The idea is that you functionally decompose a large system into smaller subcomponents and further divide those subcomponents into smaller components until no further decomposition is possible. The end result is a hierarchical organization that describes the functioning of a system in a sufficient amount of detail to implement it. It also makes it easy to divide the implementation work by parceling out branches of the hierarchy.

Java follows the object-oriented programming methodology whereby functions only exist as a part of an object. In this role, the term function has been replaced by the term method. The key difference between object-oriented programming and procedural programming—and by default the difference between methods and functions—is the focus on data. In procedural programming, data is something you act on and functions are the tools you use to act on that data. In that arrangement, however, data is taking a back seat to the functions. Over the years, the programming community has realized that the data is the most important part of the program. The data should be protected. The primary method to protect data has been to restrict access to it and to surround it with methods (functions) that are the outside world's only access to the precious data inside. This "wrapping" of functions around data in a tight little ball is where the idea of "encapsulation" comes from. An instantiation of this encapsulated data and functions in memory is then called an object.

In general, I support the object-oriented approach to program design. I do believe that the "data is king"; however, there are times when separate, stand-alone utility functions come in handy. C++ allowed both methods and stand-alone functions. Java has simplified things by only allowing methods; however, utility functions are possible by making a method static. Source 2.14 demonstrates both class methods and static class methods.

SOURCE 2.14

```
class Coord {
        int x,y,z;

        /* methods */
        Coord() /* special method called a constructor. */
        {
                x = y = z = 0;
        }

        Coord(int inX, int inY, int inZ)
        {
                x = inX; y = inY; z = inZ;
        }

        int getX() /* an accessor method */
```

```
{
        return x;
}

int getY()
{
        return y;
}

int getZ()
{
        return z;
}

void setX(int inX) /* a mutator method */
{
        x = inX;
}

void setY(int inY)
{
        y = inY;
}

void setZ(int inZ)
{
        z = inZ;
}

public String toString()
{
        return new String("x: " + x + " y: " + y +
                        " z: " + z);
}

void scalePt(int Scale)
{
    x *= Scale;
    y *= Scale;
    z *= Scale;
}
```

```
                    /* static utility function */
                    static Coord scalePt(Coord inCoord, int Scale)
                    {
                            int aX, aY, aZ;
                            /* use methods */
                            aX = inCoord.getX();
                            aY = inCoord.getY();
                            aZ = inCoord.getZ();
                            aX *= Scale;
                            aY *= Scale;
                            aZ *= Scale;
                            Coord outCoord = new Coord(aX, aY, aZ);
                            return outCoord;
                    }
            }

            class functionTst {
                    public static void main(String args[])
                    {
                            Coord aCoord = new Coord(4,5,2);

                            /* use method */
                            String coordStr = aCoord.toString();
                            System.out.println("aCoord holds " + coordStr);

                            /* use utility function */
                            Coord scaleCoord = Coord.scalePt(aCoord,10);
                            coordStr = scaleCoord.toString();
                            System.out.println("scaleCoord holds " + coordStr);
                    }
            }
```

A run of Source 2.14 produces:

```
C:\hotjava\bin>java functionTst
aCoord holds x: 4 y: 5 z: 2
scaleCoord holds x: 40 y: 50 z: 20
```

The key difference between methods and static methods is how you are able to invoke the method (function). With methods you can only invoke the method via an instantiated object. In this sense, the object "owns" the method. It is inextricably part of the object's repertoire of actions. When you declare a method static, it is not instantiated with each object but is part of the entire class. Therefore, you invoke the method by preceding it with the class name. In essence, this allows you to make utility functions that belong to a class. If the class is public, then you have in essence, created stand-alone functions.

Just as functions have been slightly modified due to Java's object-oriented focus, so have command-line arguments. Let's see how.

2.9   COMMAND LINE ARGUMENTS

Command line arguments allow you to pass parameters to a program when it is run from the operating system. In C, this is implemented by the main( ) function being passed two arguments: argc and argv. In C, main( ) looks like this

```
int main(int argc, char *argv[]);
```

The integer variable argc represents the number of arguments passed into the program. The variable argv is a pointer to an array of character strings that contain the arguments. In C, there is always at least one argument (argv[0]) that is the name of the program being executed.

Java also allows command line arguments from the operating system; however, the interface is simpler and makes use of the String class discussed above. In Java, the command line arguments are passed to the main function as an array of Java strings. The argc variable is unnecessary since all Java arrays have a length data member. Source 2.15 demonstrates a program processing the three most common types of command line arguments.

SOURCE 2.15

```
class cmdLineTst {
    public static void main(String args[])
    {
        /* 1) no need for argc because arrays have the
            length data member. */
        System.out.println("Number of command line args is " +
                        args.length);

        /* 2) command line args in Java are just
            an array of Strings. */
        for (int i=0; i < args.length; i++)
```

```
                    System.out.println("arg #" + i + " is " +
                                    args[i]);


/* 3) IMPORTANT: java arguments do NOT include
   the program name as in C and C++. */


/* 4) flag arguments. */
for (int i=0; i < args.length; i++)
{
        if (args[i].startsWith("-"))
        {
                switch (args[i].charAt(1)) {
                        case 'a':
                                System.out.println("a flag.");
                                break;
                        case 'b':
                                System.out.println("b flag.");
                                break;
                        case 'c':
                                System.out.println("c flag.");
                                break;
                        default:
                                /* normally error,
                                here do nothing to allow other
                                tests */ ;

                }
        }
}


/* 5) word arguments. */
for (int i=0; i < args.length; i++)
{
        if (args[i].equals("-verbose"))
        {
                System.out.println("Set the verbose flag.");
        }
}


/* 6) arguments that require arguments. */
for (int i=0; i < args.length; i++)
{
        if (args[i].equals("-getNext"))
```

```
                    {
                        String nextArg = new String(args[++i]);
                        System.out.println("next Arg is " + nextArg);
                    }
                }
            }
        }
    }
```

A run of Source 2.15 produces:

```
C:\hotjava\bin>java cmdLineTst -a -b -verbose -getNext hello -c
Number of command line args is 6
arg #0 is -a
arg #1 is -b
arg #2 is -verbose
arg #3 is -getNext
arg #4 is hello
arg #5 is -c
a flag.
b flag.
c flag.
Set the verbose flag.
next Arg is hello
```

The first point to stress about Source 2.15 is the fact that Java differs from C and C++ by not including the program name in the command line arguments. This is very important for people porting C and C++ applications to Java as it will require a modification to the command line processing code. This also means that if there are no command line arguments the length of the args array would be 0.

Processing Java command line arguments is very simple due to the rich array of class methods in the String class. In Source 2.15 I demonstrate processing of one-letter flags, command words, and arguments that require further arguments.

We have now covered the majority of identical and similar features between the C language and Java. Now we will turn to features in C but purposefully left out of Java.

2.10   FEATURES REMOVED FROM C

We will focus on four key areas where functionality was removed from Java. Those areas are keywords, pointers, the preprocessor, and variable arguments. We will also discuss why these items were removed and how the same or similar functionality exists in Java.

Keywords

Here is a list of C unique statement keywords removed from Java:

goto In C, a control flow keyword that allows unconditional branching to a label further down in the current function. There have been many studies on the harmful effects of using goto's in code. The most obvious is the hard-to-follow "spaghetti code" produced by overusing goto's. Also, the elimination of the goto simplified the Java language. The fact that the Java language takes a firm stance on many programming issues is very refreshing. The Java language was designed to be very clear, straightforward and without ambiguity.

sizeof In C, a compile-time operator that returned the size, in bytes, of its argument (a data type or variable). Since the Java language precisely specifies the size of all the basic types, there is no need for the sizeof operator. Again, Java has set its stake in the ground and is sticking to it. Why is this so important? Because it is an area where the language designers have taken on the responsibility of an imperfect decision (all decisions are inherently imperfect), so that the language users (programmers) do not have to worry about it. This allows programmers to concentrate on creating useful programs and less on how to work the tools of their trade.

typedef In C, a declaration keyword that allows a type to be given an alias. This directly violates the Java design principle of simplicity. The problem with typedefs, header files, and #defines is that they cause a program to be uninterpretable without having examined all of the "hidden context" behind the program. A Java program is a Java program and all types and operators mean exactly what they should.

These C unique data types were removed from Java:

struct, **union**, **enum** In C, these keywords are used to create user-defined data types. The Java class gives you the same facilities as structs and unions so that these are redundant. In effect, these technically could have removed from C++; however, the desire for strict backward compatibility to C forced these redundancies on C++. You can obtain the same effect as enums by using constants. These are good examples of how Java stuck to its design philosophy of being a simple language by removing redundancies in C++.

This list contains C unique modifier keywords removed from Java:

auto A data type modifier that gives a variable only scope and lifetime within a block. In Java, just like C++, you can declare data types anywhere in the program (not just at the start of new blocks).

extern A data type modifier that tells the compiler that the definition of the global variable or function is found in another compilation unit. In Java, there are no global variables and all external classes are loaded dynamically by the runtime interpreter.

register A data type modifier that requests the compiler to store a local variable in a register of the CPU rather than main memory. Since Java is portable across different platforms, the number of available registers is not known and therefore this type of optimization is up to each platform-dependent implementation of the interpreter.

signed, unsigned These data type modifiers specify whether an int or char is signed or unsigned. In Java the types are simpler and of fixed size and sign.

volatile A type modifier that tells the compiler a variable may be externally modified unpredictably. This will prevent the compiler from performing certain optimizations. Because of its portability across platforms, there is no equivalent of this in Java.

Pointers

Having written two books on pointers, I of course, feel they are a very important part of C and C++; however, as I stated in the introduction, we are at a point in the software industry where reliability and portability far outweigh any gains in speed or flexibility through the use of pointers. The risks of pointers are well documented. In my first book, *C Pointers and Dynamic Memory Management*, I documented many pitfalls of pointer programming, such as dangling pointers, memory leaks, forgetting the NUL terminator in a string, requesting the wrong number of bytes from malloc( ), array overruns, incorrect operator precedence in malloc( ) calls, and dereferencing a NUL pointer.

Although Java does not explicitly have a pointer variable—because all arrays and Java objects are heap-based—an uninstantiated array or object is similar to a pointer. Much of the requirements of a pointer can be fulfilled with an uninstantiated object. Source 2.16 demonstrates how Java's uninstantiated arrays and objects perform some of the functionality delegated to pointers in C.

SOURCE 2.16

```
class simpleObject {
        int a;
        public simpleObject left, right;

        simpleObject(int inA)
        {
                a=inA;
                left = right = null;
        }

        int getA()
        {
                return a;
        }

        void setA(int inA)
        {
                a = inA;
        }

        public String toString()
        {
                return new String("a: " + a);
        }
}

class PointerEquiv {
        static void swap(Object a, Object b)
        {
                Object tmp = a;
                a = b;
                b = tmp;
        }
```

```
public static void main(String args[])
{
        /* 1) Like pointers, all objects and arrays
            are dynamically allocated. */
        int arr[] = new int[10];
        simpleObject myObj = new simpleObject(5);

        /* 2) An uninitialized array or object is implemented
            via a handle (pointer pointer) that can point
            to another object. */
        int arr2[] = arr;
        simpleObject yourObj = myObj;
        System.out.println("yourObj is " + yourObj.toString());

        /* 3) null is a reserved keyword identical to
            NULL in usage. */
        int arr3[] = null;
        arr = null; /* causes arr and arr2 to point to null */

        /* 4) Arrays and Objects are placed on the stack as
            a handle (not pass by value).  However, there is
            no Pass by Reference in Java at this time. */
        simpleObject otherObject = new simpleObject(20);
        System.out.println("Before swap, myObj is " + myObj.toString() +
                        " otherObject is " + otherObject.toString());
        swap(myObj, otherObject);
        System.out.println("After swap, myObj is " + myObj.toString() +
                        " otherObject is " + otherObject.toString());

        /* 5) There is no explicit free or delete.  Java
            memory is garbage collected. */
        System.gc();  /* force garbage collection to occur NOW. */

        /* 6) Since all Java objects are descendants of a
            single Object class.  An unitialized Object
            can act like a void pointer. */
        Object voidp = otherObject;
        ((simpleObject) voidp).setA(100);
        System.out.println("voidp points to " +
                        ((simpleObject) voidp).toString());
        System.out.println("Just as otherObject now is " +
                        otherObject.toString());
```

```
/* 7) Self-referential structures are possible by
       using non-instantiated objects. */
simpleObject root = new simpleObject(1000);
root.left = new simpleObject(500);
root.right = new simpleObject(2000);

/* 8) There is NO equivalent to function pointers
       in Java. Safety prevailed as a design goal. */
    }
}
```

A run of Source 2.16 produces:

```
C:\hotjava\bin>java PointerEquiv
yourObj is a: 5
Before swap, myObj is a: 5 otherObject is a: 20
After swap, myObj is a: 5 otherObject is a: 20
voidp points to a: 100
Just as otherObject now is a: 100
```

As you see demonstrated in Source 2.16, Java's heap-based arrays and objects give you the following pointer functionality:

1. Dynamic initialization.
2. The ability for multiple uninstantiated objects to point to the same object.
3. The ability to use a check for null as a terminator in self-referential abstract types and as meaning "uninitialized object."
4. Freedom from worrying about explicitly freeing memory by using garbage collection. This allows more rapid yet safe prototyping.
5. Since all objects are inherited from a single root object (we will discuss inheritance in more detail in the next chapter), an uninstantiated variable of class Object acts like a void pointer in that it can be casted to point to any object.
6. Self-referential abstract types like linked lists, trees, and graphs can be implemented.

Java has no way of implementing two current pointer functions:

1. Pass by reference. Although arrays and objects are passed by reference, a local copy is made in the called function. The need for this is

minimized through the use of objects and object-oriented design whereby most methods act on the objects data members and do not need to modify variables in the caller. If it is necessary to modify a caller's variable, the method's return value can be used.

2. Function pointers. Although very useful as callbacks in GUI functions and in parser dispatch tables, some of the benefit of function pointers can be gained through using virtual functions and inheritance (discussed more in the next chapter). As for the function dispatcher, this can be achieved by using an uninstantiated variable of class Object and run-time type identification. All of the techniques mentioned above will be discussed in the next chapter.

Preprocessor

The C preprocessor processes a C source file before it is passed to the compiler. It generally provides two capabilities: text replacement and conditional compilation. It is important to understand that the functions the preprocessor performs have been criticized as not truly being benefits at all, especially with the fact that the majority of a code's lifetime is spent in the maintenance phase.

Bjarne Stroustrup, creator of C++, gives the following warning about preprocessor macros:

> Don't use them if you don't have to. It has been observed that almost every macro demonstrates a flaw in the programming language, in the program, or in the programmer. Because they rearrange the program text before the compiler proper sees it, macros are also a major problem for many programming tools, so when you use macros you should expect inferior service from tools such as debuggers, cross reference tools, and profilers.[2]

The primary problem with a preprocessor can be summed up with the expression, "seeing is not believing." That means that C source code cannot be trusted until all header files have been read (including the headers that the headers include) and all macros expanded. This chore becomes impractical in very large programming projects. Source 2.17 is an example of source code that is not what it appears to be through the misuse of macros.

---

[2]Bjarne Stroustrup, *The C++ Programming Language*, Second Edition (Reading, MA: Addison-Wesley, 1991), p. 138.

SOURCE 2.17

```c
/* obfuscate.c */
#include <stdio.h>
#include "obfuscate.h"

void _funcB(void)
{
    println("What function am I?");
}

void main()
{
    int a=10, b=5;

    if (b < a)
    {
        printf("b is less than a.\n");
    }
    else
    {
        printf("a is less than b.\n");
    }
}

/* obfuscate.h */
#define a b
#define b a
#define else ;
#define PI 6.28

#ifdef configureB
#define _funcA _funcB
#else
#define _funcB _funcA
#endif
```

A run of Source 2.17 produces:

```
b is less than a.
a is less than b.
```

As is evident, Source 1.17 is not only ridiculous but produces ridiculous outputs that don't make sense. Of course, this is an exaggeration; however, I have seen code that comes close to being that bad. Many modern compilers allow you to preprocess your source code and examine the product. Source 2.18 is the tail end (without all the preprocessed macros for the header files) of the preprocessed version of Source 2.17.

SOURCE 2.18

```
void _funcA(void)
{
println("What function am I?");
}
void main()
{
int a=10, b=5;
if (b < a)
{
printf("b is less than a.\n");
}
;
{
printf("a is less than b.\n");
}
}
```

The other capability that the preprocessor gave C programmers was conditional compilation. This is performed using #ifdefs and was useful in debugging. This same functionality can be performed in Java by using a boolean variable as a debug flag. Not having to worry about what the preprocessor will do to your code speeds up the programming process and increases productivity.

Variable Arguments

Variable arguments give C and C++ programs the ability to pass a variable number of arguments to a function. Source 2.19 is a C program that demonstrates the use of variable arguments.

SOURCE 2.19

```c
#include <stdio.h>
#include <stdarg.h>

long sum(int numInts, ...)
{
    long total = 0;
    int i=0;
    va_list args;
    va_start(args, numInts);

    for (i = 0; i < numInts; i++)
        total += va_arg(args, int);

    va_end(args);
    return total;
}

int main(int argc, char *argv[])
{
    long theTot = sum(4, 5, 10, 20, 30);
    printf("The total is %d.\n", theTot);
}
```

A run of the C Source 2.19 produces:

```
The total is 65.
```

Variable arguments are especially useful in creating generic utility functions in C. The flexibility that variable arguments provide in C can be achieved in Java through the use of the Vector class. The Vector class is a Java implementation of a generic dynamic array. A Vector can hold objects of any type and does not have to be homogenous. A Vector turns out to be perfect to achieve all the benefits of variable arguments. Source 2.20 demonstrates the use of the Java Vector class for passing a variable number of arguments to a method.

SOURCE 2.20

```
import java.util.Vector;
class VarArgs {
      static long sum(Vector ints)
      {
            long total = 0;
            for (int i=0; i < ints.size(); i++)
                  total += ((Integer)ints.elementAt(i)).intValue();
            return total;
      }

      public static void main(String args[])
      {
            Vector intVec = new Vector(3);
            intVec.addElement(new Integer(5));
            intVec.addElement(new Integer(10));
            intVec.addElement(new Integer(20));
            intVec.addElement(new Integer(30));
            long theTot = sum(intVec);
            System.out.println("The total is " + theTot);
      }
}
```

A run of Source 2.20 produces:

```
C:\hotjava\bin>java VarArgs
The total is 65
```

Although it takes a few extra lines of code to set up the Vector, the use of the Vector class proves simpler than the variable argument macros. As for length, there are eighteen lines of code in the C program and twenty lines of code in the Java program. Again, Java maintains its simplicity yet does not sacrifice any functionality.

Although this chapter covered C language features removed from Java, I believe we have shown how these features were redundant or how similar functionality is provided via another Java language feature. Now that we have finished covering the similarities and difference between the languages, we will explore how the Java class hierarchy gives you identical or similar functionality as the C standard library.

2.11   THE C STANDARD LIBRARY

Although C is not an object-oriented language, the C standard library is probably the greatest reuse success story to date. The C standard library has provided a wealth of useful functions used in every C program for nearly twenty years. The library consists of fifteen header files that roughly divide the library into functional parts as well as declare all the functions accessible to the C programmer. We will discuss each header file and some of the more commonly used functions, then follow up with how that functionality is achieved in the Java Standard Library. The Java Standard Library (also known as the Java environment or Java class hierarchy) is demonstrated in great detail in Chapter 4. References to Chapter 4 for specific code examples will be made instead of duplicating the code here.

<assert.h>

The purpose of this header is solely to implement the assert macro. The assert macro allows a diagnostic predicate (an expression that evaluates to true or false) to be put in your code. The assert macro is used like this:

```
assert( i < 10);
```

If the assert expression evaluates to false, a text line is printed ("Assertion failed: expression, file xyz, line nnn") and the program terminates abnormally. The utility of assert expressions is for testing and debugging of source code. You can turn off assertions by defining the macro NDEBUG.

Since Java is not preprocessed there is no direct correlation for the assert macro. It is also debatable whether it is needed at all in an object-oriented language that supports encapsulation and exception handling. There is no reason to sprinkle your code with assertions about the values of variables because data members of properly implemented objects are always in a stable state.

<ctype.h>

The purpose of this header is to define a set of macros that perform tests on a character and translation of a character (i.e., toupper(c)). This header is very common in any program that parses or manipulates text. The three most common macros in the set are isalpha(c), isdigit(c), and isspace(c). It is important to remember that this header only works on the ascii character set that is normally an 8-bit representation of a character. The impact of this is that these macros cannot be used for international characters that are part of the UNICODE standard.

The Java Character class (see section 4.2, Primitive Types as Classes) provides some of the same functionality as the macros in ctype.h for the UNICODE character set. The Character class has methods for isDigit(c), isSpace(c), toLowerCase(c) and others.

<errno.h>

The purpose of this header is to provide macros for the reporting of errors. Unfortunately, the only reliable use of the errno macro is a test where equality to zero means no error and equality to any non-zero value means error. Beyond that, the actual error codes for different functions varies widely by implementation. The Java exception model (see section 4.2, Exceptions) is far superior for both the reporting and handling of errors. In fact, the Java language has taken a bold step forward in error handling by forcing a function that throws an exception to add a throws clause to the function declaration like this:

```
public int read() throws IOException
{
    . . .
}
```

<float.h>

The purpose of this header is to define properties of floats, doubles, and long so that your programs can avoid overflow, underflow, and significance loss during floating point arithmetic. Java's implementation of float and double is fixed and in conformance with the IEEE 754 standard for floating-point arithmetic.

<limits.h>

This header is used to define macros for the ranges of numeric types in C. This is unnecessary in Java since all types are of fixed, platform-independent sizes.

<locale.h>

This header declares two functions and one type, and defines several macros that store information on properties related to a local culture (i.e., monetary formatting, time, and numeric formatting). The contents of the type lconv will also affect other library functions with respect to scanning input and formatting output. There is currently no direct equivalent to this in Java; however, Java does have standard system properties (see section 4.2, System Information) where locale properties could be stored.

<math.h>

This header serves the purpose of providing common mathematical functions to C programmers like sin( ), exp( ) and sqrt( ). The Java Math class (see section 4.2, Math Functions) serves the same purpose and almost all of the functions are identical.

<setjmp.h>

The purpose of this header is to define a macro setjmp, a type jmp_buf, and a function longjmp( ) that implement a nonlocal goto (a goto outside of the current function). Since the use of goto in programming is widely recognized as a poor practice, the only acceptable use for the setjmp/longjmp combination was for implementing a crude form of exceptions. The Java exception facilities are far superior (see section 4.2, Exceptions).

<signal.h>

The purpose of this header is to define a function, type, and macros for the handling and raising of signals. A signal is an extraordinary event (also known as an exception) that can occur because of erroneous actions in your program (i.e., divide by zero) or from the operating system (a termination signal from a control-c typed at the console). The signals common to all implementations are:

SIGABRT (signal ABORT) Abnormal termination

SIGFPE (signal Floating Point Exception) An erroneous arithmetic operation

SIGILL (signal Illegal) An illegal instruction

SIGINT (signal Interrupt) Receipt of an interactive attention signal

SIGSEGV (signal Segmentation Violation) An invalid access to memory

SIGTERM (signal Terminate) A termination request sent to the program

The functionality of signal.h is subsumed by the Java Exception classes. Java exceptions can be thrown by Java code and the Java run-time.

<stdarg.h>

The purpose of this header is to declare a type and define three macros that process a variable number of arguments passed into a function. The three macros defined are va_start( ), va_arg( ), and va_end( ). As discussed in section 2.10, although Java does not currently support variable arguments, it is easy to replicate this functionality by using the Vector class (see section 3.2, Classes).

<stddef.h>

The purpose of this header is to define macro definitions that do not fit into the specific areas covered by floats.h, limits.h, and stdarg.h. Synonyms for the primitive types are defined like ptrdiff_t, size_t, and wchar_t. Since all Java types are platform-independent fixed sizes this header is unnecessary in Java.

<stdio.h>

The purpose of this header is to define a large assortment of functions that perform input and output. This is a large and very well known (and very popular) portion of the standard library. C programmers will be happy to know that Java supports the full range of I/O provided in the stdio.h. The Java io package (see section 4.2, io Package) has a wealth of classes that implement reading and writing to streams and files. Java also has System.in and System.out, which are nearly identical to stdin and stdout.

<stdlib.h>

This header serves a variety of purposes for functions and macros that did not fit into other headers in the standard library. Dr. Plauger, in his classic book *The Standard C Library*,[3] organizes the functions of this header into six groups:

---

[3]P.J. Plauger, *The Standard C Library* (Englewood Cliffs, N. J.: Prentice Hall, 1992).

- Integer Math (abs, div, labs, and ldiv). Some of these functions (the abs( ) functions) are implemented in the Java Math class (see section 4.2, Math Functions).
- Algorithms (bsearch, qsort, rand and srand). The rand functions are implemented in the Java's Random class (see section 4.2, Miscellaneous Utilities). The search and sort algorithms are not currently part of the Java class hierarchy.
- Text Conversions (atof, atoi, atol, strtod, strtol, and strtoul). These conversions from strings to primitive types are implemented in the Java type wrappers (i.e., Integer, Float, . . . see section 4.2, Primitive Types of Classes).
- Multibyte Conversions (mblen, mbstowcs, mbtowc, wcstombs, and wctomb). This type of conversions is not necessary in Java due to its support of the UNICODE character set.
- Storage Allocation (calloc, free, malloc and realloc). Dynamic allocation is performed in Java with the new operator. Explicit deallocation (like free( )) is not necessary due to Java's runtime automatically reclaiming unused allocated memory via garbage collection.
- Environmental Interactions (abort, atexit, exit, getenv, and system). This functionality is provided by the Java System class (see section 4.2, System Information).

<string.h>

The purpose of this header is to provide a set of functions to manipulate text as arrays of characters. Commonly used functions in this header are: strcpy( ), strcmp( ), strstr( ), and strtok( ). The weakness of all these functions is their use of pointers (which also makes them efficient) and their reliance on the NUL-terminator. If an array overrun has stomped on memory and removed the NUL-terminator, the behavior of these routines is undefined. Java supports all the functionality supported by this header with the String and StringBuffer classes (see section 4.2, Strings).

<time.h>

The purpose of this header is to define structures, macros, and functions for representation and manipulation of times and dates. C programmers will be very satisfied with the Java Date class (see section 4.2, Miscellaneous Utilities), which provides all the functionality of this header and is structured almost identically like the tm struct.

Figure 2.3 summarizes the above discussion and compares the C Standard Library to the Java Standard Library.

C header	Java package or class
assert.h	Not Applicable
ctype.h	Character class (3.2.1.1)
errno.h	Exception class (3.2.1.8)
float.h	inherent in language definition
limits.h	inherent in language definition
locale.h	System Properties (3.2.1.4)
math.h	Math class (3.2.1.5)
setjmp.h	Exception class (3.2.1.8)
signal.h	Exception class (3.2.1.8)
stdarg.h	Vector class (3.2.2.1)
stddef.h	inherent in language definition
stdio.h	io Package (3.2.3)
stdlib.h	Math class (3.2.1.5)
	Random class (3.2.2.2)
	type wrapper classes (3.2.1.1)
	System class (3.2.1.4)
string.h	String class (3.2.1.3)
	StringBuffer class
time.h	Date class (3.2.2.2)

FIGURE 2.3   Correlation of the C Standard Library to the Java Standard Library.

CHAPTER 3

Comparing Java
to C++

Design. As I write a program, I should use a language that minimizes the distance between the problem-solving strategies that I have in my head and the program text I eventually write on paper.

—Jon Bentley, *Programming Pearls*

OBJECTIVE

This chapter will compare and contrast the Java language to C++. All major elements of C++ will be examined and all differences will be highlighted. This chapter will also serve as a good foundation on object-oriented programming for C programmers.

The C++ programming language was designed and developed by Bjarne Stroustrup in the Computer Science Research Center at AT&T Bell Labs in Murray Hill, New Jersey. Originally called C with Classes, C++ is a superset of the C language that adds object-oriented facilities. C++ has maintained backward compatibility with C. This backward compatibility has led to a few redundancies and some of the dangers of C, such as array overruns. In the object-oriented direction, C++ has added support for some features that make code extremely difficult to follow and maintain, such as operator overloading, multiple inheritance, and templates. This chapter will introduce C programmers to object-oriented programming as well as compare and contrast all of the major features of C++ to Java.

3.1   OBJECT-ORIENTED PROGRAMMING

There is a very basic idea behind object-oriented programming: Make the computer language resemble the way things work in the real world. Real-world objects like people, places, and things are what our programs are about. If your program tracks office supplies, then your computer language should talk about office supplies. Most real-world objects are defined in terms of characteristics (or attributes) that describe the object and behaviors (or actions) the object can perform. The object-oriented technique that allows us to model real-world objects in our programs is called *encapsulation*.

The real-world objects like people, animals, and motorcycles are often understood by grouping them in a set of objects that all share common characteristics and behaviors. Humans are part of the group called mammals because we share characteristics and behaviors with other mammals. Expressed another way, a human *is a* mammal. The object-oriented technique that allows us to organize objects hierarchically is called *inheritance* and is modeled after biological inheritance.

The last major contribution of object-oriented programming is its mimicking of how real-world objects describe the actions they perform. Real-world objects often perform the same type of action yet perform it in their own slightly different way. A boy runs, a dog runs, a stream runs, and a car runs. All those real-world objects use the verb "run" to describe one of their actions. The object-oriented technique that allows us to use one name for many different implementations of an action is called *polymorphism*. Now that we have an intuitive understanding of the three characteristic traits of all object-oriented languages (encapsulation, inheritance, and polymorphism), we will examine each in more technical detail.

Encapsulation

Encapsulation is a technique that extends the concept of abstraction from a strictly data phenomena to both data and functions. If you think of the data abstraction used in C, the structure, then it is easy to grasp the idea that a class encompasses what a structure did and then extends the concept to include the binding of functions into the single entity. See Source 3.1 for a comparison of a C structure to a C++ class. A class binds both data and functions into a single entity, creating a brand new abstraction called an object.

SOURCE 3.1

```
// encapsulate.cpp

// a C structure is only an abstraction of attributes
struct car {
    char make[60];
    char model[60];
    int top_speed;
    float price;
};

// a C++ class is an abstraction of both attributes and actions
class automobile {
    private:
            // some attributes
            char make[60];
            char model[60];
            int top_speed;
            float price;

    public:
            // some actions
            int run()
            {
                    int travelling_speed=0;

                    // do something

                    return travelling_speed;
            }

            void breakDown()
            {
                    // fix it
            }
};

int main(int argc, char **argv)
{
    struct car data_abstraction;

    automobile a_real_world_object;
```

```
                return 0;
        }
```

There is a very definite relationship between a C structure and a C++ class. In fact, in C++ the structure concept has been expanded to include member functions. This was elegantly stated in the *Annotated C++ Reference Manual*:

> Thus the C++ class concept can be seen as a generalization of the C notion of a structure or—looking at it the other way—the C concept of a structure is a simple variant of the C++ class concept. In particular, C structures do not support member functions of any kind. Having a C struct be a simple variant of a C++ class has important implications for cooperation between C and C++ programs.[1]

After examining Source 3.1 you may have noticed that a Java class is slightly different from a C++ class. Source 3.2 is an example of a Java class.

SOURCE 3.2

```java
import java.lang.Math;
import java.io.DataInputStream;

class loan {
        private float principal = 0;
        private float interestRate = 0;
        private int numYears = 0;

        loan(float thePrincipal, float theInterest,
                int theYearsToRepay)
        {
                principal = thePrincipal;
                interestRate = theInterest;
                numYears = theYearsToRepay;
        }
```

---

[1] Margaret A. Ellis and Bjarne Stroustrup, *The Annotated C++ Reference Manual* (Reading, MA: Addison-Wesley Publishing Company, 1990), p. 165.

```java
        // accessor methods
        float getPrincipal()
        {
                return principal;
        }

        float getInterestRate()
        {
                return interestRate;
        }

        int getYears()
        {
                return numYears;
        }

        double calculatePayment()
        {
                // assuming monthly payments
                double interest = interestRate/100;
                double payment = (interest * principal/12) /
                                (1 - Math.pow(interest/12 + 1,
                                        -12*numYears));
                return payment;
        }
}

class tstLoan {
        public static void main(String args[])
        {
                Float principal = new Float(0);
                Float interest = new Float(0);
                int theYears = 0;
                try {
                        DataInputStream dis = new DataInputStream(System.in);
                        System.out.print("Enter Principal of Loan: ");
                        System.out.flush();
                        String principalStr = dis.readLine();
                        principal = Float.valueOf(principalStr);
                        System.out.print("Enter annual Interest rate percentage (i.e., 9.5): ");
                        System.out.flush();
                        String interestStr = dis.readLine();
```

```
            interest = Float.valueOf(interestStr);
            System.out.print("Enter number of years of Loan: ");
            System.out.flush();
            String yearsStr = dis.readLine();
            theYears = Integer.parseInt(yearsStr);
    } catch (java.io.IOException e)
      {
            System.out.println("IO error. Rerun program.");
            System.exit(1);
      }

    loan theLoan = new loan(principal.floatValue(),
                            interest.floatValue(),
                            theYears);

    double monthlyPayment = theLoan.calculatePayment();
    System.out.println("Your monthly payment is : " +
                            monthlyPayment);

    }
}
```

A run of Source 3.2 produces:

```
C:\java\bin>java tstLoan
Enter Principal of Loan: 150000
Enter annual Interest rate percentage (i.e., 9.5): 7
Enter number of years of Loan: 30
Your monthly payment is : 997.954
```

You will notice in Source 3.2 that all Java variables and methods must be separately type-modified with a public, private, or protected keyword. We will go into more detail on access modifiers in the next section.

The last general concept to understand about an object is that a class is not an object. A class is the definition (or description) of what makes up an object. A class describes the encapsulation. The actual object comes into existence when the class is instantiated into an actual implementation of the class in memory. Many objects can be instantiated from a single class description. So, it is easy to see how encapsulation of data and functions together gives us the ability to create new data types that very closely resemble the characteristics and behaviors of real-world objects. An object's characteristics and behaviors may be very similar to other objects that are related closely to it. An example of this is how your characteristics (hair color, eye color, body type, facial features) may be very similar to those of your father or mother. In the real world, we would say that you inherited some of your characteristics and behaviors from your parents. The real-world concept of inheritance has been included in object-oriented programming.

Inheritance

Inheritance is the ability for a class, called a derived class or subclass, to acquire the characteristics and behaviors of another class, called a base class or superclass. The most common method of using inheritance is to create class hierarchies that move from the most general concept at the root of the tree to the most specific representation of that generic concept at the leaves of the tree. Figure 3.1 is an example of a class hierarchy.

Figure 3.1 demonstrates a class hierarchy that describes different modes of transportation. It is very important to understand the relationship between classes in the class hierarchy. Starting from the "leaves" of the tree, each subclass has an "is a" relationship to its parent or superclass. A Yamaha is a motorcycle. A motorcycle is a private transport. A private transport is a form of transportation. We will examine the "is a" relationship again in section 3.3. Source 3.3 demonstrates inheritance using cartesian coordinates.

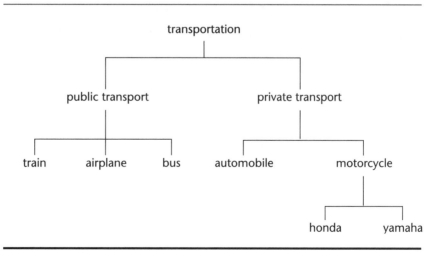

FIGURE 3.1   A class hierarchy.

SOURCE 3.3

```
class Coordinate {
      protected int x,y;

      Coordinate(int inX, int inY)
      {
            x = inX; y = inY;
      }

      int getX()
      {
            return x;
      }

      int getY()
      {
            return y;
      }
}

class Coordinate3d extends Coordinate {
      protected int z;

      Coordinate3d(int inX, int inY, int inZ)
      {
            super(inX, inY);
            z = inZ;
      }

      int getZ()
      {
            return z;
      }
}

class coordTst {
      public static void main(String args[])
      {
            Coordinate3d myCoord = new Coordinate3d(10,20,30);
            System.out.println("x: " + myCoord.getX());
            System.out.println("y: " + myCoord.getY());
            System.out.println("z: " + myCoord.getZ());
      }
}
```

A run of Source 3.3 produces:

```
C:\java\bin>java coordTst
x: 10
y: 20
z: 30
```

There are three key points to understand about Source 3.3:

1. Coordinate is the superclass and Coordinate3d is the subclass.
2. Java uses the keyword "extends" to signify that the subclass is inheriting the capabilities and characteristics of the superclass. The keyword "extends" is significant in that it clearly denotes the purpose of inheritance: code reuse. The concept of reusing an existing class but "extending" its characteristics or behavior to your specific situation is the reason why you should effectively use inheritance in your programming. Building a class hierarchy that is designed with reuse in mind is no trivial task; however, once accomplished it will pay for itself many times over.
3. The Coordinate3d class has access to the Coordinate methods just as if they were part of Coordinate3d. This is demonstrated by the call to getX( ) and getY( ) from the variable myCoord.

Polymorphism

Polymorphism, the last major tenet of object-oriented programming, is a fancy word that stands for "many forms." In C++ and Java it is a technique that implements a "single interface" for "many implementations." Just as with the other object-oriented concepts, the whole idea of polymorphism is based on a very common real-world phenomena. In real-world languages, it is very common to use a single action verb with many different nouns. For example,

The Army sergeant barked the orders.
The dog barked at the passing cars.

It is also common to combine a single action verb with different adverbs or prepositional phrases that modify how the action is performed.

The boy cried out in pain.
The bride cried for joy.
The baby cried softly.

Both Java and C++ have implemented both types of this polymorphic description of actions. Of course, in programming, the action verbs are function calls or methods. Source 3.4 demonstrates one form of poly-morphism.

SOURCE 3.4

```
class sillyMath {
        int a;

        sillyMath(int inA)
        {
                a = inA;
        }

        int add(int b)
        {
                return a + b;
        }

        float add(float b)
        {
                return ((float)a + b);
        }

        double add(double b)
        {
                return ((double)a + b);
        }
}

class polyTst {
        public static void main(String args[])
        {
                sillyMath num = new sillyMath(10);
                int c=10;
                float d = (float) 30.2;
                double e = 459998.8;

                System.out.println("adding an int  : " + num.add(c));
                System.out.println("adding a float : " + num.add(d));
                System.out.println("adding a double: " + num.add(e));
        }
}
```

A run of Source 3.4 produces:

```
C:\java\bin>java polyTst
adding an int   : 20
adding a float : 40.2
adding a double: 460009
```

Source 3.4 implements polymorphism in a single class by allowing one method name, add( ), to be used for multiple implementations of the add operation. The way the compiler distinguishes between add functions is based on the type of the arguments. The return type is not considered and cannot be used to differentiate between two methods with the same name. Additionally, two methods with the same name must have arguments that vary in either type or number. In section 3.3, Inheritance, we will demonstrate the second form of polymorphism in Java: virtual functions.

This completes your introduction to the key principles of object-oriented programming. We will now move on to a detailed comparison of the major elements of C++ with Java.

3.2   CLASSES

The Java class is identical to the C++ class in general form. Both Java and C++ classes have data members, methods, and access specifiers. We will examine each of these "class basics" in the following paragraphs. The most prominent differences between Java classes and C++ classes are the omission of the scope resolution operator from Java and the C++ ability to list multiple variables under a single C++ access specifier. Figure 3.2 shows a C++ class and Java class side by side.

As is very clear from Figure 3.2, C++ programmers will feel very comfortable with the fact that Java classes are nearly identical to C++ classes. The object-oriented community is in agreement that the concept of a class is the central tenet of object-oriented programming. As *The C++ Annotated Reference Manual* states, "'Class' is the key concept of C++."[2] The class will be central to every Java program you create. For C++ programmers this is the central reason why Java code is

---

[2]Margaret A. Ellis and Bjarne Stroustrup, *The Annotated C++ Reference Manual*, p. 165.

C++ Class	Java Class

```
class Entity{                          class Entity{
  protected:                             protected String name;
    char*name;                           protected int x;
    int x,y;                             protected int y;
  public:                                public Entity()
    Entity();                            {
    ~Entity();                             x=y=0;
    void setName(char*inName);             name=null;
    void setXY(int inX,int inY);         }
};

Entity::Entity()                         public void finalize()
{                                        {
    x=y=0;                                 //code here
    name=NULL;                           }
}

Entity::~Entity()                        public void setName(String inName)
{                                        {
    //code here                            //code here
}                                        }

void Entity::setName(char*inName)        public void setXY(int inX,int inY)
{                                        {
    //code here                            //code here
}                                        }
void Entity::setXY(int inX,int inY)    }
{
    //code here
}
```

FIGURE 3.2   Comparing a C++ class to a Java class.

immediately recognizable and "looks like C++." Let's now compare the basic constructs of a Java and C++ class as displayed in Figure 3.2. The basic constructs are the class declaration, class data members, access specifiers, and class methods.

Class Definition

Both the C++ and Java versions in Source 3.2 define the Entity class. A class definition is the template that describes all of the data members or instance variables and methods of an object. You can instantiate many objects from one class definition. Before we dissect the class into its component parts, we need to clearly understand the distinction between definition and declaration. As you will see, there is some confusion relating to class declaration versus class definition. Luckily, Java has simplified the problem for us.

Declaration versus Definition

In ANSI C, the distinction between a declaration and a definition was the allocation of storage space. As stated by Kernighan and Ritchie, "Declarations specify the interpretation given to each identifier; they do not necessarily reserve storage associated with the identifier. Declarations that reserve storage are called definitions."[3] In other words, if I use a variable that was defined in another C source file, I would declare it like this:

```
extern int NumberOfParts;    /* a variable declaration */
```

The extern keyword specifically states to the linker that the storage space for this variable is reserved elsewhere; however, the name "NumberOfParts" is declared here so the compiler can reserve the name in this namespace and know the type of the variable to perform necessary type checking if I pass it into a function or use the variable in an expression. For primitive types and functions, the difference between a declaration and a definition is very clear. It has stayed consistent with ANSI C. The vagueness and confusion come in when we look at classes.

In *The Annotated C++ Reference Manual* (ARM), Dr. Bjarne Stroustrup kept the original C meanings for declarations and definitions but did not necessarily agree with them for class declarations (he would have preferred to call them class definitions). This is exemplified by the comment in the ARM: "Except for historical reasons, a class declaration would have been called a class definition."[4] Since a definition is

---

[3]Brian W. Kernighan and Dennis M. Ritchie, *The C Programming Language*, p. 210.

[4]Margaret A. Ellis and Bjarne Stroustrup, *The Annotated C++ Reference Manual*, p. 164.

also a declaration, the question becomes: When is a class defined? When you specify the data and function members of a class, you are not reserving memory as you do when you instantiate an object of that class. On the other hand, you are not reserving storage space when you "define" a function. A function is defined when you specify the statements within the function block. Therefore, using a function definition as a precedent, you could argue (as Dr. Stroustrup did), that a class is defined when you specify all the members in the member list within the class block ({ }).

In the proposed C++ international standard, the function precedent for class definition was adopted.

> A class definition introduces the class name into the scope where it is defined and hides any class, object, function, or other declaration of that name in an enclosing scope. ...A declaration consisting solely of class-key identifier is either a redeclaration of the name in the current scope or a forward declaration of the identifier as a class name. It introduces the class name into the current scope. [5]

Using the above definitions, a class is defined when we describe its data members and methods within its enclosing braces. This means that:

```
class Entity;     // a class declaration
```

and

```
class Entity {    // a class definition
    private:
        // data members
    public:
    // methods
};
```

Java has simplified matters by only having class and variable definitions. There are no sole declarations in Java. It is understood that class definitions and variable definitions are also class declarations

---

[5]Working Paper for Draft Proposed International Standard for Information Systems—Programming Language C++, Doc No: X3J16/95-0087, 28 April 1995, p. 9-2.

and variable declarations. To conclude this discussion, in Java, all classes, data members, and variables within methods are defined. And that definition is both the act of reserving a name in the enclosing scope and reserving storage space for primitive data types. For user-defined data types, definition is the announcement to the compiler of all the data members and methods in the class.

Now we are ready to discuss the individual components of a class: data members, access specifiers, and methods.

Data Members

Just as in C++, a Java class can have both primitive data types and other classes as data members. The data members of a class are identical to the data members of a C structure except in how class data members can be hidden and protected. Data hiding is a very important principle of object-oriented programming. The best way to think of this is that an object is composed of a private internal state (composed of its private data members) and a public set of operations it can perform. Let's examine how we hide and protect the data members using the access specifier keywords.

Access Specifiers

Access specifiers are similar in meaning for both C++ and Java. The *private* specifier denotes a variable or method as being private to the class and may not be accessed outside the class. The only way to gain access to the variable or method is by calling one of the public class methods. The *protected* specifier denotes a variable or method as being public to subclasses of this class but private to all other classes outside the current package. This allows derived classes the ability to directly access protected variables of its parent. This is a good idea as it makes extending classes easier. The concept of a Java package has changed the meaning of the protected access specifier. All classes within the same package have access to protected variables regardless of whether they are subclasses. To achieve the original C++ meaning inside a package you must use "private protected." Packages are discussed in detail in Section 5.1. The *public* specifier denotes a variable or method as being directly accessible from all other classes. Public data members of a class are accessed just like structure variables; however, public data members violate the principle of data hiding and are not recommended for object-oriented programming. Remember that the "data is king" and we must protect it.

Methods

The methods (or member functions) are the actions that a class can perform. There are some special class methods called constructors and destructors that we will discuss later. The regular class methods (the methods setName( ) and setXY( ) in Figure 3.2) are identical in Java and C++, except for the omission of the scope resolution operator (::) in Java. In C++ the scope resolution operator is most often used to separate the function definitions from the function declarations. In C++ it is common to put the class declarations in the header file and the function definitions in the source file. In Java, all methods in a Java class must be declared within the class; therefore, the scope resolution operator is unnecessary. It is important to stress the fact that Java does not inline functions. In C++, including the function definition in the class automatically inlines the function. An "inline" function is a technique that inserts the function definition in place of every function call in your program. Inlining functions increases the speed of your program by eliminating the overhead of the function call (this overhead involves pushing and popping data from the application stack). Since there are also no header files in Java, this makes the scope resolution operator doubly unnecessary. Now let's examine a complete example of a Java class. Source 3.5 demonstrates a line segment class.

SOURCE 3.5

```
import java.lang.Math;
import java.awt.Point;

class lineSegment {
        protected Point pts[];

        // constructor
        lineSegment()
        {
                pts = null;
        }

        // overloaded constructor
        lineSegment(int x1, int y1, int x2, int y2)
        {
                pts = new Point[2];
                pts[0] = new Point(x1,y1);
```

```
                pts[1] = new Point(x2,y2);
        }

        // accessor method
        Point getPoint(boolean first)
        {
                return (first ? pts[0] : pts[1]);
        }

        // mutator method
        void setPoint(boolean first, int inX, int inY)
        {
                if (first)
                {
                        pts[0].x = inX;
                        pts[0].y = inY;
                }
                else
                {
                        pts[1].x = inX;
                        pts[1].y = inY;
                }
        }

        // calculate slope
        double calculateSlope()
        {
                return ( (pts[0].y - pts[1].y) /
                        (pts[0].x - pts[1].x) );
        }

        // calculate the length of the line segment
        double length()
        {
                int a = Math.abs(pts[0].x - pts[1].x);
                int b = Math.abs(pts[0].y - pts[1].y);
                double c = Math.sqrt( (a*a) + (b*b) );
                return c;
        }
}

class lineTst {
```

```
public static void main(String args[])
{
        lineSegment aSegment = new lineSegment(0,0,4,4);
        Point one = aSegment.getPoint(true);
        Point two = aSegment.getPoint(false);
        double segSlope = aSegment.calculateSlope();
        double segLength = aSegment.length();
        System.out.println("Slope of segment is  :" + segSlope);
        System.out.println("Length of segment is :" + segLength);

}
}
```

A run of Source 3.5 produces:

```
C:\java\bin>java lineTst
Slope of segment is  :1
Length of segment is :5.65685
```

Source 3.5 demonstrates four basic topics about Java classes: overloading constructors, accessor and mutator methods, the new operator and object creation, and how to call class methods. Let's discuss each topic in detail.

Overloading Constructors

A constructor is a special class method that is run automatically when an object is instantiated. The purpose of a constructor is to insure that an object is always properly initialized before the object is used in any way. A very common error in C and C++ is to use a pointer variable before it is properly initialized, causing either an immediate or delayed program crash. The constructor is to be used to insure that an object is ready for use once it is instantiated. The format of a constructor (as demonstrated by the lineSegment( ) methods in Source 3.5) is the class name and optional function arguments. There is no return type from a constructor.

We already discussed how function overloading is a form of polymorphism. In the same manner a constructor can be overloaded to provide different ways to construct an object. Source 3.5 demonstrates the overloading of constructors with two ways to create a lineSegment object.

Accessors and Mutators

Although not required, there are two categories of class methods that aid data hiding and protection in object-oriented programming. These categories are accessor methods and mutator methods. Accessor methods are methods that retrieve the current value of class data members. Mutator methods are methods that allow internal state variables to be modified. You should be cautious when providing mutator methods and only provide them if there is a valid requirement for an external class to know about and be able to influence the internal state of the object. Most objects should not need mutator functions.

The New Operator and Object Creation

In C++ there are generally three different ways to create an object: define a global object that is created at the program startup, define an object at the beginning of a function that is created on the application stack, and define a pointer to the object and allocate the object in the free store (known as the heap in C). Java simplifies object creation by providing only one method to create all objects: on the heap via the new operator. The new operator is very similar but not identical to the C++ new operator. The Java new operator must include an objects constructor call, whereby a C++ new can just have the class name (which defaults to calling the no argument constructor). Source 3.5 demonstrates the creation of a lineSegment object using the new operator.

Calling Class Methods

Calling a class method in Java is identical to the way C++ methods are accessed from an instantiated object. Java uses the "dot operator" (.) in conjunction with the object name to specify which class method is to be called. In Source 3.5 the class method getPoint( ) is invoked in this fashion:

```
Point one = aSegment.getPoint(true);
```

In C++ there is a different way to access class methods from a class pointer which uses the "arrow operator" (->). This method does not exist in Java since Java consciously did not include pointers in the language.

Now we will discuss several other characteristics of classes to include: class assignment, the this variable, static members and methods, and run time type information.

Class Assignment

In C++ and Java, the definition of a class is the defining of a new data type that has many of the same properties as the primitive data types. We will learn that Java differs from C++ in not adding features to the language that make classes have the ability to exactly mimic the primitive data types. We will explain this later, when we talk about how Java consciously left out operator overloading. For now, let's examine one commonality between user-defined types and primitive types: class assignment.

In C++ and Java you may assign classes of the same type to one another. Source 3.6 demonstrates class assignment in Java.

SOURCE 3.6

```
class simpleObject {
        private int a;

        simpleObject(int inA)
        {
                a = inA;
        }

        int getA()
        {
                return a;
        }
}

class classAssign {
        public static void main(String args[])
        {
                simpleObject myObject = new simpleObject(10);
                System.out.println("myObject a: " + myObject.getA());
                simpleObject yourObject = new simpleObject(20);
                System.out.println("yourObject a: " + yourObject.getA());

                yourObject = myObject; // assignment
                System.out.println("yourObject a: " + yourObject.getA());
        }
}
```

A run of Source 3.6 produces:

```
C:\java\bin>java classAssign
myObject a: 10
yourObject a: 20
yourObject a: 10
```

Although Source 3.6 would be nearly identical in C++ and Java, the languages arrive at the same solution via different paths. In C++, a copy constructor would be called to copy the values of myObject into yourObject. In Java, there are no copy constructors because all objects are accessed via handles (pointer pointers). This means that the above assignment of one object to another is actually a copying of the pointer pointer to myObject into the pointer pointer to yourObject. The effect of this pointer copying is that you have two handles to Objects pointing at the same instantiation of an object.

Now let's move on to another Java class feature that is identical in both Java and C++: the this variable.

The This Variable

In Java and C++, the this variable is used in exactly the same manner. The this variable represents the currently executing object. In C++, the this variable is a pointer to the current object. In Java it is a non-instantiated object (or reference or handle) to the current object. No matter what the semantics, the this variable is very useful in allowing you to pass the current object to another object's constructor or method. Source 3.7 demonstrates multiple uses of the this variable. Although Source 3.7 is longer than normal examples, it is a much more useful example that you can reuse in your own coding efforts.

SOURCE 3.7

```java
// using the this reference to share info between classes
import java.io.DataInputStream;
import java.lang.Thread;
import java.lang.ThreadGroup;
import java.io.IOException;
import java.awt.Frame;
import java.awt.Panel;
import java.awt.TextField;
```

```
import java.awt.Event;
import java.awt.Button;

class getFilename extends Frame {
        private TextField fileEntry;
        private mainLoop theDriver;
        private Thread theCaller;

        getFilename(mainLoop aDriver, Thread aCaller)
        {
                super("Enter File Name");
                theDriver = aDriver;
                theCaller = aCaller;

                fileEntry = new TextField(40);
                Panel p = new Panel();
                p.add(new Button("OK"));
                p.add(new Button("Cancel"));
                add("Center",fileEntry);
                add("South", p);
                move(120,100);
                pack();
                show();

                // suspend the caller
                aCaller.suspend();
        }

        public boolean handleEvent(Event evt)
        {
                switch (evt.id) {
                        case (Event.ACTION_EVENT) :
                                if ("Cancel".equals(evt.arg))
                                {
                                        dispose();
                                        theCaller.resume();
                                        return true;
                                }
                                else if ("OK".equals(evt.arg))
                                {
                                        theDriver.setFile(new String(fileEntry.getText()));
                                        dispose();
```

```
                                               theCaller.resume();
                                               return true;
                                       }
                                  break;
                        default:
                             return false;
                }
            return true;
        }
}

class configMode extends Thread {
        private mainLoop theDriver;
        private String configFile;

        configMode(mainLoop aDriver)
        {
                theDriver = aDriver;
        }

        public void run()
        {
                // set the mode
                theDriver.setMode(mainLoop.CONFIG_MODE);

                // process one config file
                getFilename configFile = new getFilename(theDriver, this);
        }
}

class processMode extends Thread {
        private mainLoop theDriver;
        private boolean done;

        processMode(mainLoop aDriver)
        {
                theDriver = aDriver;
                done = false;
        }

        public void run()
        {
```

```
                    while (!done)
                    {
                            if (theDriver.getMode() == mainLoop.PROCESS_MODE)
                            {
                                    System.out.println("In process mode.");
                                    // get a file to process
                                    getFilename aFile = new getFilename(theDriver, this);

                                    if (theDriver.getFile() != null &&
                                        (theDriver.getFile()).equals("Done"))
                                    {
                                            done = true;
                                            theDriver.setMode(mainLoop.QUIT_MODE);
                                    }
                                    else
                                    {
                                        try {
                                            sleep(1000); // use file in Driver
                                        } catch (Exception e) { }
                                    }
                            }
                            else
                            {
                                try {
                                    // sleep a second
                                    sleep(1000);
                                } catch (Exception e) { }
                            }
                    }
            }
}

class mainLoop {
        public static final int CONFIG_MODE = 0;
        public static final int PROCESS_MODE = 1;
        public static final int QUIT_MODE = 2;
        private String currentFile;
        private int Mode;
        private boolean quitting_time;

        mainLoop()
        {
```

```
Mode = -1;
quitting_time = false;

// kick off Threads
configMode cMode = new configMode(this);
cMode.start();
processMode pMode = new processMode(this);
pMode.start();

// sleep a little
try {
        Thread.sleep(5000);
    } catch (Exception e) { }

while (!quitting_time)
{
        switch (Mode) {
                case CONFIG_MODE:
                        System.out.println("Main in CONFIG MODE");
                        System.out.println("Current File : " +
                                                this.getFile());

                        // do something with config file
                        if (this.getFile() != null)
                            this.setMode(PROCESS_MODE);
                        break;
                case PROCESS_MODE:
                        System.out.println("Main in PROCESS MODE");
                        System.out.println("Current File : " +
                                                this.getFile());

                        // do something with Current File

                        break;
                case QUIT_MODE:
                        System.out.println("Main in QUIT_MODE");
                        quitting_time = true;
                        continue;
        }

        // sleep a little
        try {
```

```
                              Thread.sleep(5000);
                } catch (Exception e) { }
            }
        }

        void setFile(String fname)
        {
            currentFile = new String(fname);
        }

        String getFile()
        {
            return currentFile;
        }

        void setMode(int inMode)
        {
            Mode = inMode;
        }

        int getMode()
        {
            return Mode;
        }
}

class tstThis {
    public static void main(String args[])
    {
        new mainLoop();
        System.exit(0);
    }
}
```

A run of Source 3.7 produces:

```
C:\java\bin>java tstThis
Main in CONFIG MODE
Current File : null
Main in CONFIG MODE
Current File : configureIt
In process mode.
```

```
Main in PROCESS MODE
Current File : process1
In process mode.
Main in PROCESS MODE
Current File : process1
In process mode.
Main in PROCESS MODE
Current File : process2
Main in QUIT_MODE
```

Source 3.7 also produces a simple pop-up window as seen in Figure 3.3.

Source 3.7 has many interesting components that were used to demonstrate a real-world requirement for a this pointer. We will go over the function of the program in general and then cover all of the major highlights of the program.

Source 3.7 is a skeleton or framework of a larger program. This was necessary because a real-world requirement for the this pointer is in the context of a large program that requires sharing between diverse functional components. Source 3.7 uses four key objects: a getFilename object that presents the dialog in Figure 3.3 to get a file name from the user, a configMode object that handles any program configuration issues and also uses the getFilename object, a processMode object that would actually be the main workhorse of the program, and last, a mainLoop object that uses a finite state machine to control the overall program flow.

As a skeleton of a larger program, as well as including an element of a graphical user interface, Source 3.7 includes three new topics that need a brief introduction: the extends keyword, exceptions, and threads. The extends keyword is used to implement inheritance in Java. Inheritance is used extensively in the platform-independent abstract window toolkit that is part of the Java environment. Inheritance also plays a major role in C++ and is therefore discussed in detail in the next section. Exceptions are a C++ and Java method of

FIGURE 3.3   Filename dialog.

error-handling. They will be discussed in detail in section 3.5. Last, threads are not supported in C++ but are supported in Java. Although a discussion of threads does represent a slight divergence in our current conversation, they are such a cool language feature of Java that I believe they cannot be discussed too much.

Threads are a method for implementing multiprocessing within a single program, and a powerful mechanism for increasing the interactivity and asynchronous execution of your programs. In order to understand threads, it is easier if you first understand the concept of a process within a preemptive, multi-tasking operating system (like UNIX, Windows NT, and Windows 95). I have found no better explanation than that provided by Andrew Tanenbaum in his book, *Operating Systems: Design and Implementation*.

> The difference between a process and a program is subtle, but crucial. An analogy may help make this point clearer. Consider a culinary-minded computer scientist who is baking a birthday cake for his daughter. He has a birthday cake recipe and a kitchen well-stocked with the necessary input: flour, eggs, sugar, and so on. In this analogy, the recipe is the program (i.e., an algorithm expressed in some suitable notation), the computer scientist is the processor (CPU), and the cake ingredients are the input data. The process is the activity consisting of our baker reading the recipe, fetching the ingredients, and baking the cake.
>
> Now imagine that the computer scientist's son comes running in crying, saying that he has been stung by a bee. The computer scientist records where he was in the recipe (the state of the current process is saved), gets out a first aid book, and begins following the directions in it. Here we see the processor being switched from one process (baking) to a higher priority process (administering medical care), each having a different program (recipe vs. first aid book). When the bee sting has been taken care of, the computer scientist goes back to his cake, continuing at the point where he left off.
>
> The key idea here is that a process is an activity of some kind. It has a program, input, output, and a state. A single processor may be shared among several processes, with some scheduling algorithm being used to determine when to stop work on one process and service a different one.[6]

---

[6]Andrew S. Tanenbaum, *Operating Systems: Design and Implementation* (Englewood Cliffs, N.J.: Prentice-Hall, 1987), p. 47. Reprinted here with permission.

The above analogy is absolutely beautiful. Andrew Tanenbaum is a well-known computer scientist and a superb writer. All computer programmers would be well-advised to read all of his works. Now, Andrew has given us a very clear understanding of a running process on a computer system and how a multi-tasking operating system continually switches between processes. We also have a clear understanding of the difference between a process (a running program) and a program (the instructions for the CPU). Threads perform the same task-switching as do processes, except that threads all execute within a single process. Each process in a multi-tasking operating system is assigned its own memory area, registers, and application stack; however, no matter how many threads are started, each shares the resources of the one process. This actually makes it easier and more efficient for threads to share information. Source 3.7 uses threads to implement each major functional mode of our program. Both of these threads use the mainLoop object as their driver so they are required to pass back information to the mainLoop object. This requirement for passing back information is the main reason why one object needs to pass itself to another object. Now let's move on to how Source 3.7 uses the this variable.

Source 3.7 primarily uses the this variable in two ways:

1. To pass the currently executing object to another object. This is done from several of the objects like this:

```
configMode cMode = new configMode(this);
```

You will also notice that the configMode's object expects a mainLoop object to be passed to it.
2. Within the currently executing objects method. This is not done for any other reason except to illustrate what the this pointer is, as in the call:

```
this.getFile();
```

which could just have easily been:

```
getFile();
```

Now let's move on to static members and methods of a class.

Static Members and Methods

Static methods were discussed in Chapter 1 as a way to implement utility functions within Java's object-oriented framework. In this section, we will examine how static variables and methods work in C++ and in object-oriented programming in general. Last, we will examine a program that demonstrates both static class data members and methods.

If a member of a class is defined as static, it means that that data member or method belongs to the entire class. The storage space for the static data member is reserved in the static or global space and not reserved with each instantiation of the object as is the case with non-static data members. There is a slight difference between static data members in C++ versus Java. In C++, you may only declare static data members and then define them outside of the class. In Java, since there are no declarations, you define the static data member right in the class definition. Source 3.8 demonstrates the use of static variables and methods.

SOURCE 3.8

```java
// static variables
class Entity {
        static long totalEntities = 0;
        private long eId;

        // other Entity attributes

        public Entity()
        {
                eId = totalEntities++;
                System.out.println("Total # of entities: " +
                                        totalEntities);
        }
}

// static methods
class myMath {
        static int fibonacci(int n)
        {
                if (n == 0 || n == 1) return n;
                return (fibonacci(n - 1) + fibonacci(n - 2));
        }
}

class tstStatic {
```

```
public static void main(String args[])
{
        System.out.println("Case 1: use of static variables.");
        Entity eArray[] = new Entity[5];
        for (int i=0; i < eArray.length; i++)
                eArray[i] = new Entity();

        System.out.println("Case 2: use of static methods.");
        System.out.println("fibonacci(14) is : "
                                + myMath.fibonacci(14));

}
}
```

A run of Source 3.8 produces:

```
C:\java\bin>java tstStatic
Case 1: use of static variables.
Total # of entities: 1
Total # of entities: 2
Total # of entities: 3
Total # of entities: 4
Total # of entities: 5
Case 2: use of static methods.
fibonacci(14) is : 377
```

Source 3.8 uses both a static data member and a static method.
The static data member is used for a very common purpose: when you
have data about a class that is not specific to any object but applies to
the whole class. In the Entity class we use a static data member to
count the total number of entities that get instantiated. It should be
clear how a count of all entities is a piece of information only relevant
to the entire class. With this same logic, we could have written a static
method called getTotalEntities( ) that returned the count of the total
number of entities. In fact, only a static method can operate on static
data. Last, since static methods are not instantiated with an object,
the this variable cannot be used with static methods.

Source 3.8 also demonstrates a static "utility" function in the
myMath class. A static method is needed when a method has no relation to a specific object. In our example, our utility function works on
the primitive types and therefore has no relationship to any user-
defined object. Given a desired number, the utility function returns
the value of that position in the fibonacci sequence. The fibonacci

sequence is a sequence of numbers defined by Leonardo of Pisa where each successive number is formed by the addition of the two previous numbers. The fibonacci sequence holds a mystique in the mathematical community, as is clear from the book *The Joy of Mathematics*, where Theoni Pappas states that the fibonacci sequence appears in:

I.   The Pascal triangle, the binomial formula & probability
II. the golden ratio and the golden rectangle
III. nature and plants
IV. intriguing mathematical tricks
V.   mathematical identities.[7]

Run Time Type Information (RTTI)

Run time type information is the ability to determine the type of an object at run time. In the forthcoming C++ standard, Run Time Type Information is supported using the typeid operator. Source 3.9 demonstrates the use of RTTI in C++. Pay particular attention to the use of the typeid operator.

SOURCE 3.9

```
// RTTI.cpp - a demonstration of RTTI in C++
#include <typeinfo.h>
#include <iostream.h>
#include <stdlib.h>
#include <stdio.h>
#include <string.h>

class graphicImage {
        protected:
            char name[80];
            int pixelsHigh, pixelsWide;
            unsigned char **bitmap;

            public:
        graphicImage()
        {
```

---

[7]Theoni Pappas, *The Joy of Mathematics* (San Carlos, CA: Wide World Publishing, 1986), p. 29.

```cpp
                pixelsHigh = pixelsWide = 0;
                strcpy(name,"graphicImage");
        }

        graphicImage(char * filename)
        {
                // process file, store bitmap
                cout << "Process " << filename << endl;
        }

        virtual void display()
        {
                    cout << "Display a generic image." << endl;
                for (int i=0; i < pixelsHigh; i++)
                        for (int j=0; j < pixelsWide; j++)
                                ; // draw each pixel
        }

        char* getName()
        {
                return name;
        }
};

class GIFimage : public graphicImage {
        // GIF data members

         public:
        GIFimage()
        {
                // GIF constructor
                strcpy(name,"GIFimage");
        }

        void display()
        {
                // display the GIF file in a GIF-specific way
                cout << "Display a GIF file." << endl;
        }
};

class PICTimage : public graphicImage {
```

```cpp
        // PICT data members

     public:
     PICTimage()
     {
             // PICT constructor
             strcpy(name,"PICTimage");
     }

     void display()
     {
             // display the PICT in a PICT-specific way
             cout << "Display a PICT file." << endl;
     }
};

void processFile(graphicImage *type)
{
    if (typeid(GIFimage) == typeid(*type))
    {
        ((GIFimage *)type)->display();
    }
    else if (typeid(PICTimage) == typeid(*type))
    {
        ((PICTimage *)type)->display();
    }
    else
        cout << "Unknown type! <" << (typeid(*type)).name()
            << ">" << endl;
}

void main(int argc, char **argv)
{
    graphicImage *gImage = new GIFimage();
    graphicImage *pImage = new PICTimage();

    processFile(gImage);
    processFile(pImage);
}
```

A run of Source 3.9 produces:

```
Display a GIF file.
Display a PICT file.
```

As you can see from Source 3.9, the program has the ability to tell what type of type you passed the function using RTTI. Java also implements RTTI using the instanceof operator. In Source 3.10 we implement the exact same program as in Source 3.9 in Java.

SOURCE 3.10

```
import java.awt.Color;

class graphicImage {
        protected String name;
        protected int pixelsHigh, pixelsWide;
        protected Color bitmap[][];

        graphicImage()
        {
                pixelsHigh = pixelsWide = 0;
                name = new String("graphicImage");
        }

        graphicImage(String filename)
        {
                // process file, store bitmap
                System.out.println("Process " + filename);
        }

        void display()
        {
                System.out.println("Display a generic image.");
                for (int i=0; i < pixelsHigh; i++)
                        for (int j=0; j < pixelsWide; j++)
                                ; // draw each pixel
        }

        String getName()
        {
                return name;
```

```
                }
        }

        class GIFimage extends graphicImage {
                // GIF data members

                GIFimage()
                {
                        // GIF constructor
                        name = new String("GIFimage");
                }

                void display()
                {
                        // display the GIF file in a GIF-specific way
                        System.out.println("Display a GIF file.");
                }
        }

        class PICTimage extends graphicImage {
                // PICT data members

                PICTimage()
                {
                        // PICT constructor
                        name = new String("PICTimage");
                }

                void display()
                {
                        // display the PICT in a PICT-specific way
                        System.out.println("Display a PICT file.");
                }
        }

        class tstRtti {

                static void processFile(graphicImage type)
                {
                        if (type instanceof GIFimage)
                        {
                                ((GIFimage)type).display();
```

```
            }
            else if (type instanceof PICTimage)
            {
                    ((PICTimage)type).display();
            }
    }

    public static void main(String args[])
    {
            GIFimage gImage = new GIFimage();
            PICTimage pImage = new PICTimage();

            processFile(gImage);
            processFile(pImage);
    }
}
```

A run of Source 3.10 produces:

```
C:\java\bin>java tstRtti
Display a GIF file.
Display a PICT file.
```

As you can see, the functionality of the two programs is identical. In fact, except for the liberal use of pointers in the C++ program, the code looks very similar.

3.3   INHERITANCE

In C++ and Java, inheritance is the ability for a derived class to acquire the non-private data members and methods of a base class. Although the implementation works the same way in C++ and Java, the syntax used is different. Figure 3.4 is an example of C++ inheritance and Java inheritance side by side.

As stated above, the only glaring differences are the syntax used to implement inheritance and the syntax used to call the base classes constructor. Java has the more intuitive of the approaches: Java uses the keyword extends to denote that the derived class is "extending" the base class (also referred to as a superclass in other object-oriented languages). Second, Java uses the keyword super as a variable that points to the parent (or superclass) in order to call the parent's constructor. C++ overloads the colon operator for both of these purposes; however,

C++ Inheritance	Java Inheritance

<pre>//inherit.cpp
#include <iostream.h>
class Coordinate {
  protected:
    int x,y;
  public:
    Coordinate(int inX, int inY)
    {x = inX; y = inY;}
 	
    int getX()
    {return x;}
 	
    int getY()
    {return y;}
};
 	
class Coordinate3d : public Coordinate{
  protected:
    int z;
  public:
    Coordinate3d(int inX, int inY, int inZ)
         :Coordinate(inX, inY)
    {z = inZ;}
 	
    int getZ()
    {return z;}
};
 	
void main(int argc, char**argv)
{
  Coordinate3d my Coord(10,20,30);
cout << "x: " << myCoord.getX() << endl;
cout << "y: " << myCoord.getY() << endl;
cout << "z: " << myCoord.getZ() << endl;
}</pre>
	<pre>//inherit.java
	class Coordinate {
	  protected int x,y;
	  Coordinate(int inX, int inY)
	  {x = inX; y = inY;}
	
	  int getX()
	  {return x;}
	
	  int getY()
	  {return y;}
	}
	
	class Coordinate3d extends Coordinate {
	  protected int z;
	  Coordinate3d(int inX, int inY, int inZ)
	  {
	    super(inX, inY);
	    z = inZ;
	  }
	
	  int getZ()
	  {return z;}
	}
	
	class coordTst {
	  public static void main(String args[])
	  {
	    Coordinate3d myCoord =
	                new Coordinate3d(10,20,30);
	    System.out.println("x: " + myCoord.getX());
	    System.out.println("y: " + myCoord.getY());
	    System.out.println("z: " + myCoord.getZ());
	  }
	}</pre>

FIGURE 3.4   Comparing C++ inheritance to Java inheritance.

in defense of C++, this was primarily sticking with the C language's terse tradition.

Single Inheritance

We will examine a good example of single inheritance: how a warning dialog is created via inheritance of a class hierarchy of graphical user interface elements in Java's abstract window toolkit (AWT). Figure 3.5 is a graphical representation of the inheritance hierarchy for the creation of a warning dialog. Notice that each class only has one "parent." This is called single inheritance.

Let's start at the top and work our way down to the Warning class:

- **Component.** A component is an abstract class that represents a generic graphical user interface (GUI) object. Everything displayed in an abstract window toolkit GUI is a graphical component. The component class has data members and methods common to all graphical components, such as a screen coordinate, size, or color.
- **Container.** A component that can contain or hold other components, responsible for storing all the components in the display and laying them out on the screen in accordance with a chosen lay-

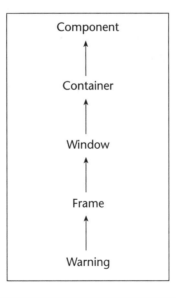

FIGURE 3.5   Single inheritance in the AWT.

out manager. The available layout managers are: BorderLayout, FlowLayout, GridLayout, and GridBagLayout. The different layout managers will be discussed in detail in Chapter 6.

- **Window.** A top-level window that has no title, no border, and no menu bar.
- **Frame.** A window that has a title and also has the ability to contain a menu bar.
- **Warning.** A frame that displays a Warning message.

Thus, the reason inheritance is so useful is because a Warning IS A frame, which IS A window, which IS A container, which IS A component. And, of course, our simple Warning class benefits by inheriting all of the characteristics and methods of every class above it. That's like adding the hubcaps to a Ferrari and saying, "Look what I built!"

Source 3.11 implements the Warning class using inheritance.

SOURCE 3.11

```
import java.awt.Frame;
import java.awt.Event;
import java.awt.Button;
import java.awt.Graphics;
import java.awt.Color;
import java.awt.Panel;

class Warning extends Frame {
        private String message;

        Warning(String title, String WarningMessage)
        {
                super(title);
                message = new String(WarningMessage);
                Panel p = new Panel();
                Button okButton = new Button("OK");
                p.add("Center", new Button("OK"));
                add("South",p);
                resize(200,100);
                move(50,50);
                setForeground(Color.black);
                setBackground(Color.white);
                show();
        }
```

```
    public boolean handleEvent(Event evt)
    {
            switch (evt.id) {
                    case Event.ACTION_EVENT:
                            if ("OK".equals(evt.arg))
                            {
                                    System.exit(1);
                            }
                            else
                                    return false;
                    break;
                    default:
                            return false;
            }
            return false;
    }

    public void paint(Graphics g)
    {
            g.drawString(message,10,40);
    }
}

class AlertTst {
    public static void main(String args[])
    {
            Warning anError = new Warning("Error", "A serious Error");
    }
}
```

A run of Source 3.11 produces the output shown in Figure 3.6.

Source 3.11 demonstrates single inheritance in Java. For now do not concern yourself with the specific implementation of the windows and event handling. That is covered in great detail in Chapter 6, Abstract Window Toolkit. So, by now you should know the two key Java constructs to implementing single inheritance: the extends keyword and the super variable. The super variable contains a reference to the superclass of the current object. It is conceptually identical to the this variable.

One last point to understand about inheritance is how it differs from containment. As I have said earlier, inheritance establishes an

FIGURE 3.6   A Warning alert box.

"IS A" relationship between a parent and child object. An "IS A" relationship is a relationship characterized by belonging to the same group and therefore sharing the same characteristics and behaviors. Inheritance forms a relationship of membership; however, there are other relationships between objects. If you are designing a program with a car object, a steering wheel object, a Honda Civic object and a wheel object, what relationships do these objects have to each other? Should the steering wheel object extend the car object? I hope you said no. The relationship between a car and a steering wheel is a "HAS A" relationship. A car HAS A steering wheel. Putting the objects in English sentences with "has a" or "is a" will quickly tell you whether you should use inheritance or not. Figure 3.7 depicts both the IS A and HAS A relationships between objects.

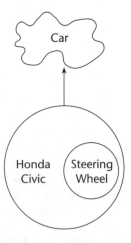

FIGURE 3.7   IS A versus HAS A relationships.

The diagram shows that a Honda Civic is a car but contains (or has) a steering wheel. The other interesting thing to note about the "car" in Figure 3.7 is that it is depicted with an amorphous shape. This graphically represents that car is an abstract idea that would do well to be implemented as an abstract class. This brings us to our next section.

Abstract Classes and Virtual Functions

An abstract class is a class created solely for the purpose of being extended. It is akin to an abstract idea that a physical implementation is derived from. You cannot instantiate an object from an abstract class. If you attempt to, a compiler error will result. Java has both abstract classes and abstract methods. A Java abstract method is a method that has no body and MUST be overriden in all subclasses derived from the class with the abstract method. In C++, abstract methods are called pure virtual functions and are declared like this:

```
class B {
    public:
        B();
        virtual int getNum() = 0;   // a pure virtual function
};
```

In C++, a class that has one or more virtual functions in it is considered abstract, although there is no abstract keyword in C++. As you can see, Java is simpler in that an abstract class and method both use the abstract keyword as they are similar concepts.

Source 3.12 demonstrates both an abstract Shape class and an abstract method. The program then extends the shape class with three specific shape classes: a square, a triangle, and a hexagon. To make this program more interesting, I made it graphical. Again, do not worry about not understanding all the aspects of the graphical user interface. It is explained in detail in Chapter 6 (If you can't wait, go ahead and jump ahead to that chapter).

SOURCE 3.12

```
import java.awt.*;
import java.lang.Math;
import java.util.Random;


abstract class Shape {
```

```
        protected Point pts[];
        protected Point Center;

        abstract void calculatePoints();
}

class Square extends Shape {
        drawWindow dw;
        int theWidth;

        Square(drawWindow win, Point center, int width)
        {
                dw = win;
                pts = new Point[4];
                Center = center;
                theWidth = width;

                for (int i=0; i < pts.length; i++)
                        pts[i] = new Point(0,0);
        }

        void calculatePoints()
        {
                int radius = theWidth/2;
                pts[0].x = Center.x - radius;
                pts[0].y = Center.y - radius;
                pts[1].x = Center.x - radius;
                pts[1].y = Center.y + radius;
                pts[2].x = Center.x + radius;
                pts[2].y = Center.y + radius;
                pts[3].x = Center.x + radius;
                pts[3].y = Center.y - radius;
                dw.setPoints(pts);
        }
}

class Triangle extends Shape {
        drawWindow dw;
        int Base, Height;
        int Angle;
```

```
Triangle(drawWindow win, Point center, int base, int height,
                        int baseAngle)
{
        dw = win;
        Center = center;
        Base = base;
        Height = height;
        Angle = baseAngle;
        pts = new Point[3];
        for (int i=0; i < 3; i++)
                pts[i] = new Point(0,0);
}

void calculatePoints()
{
        int halfBase = Base/2;
        int halfHeight = Height/2;

        // create base
        pts[0].x = Center.x - halfBase;
        pts[0].y = Center.y + halfHeight;
        pts[2].x = Center.x + halfBase;
        pts[2].y = Center.y + halfHeight;

        // now the apex
        if (Angle == 90)
        {
                pts[1].x = Center.x - halfBase;
                pts[1].y = Center.y - halfHeight;
        }
        else if (Angle < 90)
        {
                int adjacent_angle = 90 - Angle;
                int opposite_angle = 180 - (adjacent_angle + 90);
                double radians = ((double)opposite_angle/180.0 * Math.PI);
                double theTan = Math.tan(radians);
                pts[1].x = (int) (pts[0].x +
                        ((double)(Height)/theTan));
                pts[1].y = Center.y - halfHeight;
        }
        else if (Angle > 90)
        {
```

```
                    int adjacent_angle = 180 - Angle;
                    double radians = (double)adjacent_angle/180.0 * Math.PI;
                    double theTan = Math.tan(radians);
                    pts[1].x = (int) (pts[0].x -
                                ((double)(Height)/theTan));
                    pts[1].y = Center.y - halfHeight;
            }
            dw.setPoints(pts);
        }
}

class Hexagon extends Shape {
        drawWindow dw;
        int triangleBase, triangleHeight;

        Hexagon (drawWindow win, Point center, int base, int height)
        {
                dw = win;
                Center = center;
                triangleBase = base;

                // *** triangle height is half the height of the Hex
                triangleHeight = height;

                pts = new Point[6];
                for (int i=0; i < pts.length; i++)
                        pts[i] = new Point(0,0);
        }

        void calculatePoints()
        {
                int halfBase = triangleBase/2;

                // upper and lower side are trivial
                pts[0].x = Center.x - halfBase;
                pts[0].y = Center.y - triangleHeight;
                pts[5].x = Center.x + halfBase;
                pts[5].y = Center.y - triangleHeight;

                pts[2].x = Center.x - halfBase;
                pts[2].y = Center.y + triangleHeight;
                pts[3].x = Center.x + halfBase;
```

```
                pts[3].y = Center.x + triangleHeight;

                // get points to connect sides
                double radians = 60.0/180.0 * Math.PI;
                double theTan = Math.tan(radians);
                int right_triangle_adjacent = (int)
                                ((double)triangleHeight/theTan);
                pts[1].x = pts[0].x - right_triangle_adjacent;
                pts[1].y = Center.y;
                pts[4].x = pts[5].x + right_triangle_adjacent;
                pts[4].y = Center.y;
                dw.setPoints(pts);
        }
}


class drawWindow extends Frame {
        private Point dPts[];
        Random dice;

        drawWindow()
        {
                super("draw Shapes");
                setBackground(Color.white);
                setForeground(Color.red);

                // initialize the random number seed
                dice = new Random();

                // add a menuBar
                MenuBar mBar = new MenuBar();
                setMenuBar(mBar);
                Menu FileMenu = new Menu("File");
                FileMenu.add(new MenuItem("Quit"));
                mBar.add(FileMenu);
                Menu ShapeMenu = new Menu("Shapes");
                ShapeMenu.add(new MenuItem("Square"));
                ShapeMenu.add(new MenuItem("Triangle"));
                ShapeMenu.add(new MenuItem("Hexagon"));
                mBar.add(ShapeMenu);

                // size and show
                resize(200,200);
```

```
        move(50,50);
        show();
}


public boolean handleEvent(Event evt)
{
        switch (evt.id) {
                case (Event.ACTION_EVENT) :
                        if ("Quit".equals(evt.arg))
                        {
                                dispose();
                                System.exit(0);
                        }
                        else if ("Square".equals(evt.arg))
                        {
                                setPoints(null);
                                repaint(); // clear window

                                // roll a random # between 10 and 100
                                int roll = dice.nextInt() % 100;
                                if (roll < 0) roll = -roll;
                                if (roll < 10) roll = 10;

                                Square aSquare = new Square(this,new Point(100,100),roll);
                                aSquare.calculatePoints();
                                paint(getGraphics());
                        }
                        else if ("Triangle".equals(evt.arg))
                        {
                                setPoints(null);
                                repaint(); // clear window

                                // roll 2 random #'s between 10 and 100
                                int base = dice.nextInt() % 100;
                                if (base < 0) base = -base;
                                if (base < 10) base = 10;

                                int height = dice.nextInt() % 100;
                                if (height < 0) height = -height;
                                if (height < 10) height = 10;

                                // roll a random angle between 1 and 179
```

```
                        int angle = dice.nextInt() % 179;
                        if (angle < 0) angle = -angle;
                        if (angle < 1) angle = 1;

                        Triangle aTriangle =
                                new Triangle(this, new Point(100,100),
                                                base, height, angle);
                        aTriangle.calculatePoints();
                        paint(getGraphics());
                }
                else if ("Hexagon".equals(evt.arg))
                {
                        setPoints(null);
                        repaint(); // clear window

                        // roll a random #'s between 10 and 100
                        int base = dice.nextInt() % 100;
                        if (base < 0) base = -base;
                        if (base < 10) base = 10;

                        /* calculate the height of the
                                equilateral triangle  */
                        int right_triangle_adjacent = base/2;
                        double radians = 60.0/180.0 * Math.PI;
                        double theTan = Math.tan(radians);

                        int equilateral_height = (int)
                                        (theTan * right_triangle_adjacent);

                        Hexagon aHexagon =
                                new Hexagon(this, new Point(100,100),
                                                base, equilateral_height);
                        aHexagon.calculatePoints();
                        paint(getGraphics());
                }
                break;
        default:
                return false;
        }
        return true;
}
```

```
        void setPoints(Point inPoints[])
        {
                dPts = inPoints;
        }


        public void paint(Graphics g)
        {
                if (dPts != null)
                {
                        for (int i=0; i < dPts.length - 1; i++)
                                g.drawLine(dPts[i].x, dPts[i].y,
                                        dPts[i+1].x, dPts[i+1].y);

                        g.drawLine(dPts[dPts.length-1].x,
                                dPts[dPts.length-1].y,
                                dPts[0].x,dPts[0].y);
                }
        }
}

class drawShapes {
        public static void main(String args[])
        {
                new drawWindow();
        }
}
```

A run of Source 3.12 produces the output shown in Figure 3.8.

The square shape is not shown, as its implementation is trivial. All the above shapes are subclasses of the abstract Shape class. Our abstract definition of a shape is nothing more than an array of points. It is up to the specific shape to determine how many points (using the Point class) and where those points are located. That is why we made the calculatePoints( ) method abstract so that it must be overridden. The calculatePoints( ) function for the triangle and hexagon involves some trigonometry.

Figure 3.9 depicts the trigonometric functions necessary to calculate the location of the apex point of the triangle given the base, height, and an angle greater than 90 degrees. Since we have the height of the triangle, we already have the Y coordinate of the apex point. We need to determine the length of the adjacent side of the right triangle that is adjacent to the triangle we wish to draw.

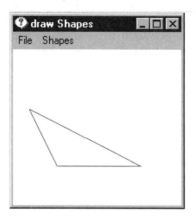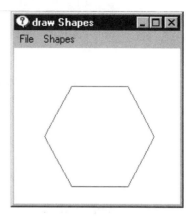

FIGURE 3.8   The drawShapes GUI.

Remembering the simple phrase my high school math teacher taught me for defining the trigonometry functions, SOH CAH TOA (say it out loud), this tells us that the sine of the angle equals the opposite over the hypotenuse, the cosine equals the adjacent over the hypotenuse and the tangent equals the opposite over the adjacent. Knowing that we have the length of the opposite side, it is apparent that we can use

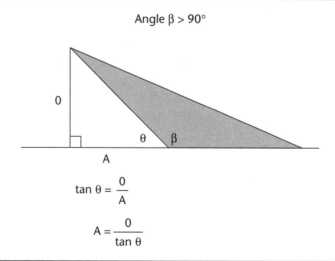

FIGURE 3.9   Calculating the apex of a triangle.

the tangent of the adjacent angle to determine the length of the adjacent side. The length of the adjacent side will give us the X coordinate of the apex point of our triangle.

We perform very similar trigonometry to calculate the apex of triangles with a base angle of less than 90 degrees and also to calculate the center left and right points of the hexagon. I hope you enjoy experimenting with this program—it was certainly fun writing it to demonstrate abstract classes and methods!

Although we have discussed abstract classes and abstract methods, we have not demonstrated how Java supports virtual functions in the way that C++ does. In C++, a virtual function in a base class is dynamically bound at run time based on the pointer value. If the pointer value points to a subclass, the subclass function with the same name will be called. If the function was not declared virtual, no run time checking of the type would occur and whatever type the pointer was declared (i.e., the base class) that is the function that would be run. In Java, all functions of the same name in both the base and derived classes are virtual. Source 3.13 demonstrates this virtual function behavior in Java.

SOURCE 3.13

```java
import java.util.Random;

class car {
        int top_speed;
        int fuel_in_gallons;

        car(int inSpeed, int inGallons)
        {
                top_speed = inSpeed;
                fuel_in_gallons = inGallons;
        }

        void howMuchFuel()
        {
                System.out.println("There is " + fuel_in_gallons +
                                " left.");
        }
}
```

```
class Honda extends car {
        String model;
        Honda(String theModel, int inSpeed, int inFuel)
        {
                super(inSpeed, inFuel);
                model = new String(theModel);
        }

        void howMuchFuel()
        {
                System.out.println("My Honda " + model +
                                    " has " + fuel_in_gallons +
                                    " left.");
        }
}

class Dodge extends car {
        String model;
        Dodge(String theModel, int inSpeed, int inFuel)
        {
                super(inSpeed, inFuel);
                model = new String(theModel);
        }

        void howMuchFuel()
        {
                System.out.println("My Dodge " + model +
                                    " has " + fuel_in_gallons +
                                    " left.");
        }
}

class tstVirtual {
        static Random dice = new Random();

        static car get_a_car()
        {
                if (dice.nextInt() % 2 == 0)
                        return new Dodge("Caravan",90,20);
                else
                        return new Honda("Civic",70,10);
        }
```

```
public static void main(String args[])
{
        car theCar;
        for (int i=0; i < 5; i++)
        {
                theCar = get_a_car();
                theCar.howMuchFuel();
        }
}
}
```

A run of Source 3.13 produces:

```
C:\java\bin>java tstVirtual
My Honda Civic has 10 left.
My Honda Civic has 10 left.
My Dodge Caravan has 20 left.
My Dodge Caravan has 20 left.
My Dodge Caravan has 20 left.
```

The key point to understand in Source 3.13 is that the type declaration of the variable theCar is as a type of base class car; however, the object instantiated is one of the subclasses (Honda or Dodge). Since the instantiated object is one of the subclasses, the subclass howMuch-Fuel( ) method is called. This is identical to the behavior of virtual functions in C++. Of course, the C++ implementation involves class pointers. Now we can move on to another area in which C++ and Java are similar: exceptions.

3.4   EXCEPTIONS

Exceptions are a robust error-handling mechanism that functions equally well in C++ and Java. In the latest draft language specification from the standards committee, C++ exception handling has been expanded and improved, resulting in a system nearly identical to Java's. You will notice that C++ has a few unique features in its exception handling mechanism and so does Java. In general, the exception handling facilities of both languages are good. Let's now examine the main elements of exception handling in both languages and demonstrate them in code.

Try Blocks and Handling Exceptions

The cornerstone of exception handling in both C++ and Java involves a try block and catch expression. The keyword try precedes a block of code that may throw an exception. It is simpler in Java to know if a function throws an exception because any function that throws an exception must explicitly state so in its function declaration using the throws keyword. C++ also allows exception specifications in its function declaration, but the absence of an exception specification can mean that the function can throw all exceptions. The closing brace of a try block must be followed by a catch expression. This catch expression is the type of the exception that the following block of code can handle. Both C++ and Java allow a catchall feature by using the following code:

```
in C++:     } catch (...)
in Java:    } catch (Exception e)
```

The catch expressions are followed by an exception handler block of code for that exception. Source 3.14 demonstrates throwing and catching exceptions as well as some C++ unique facilities for exception handling (i.e. set_unexpected( )).

SOURCE 3.14

```cpp
#include <iostream.h>
#include <stdlib.h>
#include <stdio.h>
#include <string.h>
#include <stdexcept.h>

class ResultTooLarge : public exception{
    char message[80];

    public:
    ResultTooLarge(char * msg)
    {
        strcpy(message,msg);
    }

    const char *what()
    {
        cout << "Exception: " << message << endl;
```

```
            return message;
      }
};

void my_unexpected()
{
    cout << "Catching unexpected exceptions." << endl;
}

void my_terminate()
{
    cout << "If unexpected not handled, call me." << endl;
    exit(1);
}

void badboy()  // can throw all exceptions
{
    throw ResultTooLarge("I'll throw any exception I like.");
}

void goodboy() throw (ResultTooLarge)
{
    throw ResultTooLarge("You can expect me only to throw ResultTooLarge");
}

void greatboy() throw()
{
    cout << "I don't throw ANY exceptions." << endl;
}

void main()
{
    set_unexpected(my_unexpected);
    set_terminate(my_terminate);

    int a=100, b=2;
    try {
        int result = a/b;
        if (result > 5)
        {
                char msg[80];
```

```
            sprintf(msg,"%d is too Large.", result);
            throw ResultTooLarge(msg);
        }
    } catch (ResultTooLarge e)
        {
            cout << "Caught the result too large." << endl;
            e.what();
        }
    catch (...)
        {
            cout << "Caught any exception." << endl;
        }
}
```

A run of Source 3.14 produces:

```
Caught the result too large.
Exception: 50 is too Large.
```

There are three key points to note about Source 3.14:

- The class ResultTooLarge is a subclass of the standard exception class. There are several types of standard exceptions defined in the proposed C++ standard and they are broken down into two types: logic exceptions and run time exceptions. These two types are identical to the function of the Exception and RuntimeException classes in Java. Those Java classes are discussed in detail in the next chapter, The Java Standard Library.
- The functions badboy( ), goodboy( ), and greatboy( ) demonstrate exception specifications. In my opinion, the fact that lack of a specification denotes that the function may throw any exceptions weakens the utility of the C++ exceptions specification facility as well as opens itself up to abuse. This, of course, is the most severe drawback of C++: The majority of safety features and object-oriented protections can be circumvented via either casting or pointers.
- The function set_unexpected( ) and set_terminate( ) allow you to provide last-ditch event handlers to cover two specific conditions. The unexpected( ) function will be called if an exception is thrown in a function that has an exception specification where the exception being thrown is not part of the specification. The terminate( ) function is called if no handler is found for an exception.

Now let's examine the Java exception handling facility and compare it to the code above. Source 3.15 demonstrates exception handling and throwing in Java.

SOURCE 3.15

```
import java.lang.Exception;

class ResultTooLarge extends Exception {
        ResultTooLarge(String msg)
        {
                super(msg);
        }
}

class TestExceptions {
        public static void main(String args[])
        {
                int a=100, b=2;
                try {
                        int result = a/b;
                        if (result > 5)
                        {
                                throw new ResultTooLarge(result + " is too Large.");
                        }
                } catch (ResultTooLarge e) {
                        System.out.println("Caught the result too large.");
                        System.out.println(e.getMessage());
                } finally {
                        System.out.println("Finally will always be run.");
                        System.out.println("Even if exceptions are caught.");
                }
        }
}
```

A run of Source 3.15 produces:

```
C:\java\bin>java TestExceptions
Caught the result too large.
50 is too Large.
Finally will always be run.
Even if exceptions are caught.
```

Before we get into the specific variations of Java exception handling, it should be evident that the facilities are very similar. I feel that is a good thing. Both seem to be well thought out and should be taken very seriously by every programmer.

There are three key points to understand about Source 3.15:

- The exception ResultTooLarge is a subclass of the Exception class. The Exception class extends the Throwable class. Any class that extends throwable can be thrown and caught. Classes derived from the Exception class fall into the category of errors that can be recovered from, whereas classes derived from the RuntimeException class generally cannot be recovered from.
- The Java try, throw, and catch constructs are nearly identical to their C++ counterparts.
- The Java finally keyword allows a block of code to be executed, even if any exceptions are thrown within the try block and catch blocks.

Although we have shown that many parts of C++ have been adopted by Java, there are also many parts of the language intentionally left out. We discuss these in the next section.

3.5   FEATURES OMITTED FROM C++

C++ is a large language that is growing larger with its standardization. Part of this is due to the fact that C++ has grown from being extensions to C into being a whole separate language on top of C (sort of like Windows on top of DOS). The draft standard just released by the C++ standards committee has seen the standard library leap from just iostreams and the C standard library into ten separate libraries. In a word, the C++ standard library is now huge (we will discuss this more in the next section).

Being large is not necessarily a problem, especially in relation to library routines. However, the C++ language has also grown increasingly complex. Features like operator overloading, multiple inheritance, and templates can generate very complex code that can only be enhanced or maintained by the person who created it. If that person leaves the company, the code becomes practically useless.

Lastly, not only did C++ inherit certain flaws and dangers from C—like the preprocessor and pointers—but added its own dangers and redundancies such as multiple inheritance and references. And all the features to be discussed here do not include all the new features and ambiguities in the new draft C++ standard. A discussion of some problems in the new C++ standard can be found in the January 1996 issue of *Dr. Dobb's Journal* by the well-known columnist and author Al Stevens.

The following C++ features were intentionally omitted from Java or significantly modified.

- **Destructors.** The Java language has changed the concept of an object's destruction to its finalization. The reason for this is that object destruction is most often associated with the explicit freeing of dynamic memory allocated for the object. Since Java performs garbage collection, the programmer does not explicitly deallocate memory. However, there may be some resources (ports, files, devices) that need to be released, closed, or cleaned up before they are garbage collected by the system. Therefore Java has replaced the object's destructor with a finalize( ) function. Source 3.16 demonstrates finalization in Java.

SOURCE 3.16

```
class simpleObject {
        int a;

        simpleObject()
        {
                System.out.println("Constructing simpleObject.");
                a = 5;
        }

        void setA(int inA)
        {
                System.out.println("Using a simpleObject.");
                a = inA;
        }

        protected void finalize()
        {
                System.out.println("Finalizing simpleObject.");
                a = 0;
        }
}

class tstFinalize {
```

```
public static void main(String args[])
{
        simpleObject myObject = new simpleObject();

        myObject.setA(100);
        myObject = null;
        System.gc();
        System.runFinalization();
}
}
```

A run of Source 3.16 produces:

```
C:\java\bin>java tstConstructor
Constructing simpleObject.
Using a simpleObject.
Finalizing simpleObject.
```

In Source 3.16 the object had to be forced to be finalized. Normally, objects would not be garbage collected until either the program was idle (the Java garbage collector is a low-priority thread), or a memory request could not be satisfied. Since neither situation applied in our simple program, I forced the system to garbage collect via a call to System.gc( ). However, just because the garbage collector ran, there was still no need for the program to immediately finalize the object. Instead, it sat on the finalization queue awaiting finalization if the resource was needed (which it wasn't). Therefore, to force finalization I called System.runfinalization( ).

- **Operator Overloading.** This is a C++ construct that allows the primitive operators to be overloaded to work with classes. This can lead to elegant code that lets you use the + operator to add matrix classes, coordinates, and other objects where addition makes sense. However, all of a sudden you have programmers getting carried away with the feature and overloading the minus operator to remove components from a GUI. Or you have an overloaded right shift operator (>>) used to mean fast-forward through a linked list because "it sort of resembled the fast-forward button on my VCR." The bottom line is that it is actually more intuitive and not open to interpretation to use descriptive method names for operations involving objects. And with Java allowing method and variable names of any length, there is no excuse not to be descriptive.

- **Templates.** The idea behind templates is an excellent one, allowing classes and methods to be type independent or generic. Unfortunately, many of the other C++ features like multiple inheritance, references, and operator overloading can make a template overly complicated and difficult to understand. It is as if the language polluted a fine idea that was implemented in Ada long before being implemented in C++. You may have noticed that the keyword "generic" is reserved for future use in Java. It is highly probable that you will see generic become either a method modifier or a new type. Since every Java object is inherited from the root Object class, it is not necessary to have a class be generic. The Container classes can already store a generic object by storing a uninstantiated Object. This is exactly the methodology of the Vector and other container classes.

- **Multiple Inheritance.** A C++ feature that allows inheritance from more than one parent or base class. This is another feature where the concept is sound but the implementation proves difficult and adds complexity to the language. In the end, a simpler solution like Java interfaces (explained in section 5.2) provides most of the same benefits.

- **References.** The reference is a feature that has two purposes: first, to eliminate the need for pointers, and second, to make operator overloading work. Considering the fact that good reasons have been put forth for eliminating both pointers and operator overloading, references become clearly unnecessary. Actually, the fact that references exist in C++ is a statement that the language designer was attempting to bandaid a flaw instead of eliminating it.

- **Friend Classes.** A feature that allows one class to have access to protected and private data members and methods of another class. This feature is implemented through packages (see section 5.1). In a Java package, when you do not explicitly put in an access specifier, the default access specifier is "friendly," which means that all classes and methods within the package have access to friendly methods and data.

3.6   THE C++ STANDARD LIBRARY

I mentioned in the previous section that the new C++ standard library was getting huge. Let me give you a little detail on exactly what the new library contains (from the draft standard specification):

54 standard macros from the C library

45 standard values from the C library

19 standard types from the C library

2 standard structures from the C library

208 standard functions from the C library

66 standard template classes

86 standard template operator functions

24 standard template structures

28 standard classes

144 standard template functions

12 standard operator functions

78 standard functions in the C++ library

16 additional structures in the C++ library

28 additional types in the C++ library

8 standard objects

This gives a grand total of 818 items in the Standard C++ library, all accessed via 18 C library headers and 32 C++ headers.

Naturally, no compiler vendor has yet implemented the entire standard C++ library as specified in the latest draft standard. Some have only a very small portion implemented. Regardless, it is not the primary domain of this book and is far too large to discuss. The draft specification divided the library into ten categories. We will describe each category in general terms and then refer the reader to a similar capability or package in the Java standard library if one exists.

Language Support Library

This library implements macros, objects and functions used in other parts of the library and in the C++ language. The majority of this library is composed of C standard library headers discussed already in section 2.11. The C standard library headers are:

```
<cstddef> <climits> <cfloat> <cstdlib>
<cstdarg> <csetjmp> <ctime> <csignal> <cstdlib>
```

There are four C++ headers:

- **<limits>** This header provides detailed information on the implementation of the primitive types. This type of information is platform-independent in Java and fixed.

- **<new>** This header implements the C++ dynamic allocation functions new, delete, and the array forms of the operators. The Java new operator and built-in garbage collection provide the same functionality.
- **<typeinfo>** This header provides the C++ Run Time Type Information as demonstrated for C++ and Java previously in this chapter.
- **<exception>** This header defines the bad_exception class, the unexpected( ), terminate( ), set_unexpected( ), and set_terminate( ) functions. Due to Java's stricter implementation of exceptions, these functions are not necessary in Java.

Diagnostics Library

The diagnostics library offers basically the standard exception classes added to the existing C library headers for reporting errors. The C headers are:

```
<cassert> <cerrno>
```

The C++ header that declares the standard exceptions is <stdexcept>. The standard exceptions are the following classes: exception, logic_error, domain_error; invalid_argument, length_error, out_of_range, runtime_error, range_error, and overflow_error. While this is a good start, the Java standard library has many more standard exceptions in each package of the library. We will discuss every Java exception in the next chapter.

General Utilities Library

This library has utility classes and functions that can be used both by the C++ library and user programs. There is one C header in this category, the <ctime> header, which provides date and time function. In general, this category has some similarities to the Java util package (see Chapter 4).

There are three C++ specific headers in this category:

- **<utility>** This header defines numerous template operators. There are no templates in Java.
- **<functional>** This header also defines numerous templates for basic operations (minus, plus, logical operations, etc.); no correlation to Java.

- **<memory>** This header provides templates for allocators and allocator support functions. There is no correlation to Java, which is garbage collected.

Strings Library

In addition to the C string and character headers below

<cctype> <cwctype> <cstring> <cwchar>

This category also includes a template classes for a basic_string class in the C++ <string> header. The functionality is very similar to the Java String and StringBuffer classes discussed in Chapter 4.

Localization Library

In addition to the C header <clocale> previously discussed, this category adds a C++ header <locale>. These headers provide interationalization support for character classification and string collation, numeric, monetary, and date/time formatting and parsing. This locale support is currently more robust than provided by Java. Java supports UNICODE and has some locale support in its Date class. Both Java and Netscape are committed to international support and you can expect the Java standard library to be improved in this area.

Containers Library

It is important to give credit where credit is due, and the next three sections (mostly derived from the Standard Template Library (STL) developed by Alex Stepanov, Meng Lee, and David R. Musser) are incredible achievements. It would not surprise me if Sun did not add generics just to have the STL. Hewlett-Packard has released its implementation into the public domain; you can obtain the source code via anonymous ftp from butler.hp1.hp.com.

The containers library is the part of the STL that is completely implemented already in Java. In fact, an even greater number of containers can be found at http://www.gamelan.com. The containers category has eight headers:

- **<vector> <deque> <list> <queue> <stack>** These containers are all sequences. A sequence is a finite set of elements arranged in a linear fashion. Java currently implements a Vector class and Stack class. (See Chapter 4.)

- **<map> <set>** These implement an associative container that maps keys to values. Java provides a Dictionary and HashTable class described in Chapter 4.
- **<bitset>** A sequence of individual bits. Java has a BitSet class as described in Section 4.2.

Iterators Library

In one sense, iterators are another bandaid to avoid the dangers of pointers. (Boy, all this slapping around of pointers, which I find to be crucial to complete the training of any programmer.) I admit pointers can be dangerous in the wrong hands (just like power tools) but they are worth the effort to learn. After you learn them, you will see why it is better to not program with them explicitly. This is what both Java and iterators do for you. They allow you to implicitly program with pointers instead of explicitly. And that is fine because safety and reliability should outweigh control and efficiency for most (not all) programming situations.

There is only one <iterator> header. An iterator is described in the standard as a generalization of pointers that allow data structures to be sequenced through in a uniform manner. This same definition could be used to describe the Enumeration interface in Section 4.2. I also demonstrate in Section 5.1 how to implement the Enumeration interface for a list package.

Algorithms Library

This is probably the only area where the C++ library outshines the Java standard library (again, thanks to the STL). This category has four types of generic algorithms: nonmutating sequence operations, mutating sequence operations, sorting operations, and the C standard library algorithms (binsearch, quicksort, etc.). I expect all of these to be implemented and incorporated into the Java standard library as new interfaces (along with some new containers).

This category consists of the <cstdlib> header and one C++ header called <algorithm>. The <algorithm> header is fairly large and packed with over a hundred useful algorithms. The header contains generic algorithms to search, sort, compare, transform, merge, unique, fill, count, copy, swap, randomly access, partition, and many other operations on container elements.

Numerics Library

The numerics library performs many functions for the manipulation of numbers. Some of this capability is also in Java but not all. In addition to the <cmath> header and <cstdlib> header, this category has three C++ headers:

- **<complex>** A comprehensive header that provides templates and functions to manipulate complex numbers. Complex numbers are numbers that can be written in the form a + bi, where a and b are real numbers and i is the imaginary unit (defined by $i^2 = -1$). There is no corresponding class or function currently in Java.
- **<valarray>** This header defines five different types of arrays (valarray, slice_array, gslice_array, mask_array, and indirect_array). Some of these capabilities are in Java's array, being a first-call object, but not close to all of them. A Java array is very similar to the val_array template class. There are no corresponding classes in Java for the slice and gslice class in this header.
- **<numeric>** This header provides generic mathematical algorithms for operations such as accumulate, calculating the inner product, partial sum, and adjacent difference. There is no corresponding interface currently in Java.

Input/Output Library

Besides the C headers <cstdlib>, <cstdio>, and <cwchar>, this category has nine C++ headers:

```
<iosfwd> <iostream>  <ios>  <streambuf> <istream>
<ostream>  <iomanip>  <sstream>  <fstream>
```

We do not need to discuss the C++ io classes in detail. Suffice it to say that both C++ and Java have robust Input/Output facilities. The Java io package is described in detail in Chapter 4.

CHAPTER 4

The Java Standard Library

Sometimes a programmer is called upon to be more a craftsman than an artist; and a craftsman's work is quite enjoyable when good tools and materials are present.

—Donald E. Knuth, *Literate Programming*

OBJECTIVE

This chapter provides a complete description and demonstration of the Java class hierarchy which, in relation to C and C++, would be considered Java's standard library. It also provides the reader with practical software tools for reuse and experimentation.

This chapter is about tools—programmer's tools. The C, C++, and now Java standard libraries all boil down to programmers creating tools to be reused by other programmers. Tools and the invention of tools should be held in the highest regard, in fact, in awe, by those of us who use them and take them for granted. Tool use itself cuts to the very foundation of the evolutionary success of humans. Tool use allows us to solve problems more efficiently and effectively. This book, as all my books, attempts to make learning a by-product of both examining the tool creation process and using your own set of software power tools for experimentation and use. It is that great tradition of craftsmanship that I strive for with this chapter on the software tools provided with Java. And a powerful set of tools they are!

This chapter is designed to first give you the "big picture," or an overview of the whole library (section 4.1), and then to narrow in on the specifics of every class in the library (section 4.2). However, do not think this chapter is some boring reference-type chapter, because after you understand the general concepts, we will be demonstrating many of the classes with complete example programs.

4.1   OVERVIEW OF THE JAVA STANDARD LIBRARY

Being a pure object-oriented programming environment, the Java standard library is in the form of a collection of classes separated into packages by functionality. Figure 4.1 reveals the functional breakdown. Technically, it is more accurate to describe these packages as the Java class hierarchy; however, I will use the term Java standard library because we are examining Java from the perspective of C and C++ programming.

This section is designed to give you an overview of each package; it breaks down the packages into function parts, and then lists the classes that make up the package. The individual classes will then be described in detail in section 4.2.

lang Package

This package of classes completes the pure object-oriented implementation of the Java language. These are classes that the Java compiler itself uses and that you can also use. Below, I further divide the classes in this package into functional areas. This division is not enforced in any way but makes understanding the package easier.

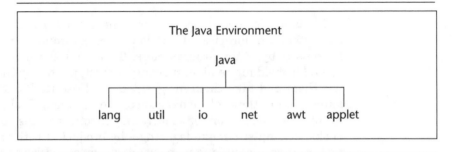

FIGURE 4.1   The Java standard library.

Primitive Types as Classes. Except for the primitive data types, everything in Java is an object that is a subclass of the Object class (discussed next). This entire class hierarchy or standard library manipulates objects. It is therefore often useful to wrap a primitive type in an "object wrapper."

Classes: Number, Character, Boolean, Double, Long, Float, Integer

Abstract Superclasses for All Objects in Java. Every object in the Java standard library is a subclass of the Object class. This commonality between all Java objects makes it easier to manipulate any user-defined object. Also, every object generated also has a Class object that stores information about the object's type. That dynamic class information can be accessed at run time. This is how Java implements run time type information (RTTI).

Classes: Class, Object

Strings. The C Standard library provides a rich set of string manipulation functions (i.e., strcpy( ), strcat( ), strtok( ), strlen( )); however, C strings fall victim to array bounds overruns and memory corruption via stray pointers. In C++, the standardization committee has fixed many of the problems of C strings by creating a safe string template class called basic_string; however, the simplicity of the safe Java strings make the C++ templatized basic_string appear not very basic at all. Java strings come in two forms—immutable (the String class) and mutable (the StringBuffer class). You will find Java strings to be very safe and simple tools.

Classes: String, StringBuffer

System Information. One of Java's key benefits is its cross-platform portability; however, sometimes even an environment designed to be portable needs to know specific properties of the computer system it is running on. Java provides classes to extract this system specific information like the path separator (a \ for Windows but a / for UNIX).

Classes: System, Process, Runtime, ClassLoader, Security-Manager

Math Functions. Every programming language provides a utility routine for common math function such as sin( ), cos( ), exp( ), and power( ).

Classes: Math

Threads. Java is very unique in its support for multi-threading at the language level. Java has classes that implement threads and groups of threads.

Classes: Thread, ThreadGroup

Run Time Errors. Java run time errors are subclasses of Throwable (just like exceptions) for abnormal events. You have the ability to catch and handle errors just as you do exceptions; however, errors are much more difficult to handle in any meaningful way.

Classes: StackOverflowError, UnknownError,
NoSuchMethodError, IncompatibleClassChangeError,
OutOfMemoryError, UnsatisfiedLinkError,
AbstractMethodError, IllegalAccessError, ThreadDeath,
VirtualMachineError, ClassCircularityError,
ClassFormatError, LinkageError, NoClassDefFoundError,
Error, VerifyError, InstantiationError, NoSuchFieldError

Exceptions. Exceptions are error conditions thrown by the Java run time that you can and should provide error handlers for.

Classes: Throwable, ArithmeticException,
ClassCastException, Exception, IllegalArgumentException,
InterruptedException, ArrayStoreException,
NullPointerException, NegativeArraySizeException,
NumberFormatException,
ArrayIndexOutOfBoundsException, RuntimeException,
SecurityException, IllegalThreadStateException,
StringIndexOutOfBoundsException,
IndexOutOfBoundsException, ClassNotFoundException,
InterruptedException, NoSuchMethodException,

util Package

This is a package of utility objects that help your programs store and manipulate other objects efficiently. Some classes in this package are similar to the C time and rand functions. The C++ standards committee has just adopted the Standard Template Library (STL) for inclusion into the C++ standard. Some of the Java container classes are similar to container templates in the STL.

Containers. Container objects are objects that hold other objects in a specific manner. The C++ STL has more container classes than does the Java util package; however, SUN Microsystems, the developer of Java, has stated that this is just the first cut of the Java environment and is committed to constantly improving it.

> Classes: HashtableEntry, Properties, Vector, VectorEnumerator, Stack, ObserverList, BitSet, Dictionary,

Miscellaneous. Java provides several other classes for random number generation, date manipulation, and string tokenizing that are just general utility classes.

> Classes: Random, Date, StringTokenizer, NoSuchElementException

io Package

Every programming language must also provide facilities for the input and output of data. The C standard library has the <stdio> header that provides well known function such as printf( ), scanf( ), fopen( ), fwrite( ), and fread( ). The C++ standard library provides a complete set of streams classes. C++ also allows overloading of the << and >> operators on those streams. The Java io package takes the middle ground between these two venerable solutions. You will find that Java has a rich set of streams classes yet provides familiar and simple access methods like println( ), read( ), and write( ).

Input Streams. Java has an impressive array of input streams that allow you to get input from a variety of sources as well as manipulate the stream in a variety of ways. There are two analogies that are extremely useful in understanding streams: first, the obvious analogy to a stream of water is the correct way to think about these streams of data. Second, think of Java streams as also providing the necessary piping to direct your data to and from wherever you want. In fact, with the FilterInputStream class you will see that we can even connect different pipes (think of different shaped pipes or pipes with special filters) that let you string together different data stream modifiers until the output is exactly what you want.

> Classes: InputStream, ByteArrayInputStream, FilterInputStream, PushbackInputStream, StringBufferInputStream, DataInputStream,

BufferedInputStream, LineNumberInputStream, SequenceInputStream, PipedInputStream, StreamTokenizer

Output Streams. Just as with Java's input streams, the output streams provide a number of different classes that output data in a variety of ways.

Classes: OutputStream, DataOutputStream, BufferedOutputStream, PrintStream, FilterOutputStream, ByteArrayOutputStream, PipedOutputStream

Files. The File classes are your data stores (or data pools) that your streams feed or use as a source. Again, the analogy to water is very useful.

Classes: File, FileInputStream, FileOutputStream, RandomAccessFile,

Exceptions. Input and output interface with the operating system and the computer hardware and are prone to error. The Java run time catches these errors and throws the appropriate exception. All of these exceptions should be caught and handled by your programs. These will be the most common exceptions that are thrown.

Classes: IOException, InterruptedIOException, FileNotFoundException, EOFException, UTFDataFormatException

net Package

The networking classes in Java have absolutely no parallel in C or C++. In fact, you will find that to be the case with the net, AWT, and applet packages. You will realize that not only is Java a better language than C or C++, but it has much more capability than either language. The net package consists of classes to communicate with both other computers (using sockets) and with internet servers (http, ftp, etc.).

Web Tools. The World Wide Web (WWW) is the most exciting thing to happen to the internet since its inception. Java provides classes to allow you to connect to and process Uniform Resource Locators (URLs).

InetAddress, URL, URLConnection, URLStreamHandler, ContentHandler

Sockets. A socket is a simple way to connect to processes on different machines via a TCP/IP network and share data. A socket is similar to a network pipe (a pipe is a file that one process writes to and another process reads from). The best analogy for understanding a socket is to think of a network file. You write to/read from a socket just like you write to/read from a file.

ServerSocket, Socket, SocketImpl, SocketInputStream, SocketOutputStream,

Exceptions. The net package has network specific exceptions that can be thrown and should be caught and handled by your Java application.

ProtocolException, SocketException, UnknownHostException, UnknownServiceException, MalformedURLException,

AWT Package

The AWT package is a set of classes that implement an abstract window toolkit (AWT). The abstract window toolkit is a set of classes that implement a platform-neutral graphical user interface (GUI). The AWT package gives you classes for windows, buttons, lists, menus, and so on. We will not discuss the AWT package in this chapter as it is covered separately in Chapter 6.

applet Package

The applet package is a set of classes that lets you create an applet. An applet is a small Java application that gets embedded in a web page and can be run by a web browser like HotJava or Netscape 2.0. We will not discuss the applet package here as it is covered separately in Chapter 7.

4.2 DETAILED DESCRIPTION OF THE JAVA STANDARD LIBRARY

Now that you have an introduction to the packages in the Java standard library, we will examine each class in each package. It is very important to be familiar with all the tools available to you when you are faced with a programming problem. Good knowledge of your available tools will prevent you from wasting time reinventing the wheel.

The format of the following section will be the same format as above; however, instead of describing the package or the general categories of classes, we will describe each class. At a minimum there will be one program to demonstrate each category of classes within each package. For a detailed listing of each class with all of its available methods, see **Appendix C**.

lang Package

This package supports the Java language. It is not required to import these classes since they are part of the language.

Primitive Types as Classes. The classes below are more than just wrapper classes as can be seen in the code that demonstrates them:

- **Character.** A wrapper class for a character. Remember that Java characters are in the 16-bit Unicode format. This class provides some of the useful methods in the C <ctype> header like isDigit( ) and isSpace( ). For a demonstration of the Character class see Source 4.4.
- **Boolean.** A wrapper class for a boolean.
- **Number.** An abstract superclass for the Double, Long, Float, and Integer classes. A very common use of all the wrapper classes is to convert a string input into a number.
- **Double.** A wrapper class for a double precision floating point number. Source 4.1 is an example of using the number wrapper classes.
- **Long.** A wrapper class for a long integer. See Source 4.1.
- **Float.** A wrapper class for a floating point number. See Source 4.1.
- **Integer.** A wrapper class for an integer. See Source 4.1.

Source 4.1 demonstrates use of the wrapper functions for types.

SOURCE 4.1

```java
import java.io.DataInputStream;
import java.util.Vector;
import java.io.IOException;


class tstNumTypes {
```

```java
public static void main(String args[])
{
        DataInputStream dis = new DataInputStream(System.in);
        int myInt;
        String IntString = null;
        String FloatString = null;

        System.out.print("Enter an Integer: ");
        System.out.flush();
        try {
          IntString = dis.readLine();
        } catch (IOException ioe)
          {
                System.out.println("IO Exception");
                System.exit(1);
          }
        myInt = Integer.parseInt(IntString);
        System.out.println("myInt : " + myInt);

        System.out.print("Enter a Float: ");
        System.out.flush();
        try {
          FloatString = dis.readLine();
        } catch (IOException ioe)
          {
                System.out.println("IO Exception.");
                System.exit(1);
          }
        Float myFloat = Float.valueOf(FloatString);
        System.out.println("myFloat : " + myFloat);

        Integer intObject = new Integer(myInt);

        // stuff num objects into a Vector
        Vector numbers = new Vector(2);
        numbers.addElement(intObject);
        numbers.addElement(myFloat);

        Integer anInt = (Integer) numbers.elementAt(0);
        Float aFloat = (Float) numbers.elementAt(1);

        System.out.println("At Vec element 0 : " + anInt);
```

```
                        System.out.println("At Vec element 1 : " + aFloat);
            }
    }
```

A run of Source 4.1 produces:

```
C:\java\bin>java tstNumTypes
Enter an Integer: 10
myInt : 10
Enter a Float: 230.333
myFloat : 230.333
At Vec element 0 : 10
At Vec element 1 : 230.333
```

Source 4.1 demonstrates two key points:

1. How to convert a string to a number using the valueOf( ) method or parseInt( ) method. There is also a parseLong( ) in the Long class.
2. How to convert the primitive types to objects for use in other Java classes (i.e., the Vector class). You will find this absolutely essential when using the container classes in the util package.

Abstract Classes for All Objects. These classes represent the root of the class hierarchy as well as a commonality between all Java objects:

- Class   This class is a runtime description of a class. Each object in the Java runtime is an instance of some class. Each class will have a corresponding instantiation of the Class class that acts as a class descriptor. Source 4.2 demonstrates the use of a class descriptor to find out the names of all the superclasses for the input class.

SOURCE 4.2

```
import java.lang.Class;
import java.lang.ClassNotFoundException;
import java.io.DataInputStream;
import java.io.IOException;

class getHierarchy {
        public static void main(String args[])
        {
            try {
```

```
            DataInputStream dis = new DataInputStream(System.in);
            System.out.print("Enter class to print hierarchy: ");
            System.out.flush();
            String ClassName = dis.readLine();
            Class aClass = Class.forName(ClassName);
            System.out.println("Class name: " + aClass.getName());
            Class superClass;
            do {
                    superClass = aClass.getSuperclass();
                    if (superClass != null)
                    {
                            aClass = Class.forName(superClass.getName());
                            System.out.println("Class name: " +
                                                    superClass.getName());
                    }
                    else
                    {
                            System.out.println("No superclass.");
                            break;
                    }
            } while (!superClass.getName().equals("java.lang.Object"));
        } catch (ClassNotFoundException cfe)
        {
            System.out.println("Class Not Found: " + cfe.getMessage());
        }
        catch (IOException ioe)
        {
            System.out.println("IO Exception.");
            System.out.println(ioe.getMessage());
        }
    }
}
```

A run of Source 4.2 produces:

```
C:\java\bin>java getHierarchy
Enter class to print hierarchy: java.awt.Frame
Class name: java.awt.Frame
Class name: java.awt.Window
Class name: java.awt.Container
Class name: java.awt.Component
Class name: java.lang.Object
```

- Object. All objects in the Java runtime are descendants (subclasses) of the Object class. It is important to understand that every class you create extends Object by default. You don't even have to specify it. In Source 4.3 Aobj is defined:

```
class Aobj {
...
}
```

Which is translated to:

```
class Aobj extends Object {
...
}
```

This gives you many advantages in manipulating objects at run time. One of the most important is the ability to supply any object for a method that requires an object of type Object. This makes creating generic container classes simple. The Object class also has a getClass( ) function that will return the Class descriptor for the current object. Source 4.3 demonstrates some of the methods provided by the Object class.

SOURCE 4.3

```
class Aobj implements Cloneable {
        int inum;
        Aobj(int inNum) { inum = inNum; }
        int getNum() { return inum; }

        public Object clone()
        {
            try {
                Object result = super.clone();
                return result;
            } catch (Exception e) { return null; }
        }
{

class Bobj {
        float fnum;
        Bobj(float inNum) { fnum = inNum; }
        float getNum() { return fnum; }
}
```

```
class tstObject {
    public static void main(String args[])
    {
            Aobj a1 = new Aobj(10);
            Aobj a2 = new Aobj(20);
            Bobj b1 = new Bobj((float)5.0);

            if (a1.equals(a2))
                    System.out.println("a1 equals a2");

            if (a1.equals(b1))
                    System.out.println("a1 equals b1");
            else
                    System.out.println("a1 does NOT equal b1");

            Aobj a3 = (Aobj) a1.clone();
            System.out.println("a1 is              : " + a1.toString());
            System.out.println("a3 is an a1 clone: " + a3.toString());
    }
}
```

A run of Source 4.3 produces:

```
C:\java\bin>java tstObject
a1 does NOT equal b1
a1 is           : Aobj[inum=10]
a3 is an a1 clone: Aobj[inum=10]
```

Strings. You will find Java's string classes extremely robust.

- String. The String class was discussed in Chapter 2. The primary purpose of the String class is to store and manipulate immutable (nonchangeable) strings. Source 4.4 demonstrates both Strings and StringBuffers.
- StringBuffer. A StringBuffer is used for mutable (changeable) strings. See Source 4.4.

SOURCE 4.4

```
import java.io.DataInputStream;
import java.io.IOException;
```

```
class tstStrings {
      public static void main(String args[])
        {
              if (args.length < 1)
              {
                      System.out.println("USAGE: java tstStrings someString");
                      System.exit(1);
              }

              String clString = new String(args[0]);
              System.out.println("Command line string is : " + clString);

              // count characters and digits
              int charCount = 0;
              int digitCount = 0;
              for (int i=0; i < clString.length(); i++)
                      if (!Character.isDigit(clString.charAt(i)) &&
                          !Character.isSpace(clString.charAt(i)))
                              charCount++;
                      else if (Character.isDigit(clString.charAt(i)))
                              digitCount++;

              System.out.println("# of Chars : " + charCount +
                                 " # of Digits: " + digitCount);

              // construct a sentence
              DataInputStream dis = new DataInputStream(System.in);
              System.out.println("Enter words, to exit type a '.'");
              String word=null;
              StringBuffer sentence = new StringBuffer();
              do {
                    try {
                       word = dis.readLine();
                    } catch (IOException ioe)
                    {
                            System.out.println("IOException.");
                            break;
                    }
                    if (!word.equals("."))
                      sentence.append(word + " ");
                    else
                      sentence.setCharAt(sentence.length() - 1, '.');
```

```
            } while (!word.equals("."));

            System.out.println("Sentence : " + sentence);
     }
}
```

A run of Source 4.4 produces:

```
C:\java\bin>java tstStrings StringsAndStringsBuffers111222areFun333444
Command line string is : StringsAndStringsBuffers111222areFun333444
# of Chars : 30 # of Digits: 12
Enter words, to exit type a '.'
Every
Good
Boy
Does
Fine.
Sentence : Every Good Boy Does Fine.
```

System Information. This category of classes provides both information from the operating system and access to some operating system services.

- System. You have seen a demonstration of one aspect of the System class in almost every program in this book. You may have guessed that I was referring to the call to System.out.println( ). The method println( ) actually belongs to the PrintStream class; however, the variable out is a public and static member of the System class. In addition to having the in, out, and error streams (known as stdin, stdout, and stderr in C or as cin, cout, and cerr in C++), the System class provides a system-independent method of accessing system functionality and information. Source 4.5 demonstrates accessing system information with the System class.

SOURCE 4.5

```
import java.util.Properties;

class sysProps {
      public static void main(String args[])
      {
            Properties props = System.getProperties();
```

```
        // list the properties
        props.list(System.out);

        // access an individual property
        System.out.println("\n Accessing individual properties.");
        String fileSeparator = System.getProperty("file.separator");
        System.out.println("File Separator is <" + fileSeparator +
                                ">");
    }
}
```

A run of Source 4.5 produces:

```
C:\java\bin>java sysProps
-- listing properties --
java.home=C:\JAVA\BIN\..
awt.toolkit=sun.awt.win32.MToolkit
java.version=JDK1.0beta
file.separator=\
line.separator=

java.vendor=Sun Microsystems Inc.
user.name=Mike Daconta
os.arch=x86
os.name=Windows 95
java.vendor.url=http://www.sun.com/
user.dir=C:\java\bin
java.class.path=C:\java\classes;c:\java\bin;c:\java\o...
java.class.version=45.3
os.version=4.0
path.separator=;
user.home=C:\JAVA\BIN\..

 Accessing individual properties.
File Separator is <\>
```

- **Process.** A class instantiated from a call to the exec( ) method in the run time class. The exec( ) call is very common in UNIX programming where it is used to spawn a new process. Remember that UNIX is a multi-tasking and multi-user system so that the CPU is constantly running many background and interactive processes such as servers, shells, and user-command programs. This will become more common in low-end systems with the pre-emptive multi-tasking capabilities now in Windows 95 and being added to the Mac OS. The process class provides methods that let you get the standard input and standard output of the process, kill the process, and get the exit value if the process has terminated.

- Runtime. This class is an adjunct class to the system class. In fact, the system class uses the Runtime class to perform some of its functions. Source 4.6 demonstrates some of the functions of the Runtime class.

SOURCE 4.6

```
class sysRuntime {
        public static void main(String args[])
        {
                Runtime sysRun = Runtime.getRuntime();
                System.out.println("Free Memory (in bytes) : " +
                                sysRun.freeMemory());
                System.out.println("Total Memory (in bytes): " +
                                sysRun.totalMemory());

        }
}
```

A run of Source 4.6 produces:

```
Free Memory (in bytes) : 3141696
Total Memory (in bytes) : 3145720
```

- SecurityManager. This class is an abstract class that allows a security policy to be created and enforced in your Java code. This class has methods that allow checks to the ClassLoader, to file creation, to applet access of packages, and much more. With security being such a ripe area of concern, this topic alone requires several chapters if not an entire separate book.
- ClassLoader. This is an abstract class that can be extended to allow the loading of classes either from a file or over a network. This mechanism will allow true dynamic distribution of objects to any machine on the network that has a Java run time (soon to be all or most computers out there).

Math functions.

- Math. The math class has already been used in many of the programs in this book. Source 4.7 demonstrates using the exp( ) static method in the Math class to calculate exponential growth.

SOURCE 4.7

```
import java.lang.Math;
import java.io.DataInputStream;
import java.io.IOException;

class growth {
        public static void main(String args[])
        {   try {
                DataInputStream dis = new DataInputStream(System.in);
                System.out.print("Enter initial Deficit: ");
                System.out.flush();
                String popStr = dis.readLine();
                long initPopulation = Long.parseLong(popStr);

                System.out.print("Enter number of years elapsed: ");
                System.out.flush();
                String yearStr = dis.readLine();
                int years = Integer.parseInt(yearStr);

                double growth = Math.exp((double)years);
                long newPopulation =
                        Math.round(( (double)initPopulation * growth));
                System.out.println("Exponential growth : "
                                                + newPopulation);
            } catch (IOException ioe)
            {
                System.out.println("IO Error");
                System.exit(1);
            }
        }
}
```

A run of Source 4.7 produces:

```
C:\java\bin>java growth
Enter initial Deficit: 100000
```

```
Enter number of years elapsed: 7
Exponential growth : 109663316
```

Threads. The Thread classes implement priority-based multiple execution contexts in a single program. This facility is one of the strongest features of Java and simplifies many programming tasks and makes GUI programming simpler and more responsive.

- Thread. This class is subclassed to produce a thread. You must override the run( ) function of the Thread class with the code you want your thread to run. Source 4.8 demonstrates how to create a thread.
- ThreadGroup. Allows you to group threads and manipulate them as an entire group. For example, you could change the priority of the whole group and enumerate through all the threads in a group. As your experience grows with threads, you will begin using the ThreadGroup class in your "thread management" strategy. Source 4.8 demonstrates accessing information about a ThreadGroup.

SOURCE 4.8

```java
import java.lang.Thread;
import java.lang.ThreadGroup;
import java.util.Random;

class dummyThread extends Thread {
        static int dummyThreadCount = 0;
        int Seconds;
        int id;

        dummyThread()
        {
                id = ++dummyThreadCount;
                Random dice = new Random(System.currentTimeMillis() +
                                        dummyThreadCount);
                Seconds = dice.nextInt() % 100;
                if (Seconds < 0) Seconds = -Seconds;
        }

        public void run()
        {
```

```
                System.out.println("Dummy Thread # " + id +
                                " is sleeping for " + Seconds +
                                " seconds.");
                try {
                        sleep(Seconds * 1000);
                } catch (Exception e) { }
        }
}

class tstThreads {
        public static void main(String args[])
        {
                Random generator = new Random();
                int numThreads = generator.nextInt() % 10;
                if (numThreads < 0) numThreads = -numThreads;

                System.out.println("Number of Threads to start: " +
                                        numThreads);
                for (int i=0; i < numThreads; i++)
                {
                        dummyThread d = new dummyThread();
                        d.start();
                }

                Thread currentThread = Thread.currentThread();
                ThreadGroup theGroup = currentThread.getThreadGroup();
                theGroup.list();  // list all threads in the group
                System.exit(0);
        }
}
```

A run of Source 4.8 produces:

```
C:\java\bin>java tstThreads
Number of Threads to start: 8
Dummy Thread # 1 is sleeping for 36 seconds.
Dummy Thread # 2 is sleeping for 77 seconds.
Dummy Thread # 3 is sleeping for 26 seconds.
Dummy Thread # 4 is sleeping for 79 seconds.
Dummy Thread # 5 is sleeping for 28 seconds.
java.lang.ThreadGroup[name=main,maxpri=10]
```

```
    Thread[main,5,main]
Dummy Thread # 7 is sleeping for 56 seconds.
Dummy Thread # 6 is sleeping for 8 seconds.
Dummy Thread # 8 is sleeping for 9 seconds.
    Thread[Thread-1,5,main]
    Thread[Thread-2,5,main]
    Thread[Thread-3,5,main]
    Thread[Thread-4,5,main]
    Thread[Thread-5,5,main]
    Thread[Thread-6,5,main]
    Thread[Thread-7,5,main]
    Thread[Thread-8,5,main]
```

Run Time Errors. The following classes extend the Throwable class and are thrown by the Java run time when an abnormal event occurs. In general, you should not bother catching these errors unless you have an intimate knowledge of the Java run time. Unless you are writing programs that stress the limits of your machine, you will probably never see any of these errors thrown. However, these errors could also be triggered from buggy applets or malicious applets. It is good to see the Java run time have extensive error checking. This will allow browser vendors to better protect your machine from viruses disguised as applets. Some of these errors could be thrown from the Java byte code verifier. You will notice that most of these errors fall into two major categories: a virtual machine error or some type of linkage error when trying to load a class.

- Error. A generic error class that other run time errors extend. Allows the storing of a detailed error message.
- ThreadDeath. This class extends Error. It is thrown when thread.stop( ) is called. You should not catch this error since it should be thrown.
- VirtualMachineError. This class extends Error. It signals that either the Virtual Machine has run out of resources or it has an unrecoverable internal error.
- StackOverflowError. This class extends VirtualMachineError. It signals an error that indicates the Java virtual machine's run time stack has overflowed. There are usually only two ways this can be caused: passing very large objects on the stack by value, which is currently impossible in Java, or runaway recursion. Source 4.9 demonstrates runaway recursion.

SOURCE 4.9

```
class badRecurse {
        static long numCalls=0;
        static void badFunc(long dummy)
        {
                numCalls++;
                if (numCalls % 1000 == 0)
                        System.out.println("numCalls : " + numCalls);
                badFunc(numCalls);
        }

        public static void main(String args[])
        {
                try {
                        badFunc(0);
                } catch (Error e)
                  {
                        System.out.println(e.toString());
                  }
        }
}
```

A run of Source 4.9 produces:

```
C:\java\bin>java badRecurse
numCalls : 1000
numCalls : 2000
numCalls : 3000
numCalls : 4000
numCalls : 5000
numCalls : 6000
numCalls : 7000
numCalls : 8000
java.lang.StackOverflowError
```

- OutOfMemoryError. This class extends VirtualMachineError. It occurs when the Java run time cannot satisfy a memory request. Source 4.10 demonstrates a program gobbling an extraordinary amount of memory and causing the VM to run out.

SOURCE 4.10

```
class badGobble {
       static long totalMemRequested=0;
       static int numBytes=0;
       static char cArray[];
       static void badGobble()
       {
              numBytes += 1000;
              totalMemRequested += numBytes;
              cArray = new char[numBytes];
              if (numBytes % 100000 == 0)
                     System.out.println("numBytes : " + numBytes);
       }

       public static void main(String args[])
       {
              try {
                     while (true)
                         badGobble();
              } catch (Error e)
                {
                     System.out.println(e.toString());
                     System.out.println("Total memory requested was: " +
                                            totalMemRequested);
                }
       }
}
```

A run of Source 4.10 produces:

```
C:\java\bin>java badGobble
numBytes : 100000
numBytes : 200000
numBytes : 300000
numBytes : 400000
numBytes : 500000
numBytes : 600000
numBytes : 700000
numBytes : 800000
numBytes : 900000
java.lang.OutOfMemoryError
Total memory requested was: 476776000
```

- UnknownError. This class extends VirtualMachineError. An unknown error with the Virtual Machine; should never occur.
- LinkageError. This class extends Error. Many subclasses extend this class. This class and all its subclasses indicate that a class has a dependency on another class; however, the latter class has incompatibly changed after the compilation of the first class. This only occurs if you change the class in some abnormal way. Normally a class is neatly defined into a private implementation and public interface. As long as the public interface does not change, or classes outside the package do not access the private implementation, you should not have any problems. However, if you violate the above rules you could see a subclass of Linkage error be thrown.
- NoClassDefFoundError. This class extends LinkageError. The Virtual Machine cannot find a class. This could occur if the <classname>.class file existed during compilation but was later accidentally deleted or moved (moved outside of the CLASSPATH environment variable). Source 4.11 demonstrates the above situation.

SOURCE 4.11

```
import noExist;

class noClass {
        public static void main(String args[])
        {
                noExist aClass = new noExist();
                aClass.noMethod();
        }
}
```

A run of Source 4.11 produces:

```
C:\java\bin>java noClass
Exception in thread "main" java.lang.NoClassDefFoundError: noExist
        at
```

- ClassCircularityError. This class extends LinkageError. A circularity has been detected during the initalization of a class. If the static initializer of class A uses a class B that has not been loaded, the run time then loads class B and tries to initialize it. If class B uses class A, an impossible to fulfill circular dependency has been created (a classic catch-22).

- ClassFormatError. This class extends LinkageError. It indicates the detection of an invalid file format while attempting to load a class.
- VerifyError. This class extends LinkageError. A verification has occurred when verifying the byte-codes of a class being loaded.
- UnsatisfiedLinkError. Extends LinkageError. This class is thrown if a native method was declared native but the run time cannot find the dynamic library to link to or has linked to the specified library but the method is not part of that library.
- IncompatibleClassChangeError. This class extends LinkageError. Several classes extend this one. Again the basic reason for this error is when a class with dependencies is changed in an incompatible way. Four specific changes will cause this exception:
  1. A variable is changed from static to nonstatic without recompiling other classes that still use the variable as static.
  2. A variable is changed from nonstatic to static without recompiling other classes that use the variable as a nonstatic.
  3. A field is deleted but is still used in other classes that access the field.
  4. A method is deleted but classes that use it are not recompiled.
- NoSuchMethodError. Extends IncompatibleClassChangeError. A method could not be found. See IncompatibleClassChangeError for the reason why.
- NoSuchFieldError. Extends IncompatibleClassChangeError. A field could not be found. See IncompatibleClassChangeError for the reason why.
- AbstractMethodError. This class extends IncompatibleClassChangeError. This is thrown if there was an attempt by the run time to call an abstract method.
- IllegalAccessError. This class extends IncompatibleClassChangeError. An illegal access has occurred.
- InstantiationError. This class extends IncompatibleClassChangeError. This class is thrown if the interpreter attempts to instantiate an abstract class or interface.

Exceptions. The purpose and use of exceptions have already been discussed. Here we will examine the Exception classes thrown by either the Java lang classes or the Java Virtual Machine.

- Exception. An exception is an abnormal condition that programs should attempt to catch and handle.
- InterruptedException. This class extends Exception. It is thrown by a thread when a thread with a higher priority has interrupted it.
- ClassNotFoundException. This class extends Exception. It is thrown if a class cannot be found.
- NoSuchMethodException. This class extends Exception. A method could not be found.
- RuntimeException. An exception thrown by the Virtual Machine that can reasonably occur. You are not forced to catch these exceptions as you are with exceptions that extend the Exception class. Source 4.12 demonstrates the requirement for catching Exceptions but not RuntimeExceptions.

SOURCE 4.12

```
class mySeriousException extends RuntimeException {
        mySeriousException()
        {
                super("A really bad exception.");
        }
}

class recoverableException extends Exception {
        recoverableException()
        {
                super("catch this");
        }
}

class throwRTE {
        public static void main(String args[])
        {
                throw new mySeriousException();
                throw new recoverableException();
        }
}
```

We are not going to run the above program, because it will not compile (this was intentional). A compile of the program produces:

```
C:\java\bin>javac throwRTE.java
throwRTE.java:20: Statement not reached.
                throw new recoverableException();
                ^
throwRTE.java:20: Warning: Exception recoverableException must be caught,
or it must be declared in the throws clause of this method.
                throw new recoverableException();
                ^
1 error, 1 warning
```

It is very important to note that when creating exceptions you should extend the Exception class. The RuntimeException class is reserved for exceptions that the Virtual Machine can throw. The only difference a run time exception makes is that you are not forced to "propagate" the exception if you do not catch it; however, you should catch all these exceptions to include the run time exceptions.

- ArithmeticException. This class extends RuntimeException. It is thrown when an arithmetic exception like a divide by zero occurs.
- ClassCastException. This class extends RuntimeException. It is thrown when an attempt is made to cast an Object of type A into an Object of type C when A is neither a C nor a subclass of C. Source 4.13 demonstrates legal and illegal casts.

SOURCE 4.13

```
class A {
        int a;
        A()
        { System.out.println("I am A"); }
}

class Ason extends A {
        int b;
        Ason()
        { System.out.println("I am son of A"); }
}

class C {
        int c;
```

```
            C()
            { System.out.println("I am C"); }
}

class tstCast {
      public static void main(String args[])
      {
            A anA = new A();
            Ason B = new Ason();
            C aC = new C();

            A A2 = (A) B;            // legal
            Ason B2 = (Ason) anA;    // legal
            // Ason B3 = (Ason) aC;  -- invalid cast
            // C C2 = (C) anA;       -- invalid cast
      }
}
```

- ArrayStoreException. This class extends RuntimeException. It is thrown when an attempt is made to store the wrong type in an array.
- NullPointerException. This class extends RuntimeException. This is one of the most common exceptions thrown. It is thrown any time a null object is used to access a method. Source 4.14 demonstrates this.

SOURCE 4.14

```
class useNull {
      public static void main(String args[])
      {
            String myName = null;

            // oops forgot to assign it a valid String
            System.out.println("My name is " + myName);

            // cannot trim a null
            myName.trim();
      }
}
```

A run of Source 4.14 produces:

```
C:\java\bin>java useNull
My name is null
Exception in thread "main" java.lang.NullPointerException
        at useNull.main(useNull.java:10)
```

- NegativeArraySizeException. This class extends RuntimeException. It is thrown if an attempt is made to create an array with a negative size.
- IllegalArgumentException. This class extends RuntimeException. It is extended further by other more specific exceptions. In general, it indicates that an illegal argument has occurred. See Number-FormatException for a specific example.
- IllegalThreadStateException. This class extends the IllegalArgumentException class. It is thrown if a thread is not in the proper state for the requested operation. As an example, it will be thrown if you try to call Thread.stop( ) before a call to Thread.run( ).
- NumberFormatException. This class extends IllegalArgumentException. It is thrown if an invalid number format occurs. This is a very common exception that is easily thrown. Source 4.15 demonstrates this exception being thrown. You should always catch and handle this exception.

SOURCE 4.15

```
import java.io.DataInputStream;
import java.io.IOException;

class badFormat {
    public static void main(String args[])
    {
        DataInputStream dis = new DataInputStream(System.in);
        System.out.print("Enter an Integer: ");
        System.out.flush();
        String numStr = null;

        try {
            numStr = dis.readLine();
        } catch (IOException ioe)
        {
            ioe.printStackTrace();
```

```
            System.exit(1);
        }


        System.out.println("numStr is : " + numStr);
        int theNum = Integer.parseInt(numStr);
    }
}
```

A run of Source 4.15 produces:

```
C:\java\bin>java badFormat
Enter an Integer: abc
numStr is : abc
Exception in thread "main" java.lang.NumberFormatException: abc
        at java.lang.Integer.parseInt(Integer.java:139)
        at java.lang.Integer.parseInt(Integer.java:159)
        at badFormat.main(badFormat.java:21)
```

- IndexOutOfBoundsException. This class extends RuntimeException. It is thrown if an index is out of bounds. This class is extended by specific classes for strings and arrays.
- ArrayIndexOutOfBoundsException. This class extends IndexOutOfBoundsException. It is thrown if an array index is out of range.
- StringIndexOutOfBoundsException. This class extends IndexOutOfBoundsException. It is thrown if a string index is out of range.
- SecurityException. This class extends RuntimeException. It is thrown if there is a violation of the security policy set by the SecurityManager class.

util Package

This package is a utility package of classes that provides common storage classes, math functions, date and time classes, and methods.

Containers. This category of classes consists of classes that perform efficient storage and retrieval of other objects. All the Java containers can store ANY Java object. There is no requirement for the containers to hold a homogeneous sequence of objects. You could use run time type information to determine the type on the fly.

- Dictionary. An abstract class that describes an associative set. An associative set maps keys to values. This class is the abstract parent of HashTable.

- HashTable. This class extends Dictionary. A hash table is an efficient random access storage technique that uses a hash function (the method HashCode( ) in this class) to change the key into an array index. If two keys map to the same index, a collision list is created. Source 4.17 demonstrates the use of HashTable.
- Properties. This class extends HashTable. A persistent hash table is created that can be saved to a stream and loaded from a stream.
- Vector. A growable array class. You have seen this demonstrated several times already. You can reexamine Source 1.7 for a demonstration of the Vector class.
- Enumeration. An interface (Section 5.2 describes interfaces in detail. In general they are a set of methods that specify a protocol that one or more classes can implement.) that describes the protocol for sequencing through a set of elements until there are no more. There are two methods declared in this interface—hasMoreElements( ) and nextElement( ). Similar in concept to the C++ iterator described in Section 3.6.
- VectorEnumerator. A final class (cannot be extended) that implements the Enumeration interface.
- Stack. This class extends Vector. It implements a First-In-First-Out queue; a data structure that lets you push( ) and pop( ) elements from a single side of queue. Source 4.16 demonstrates the use of a Stack in a simple postfix calculator.

SOURCE 4.16

```java
import java.util.Stack;
import java.io.DataInputStream;
import java.io.IOException;

class postFix {
      public static void main(String args[])
      {
              DataInputStream dis = new DataInputStream(System.in);
              System.out.println("Simple PostFix calculator.");
              String input=null;

              System.out.println("Valid operations are + - / *");
              System.out.println("Enter 'q' to quit.");

              Stack numberStack = new Stack();
```

```
do {
        System.out.print(": ");
        System.out.flush();
        try {
                input = dis.readLine();
        } catch (IOException ioe)
          {
                System.out.println("IO Error.");
                System.exit(1);
          }

        if (input.equals("+"))
        {
                if (numberStack.size() >= 2)
                {
                        Integer a = (Integer) numberStack.pop();
                        Integer b = (Integer) numberStack.pop();
                        int total = a.intValue() + b.intValue();
                        System.out.println(total);
                        numberStack.push(new Integer(total));
                }
                else
                {
                        System.out.println("In Postfix notation " +
                                        "there must be 2 numbers " +
                                        "and then an operator.");
                }
        }
        else if (input.equals("-"))
        {
                if (numberStack.size() >= 2)
                {
                        Integer a = (Integer) numberStack.pop();
                        Integer b = (Integer) numberStack.pop();
                        int total = b.intValue() - a.intValue();
                        System.out.println(total);
                        numberStack.push(new Integer(total));
                }
                else
                {
                        System.out.println("In Postfix notation " +
                                        "there must be 2 numbers " +
```

```
                                                "and then an operator.");
            }

        }
        else if (input.equals("/"))
        {
                if (numberStack.size() >= 2)
                {
                        Integer a = (Integer) numberStack.pop();
                        Integer b = (Integer) numberStack.pop();
                        if (a.intValue() != 0)
                        {
                            int total = b.intValue() / a.intValue();
                            System.out.println(total);
                            numberStack.push(new Integer(total));
                        }
                        else
                            System.out.println("Divide by 0 is illegal.");
                }
                else
                {
                        System.out.println("In Postfix notation " +
                                        "there must be 2 numbers " +
                                        "and then an operator.");
                }

        }
        else if (input.equals("*"))
        {
                if (numberStack.size() >= 2)
                {
                        Integer a = (Integer) numberStack.pop();
                        Integer b = (Integer) numberStack.pop();
                        int total = a.intValue() * b.intValue();
                        System.out.println(total);
                        numberStack.push(new Integer(total));
                }
                else
                {
                        System.out.println("In Postfix notation " +
                                        "there must be 2 numbers " +
                                        "and then an operator.");
```

```
                        }

                }
                else if (input.equals("="))
                {
                        // show top of stack
                        if (!numberStack.empty())
                        {
                                Integer tot = (Integer) numberStack.pop();
                                System.out.println("Total : " + tot);
                        }
                        else
                        {
                                System.out.println("Stack is empty!");
                        }
                }
                else if (Character.isDigit(input.charAt(0)))
                {
                        int num = Integer.parseInt(input);
                        numberStack.push(new Integer(num));
                }
                else if (!input.equals("q")) // unknown input
                {
                        System.out.println("Unknown input <" +
                                                input + ">");
                }
        } while (!input.equals("q"));
    }
}
```

A run of Source 4.16 produces:

```
C:\java\bin>java postFix
Simple PostFix calculator.
Valid operations are + - / *
Enter 'q' to quit.
: 10
: 20
: +
30
: 10
: -
```

```
20
 : 10
 : *
200
 : 2
 : /
100
 : =
Total : 100
 : q
```

- Observer. An interface that allows the class to be observable by an instance of class Observer.
- Observable. A representation of an object or "data" that is being observed by a set of observers. If the object changes all observers are notified by calling their update( ) routine (the update( ) is part of the Observer interface).
- BitSet. A growable set of bits. These bits can be set, cleared, read, ANDed, ORed, and XORed.

Miscellaneous Utilities. The rest of the utilities in this package do not belong to a specific category. They are math, date, time, and parsing utilities. As the Java standard library grows, we will be able to compartmentalize the growing set of utilities.

- NoSuchElementException. This class extends RuntimeException. It is thrown when an attempt is made to get another element in an enumeration that is empty. This can be avoided by testing the hasMoreElements( ) method as demonstrated in Source 4.17.
- EmptyStackException. This class extends RuntimeException. It is thrown when you try to pop( ) an empty Stack. This can be avoided by testing the empty( ) method of the Stack as demonstrated in Source 4.16 above.
- Random. A class that creates a pseudo-random number generator. You can either provide a seed or use the default which is the System time in milliseconds. You can choose between a uniform distribution and a gaussian (bell curve) distribution. Source 4.8 demonstrates the use of the Random class.
- Date. A very robust date and time class, the majority of the functionality of the standard C library <time.h> header. Source 4.17 is a Reminder utility that uses the Date class as a key field of the Reminder. Pay attention to this source, as in Chapter 6 we give it a graphical user interface.

- StringTokenizer. This class implements the Enumeration interface; a class that will tokenize (separate into meaningful units, like words or keywords) a String. This is a more robust version of the standard C library function strtok( ). Source 4.17 demonstrates the use of this function to parse reminders and input from the user.

SOURCE 4.17

```
import java.util.Date;
import java.io.DataInputStream;
import java.util.StringTokenizer;
import java.util.Hashtable;
import java.util.Enumeration;
import java.io.File;
import java.io.FileInputStream;
import java.io.FileOutputStream;
import java.io.PrintStream;

class Record {
        private Date reminderDate;
        private String reminderInfo;

        public Record(Date inDate, String inInfo)
        {
                reminderDate = (Date) new Date(inDate.getTime());
                reminderInfo = (String) new String(inInfo);
        }

        public String toString()
        {
                return (reminderDate.toLocaleString() +
                        "-" + reminderInfo);
        }

        static Record getRecord()
        {
            Date outDate = null;
            String outString = null;
            Record outRecord = null;
            try {
                DataInputStream dis = new DataInputStream(System.in);
                System.out.print("Enter Reminder Date as (MM/DD/YY HH:MM) : ");
```

```
System.out.flush();
String DateStr = dis.readLine();
String timeStr=null, dateStr=null;
int hours=0, mins=0, date=0, mon=0, year=0;

// tokenize date
StringTokenizer split = new StringTokenizer(DateStr);
if (split != null && split.countTokens() == 2)
{
        dateStr = split.nextToken();
        timeStr = split.nextToken();
}
else
{
        System.out.println("Malformed date string <" +
                              DateStr + ">");
        return null;
}


StringTokenizer theToks = new StringTokenizer(dateStr,"/");
if (theToks != null && theToks.countTokens() == 3)
{
        mon = Integer.parseInt(theToks.nextToken());
        mon--;  // enter from 0-11
        date = Integer.parseInt(theToks.nextToken());
        year = Integer.parseInt(theToks.nextToken());
}
else
{
        System.out.println("Malformed Date string <" +
                              dateStr + ">");
        return null;
}

theToks = new StringTokenizer(timeStr,":");
if (theToks != null && theToks.countTokens() == 2)
{
  hours = Integer.parseInt(theToks.nextToken());
  mins = Integer.parseInt(theToks.nextToken());
}
else
```

```
            {
                    System.out.println("Malformed time string <" +
                                          timeStr + ">");
                    return null;
            }

            outDate = new Date(year, mon, date, hours, mins);

            // Enter the info with this date
            System.out.print("Enter reminder: ");
            System.out.flush();
            outString = dis.readLine();

            // create the record
            outRecord = new Record(outDate, outString);

        } catch (Exception e)
          {
            e.printStackTrace();
            return null;
          }

      return outRecord;
}

static Record parseRecord(String inLine)
{
    Date outDate = null;
    String outString = null;
    Record outRecord = null;
    String DateString = null;

    try {

        StringTokenizer split = new StringTokenizer(inLine,"-");
        if (split != null && split.countTokens() == 2)
        {
                DateString = split.nextToken();
                outString = split.nextToken();
        }
        else
        {
```

```
                System.out.println("Malformed line: <" +
                                        inLine + ">");
            return null;
    }


String timeString=null;
String dateString=null;
int mn=0,dt=0,yr=0,hr=0,min=0,sc=0;
StringTokenizer dtg = new StringTokenizer(DateString," ");
if (split != null && dtg.countTokens() == 2)
{
        dateString = dtg.nextToken();
        StringTokenizer datePieces = new
                StringTokenizer(dateString,"/");
        if (datePieces != null && datePieces.countTokens() == 3)
        {
                String mnStr, dtStr, yrStr;
                mnStr = datePieces.nextToken();
                dtStr = datePieces.nextToken();
                yrStr = datePieces.nextToken();
                mn = Integer.parseInt(mnStr);
                dt = Integer.parseInt(dtStr);
                yr = Integer.parseInt(yrStr);
        }
        else
        {
                System.out.println("Malformed date: <" +
                                        dateString + ">");
                return null;
        }

        timeString = dtg.nextToken();
        StringTokenizer timePieces = new
                StringTokenizer(timeString,":");
        if (timePieces != null && timePieces.countTokens() == 3)
        {
                String hrStr, minStr, scStr;
                hrStr = timePieces.nextToken();
                minStr = timePieces.nextToken();
                scStr = timePieces.nextToken();

                hr = Integer.parseInt(hrStr);
```

```
                            min = Integer.parseInt(minStr);
                            sc = Integer.parseInt(scStr);
                }
                else
                {
                        System.out.println("Malformed time: <" +
                                            timeString + ">");
                        return null;
                }
        }
        else
        {
                System.out.println("Malformed date: <" +
                                    DateString + ">");
                return null;
        }

        mn--; // month must be between 0-11

        outDate = new Date(yr,mn,dt,hr,min,sc);

        // create the Record
        outRecord = new Record(outDate, outString);

    } catch (Exception e)
      {
        e.printStackTrace();
        return null;
      }

    return outRecord;
    }

    public Date getDate() { return reminderDate; }
    public String getInfo() { return reminderInfo; }
}

class Reminder {
    public static void main(String args[])
    {
            Hashtable reminders = new Hashtable();
```

```
DataInputStream dis = new DataInputStream(System.in);

// get the current date
Date now = new Date();
System.out.println("Now is : " + now.toLocaleString());

// Check if a Reminder File exists
File dataFile = new File("Reminder.data");
if (dataFile.exists())
{
 try {
        FileInputStream fis = new FileInputStream("Reminder.data");
        DataInputStream dis2 = new DataInputStream(fis);
        String line = null;

        while ( (line = dis2.readLine()) != null)
        {
                Record theRec = Record.parseRecord(line);
                if (theRec != null)
                {
                        // add the Record to the hashTable
                        reminders.put(theRec.getDate(),
                                     theRec.getInfo());
                }
                else
                {
                        System.out.println("Unable to get a Reminder.");
                }
        }
        fis.close();
    } catch (Exception e)
    {
                System.out.println("Unable to open Reminder.dat");
                System.exit(1);
    }
}


// Check if any Reminders for Today.
System.out.println("---Reminders for today---");
Enumeration keys,vals;
keys = reminders.keys();
```

```
vals = reminders.elements();
Date startDate = (Date) new Date(now.getTime());
startDate.setHours(0);
startDate.setMinutes(0);
Date endDate = (Date) new Date(now, getTime());
endDate.setHours(23);
endDate.setMinutes(59);

for ( ; keys.hasMoreElements(); )
{
   Date theDate = (Date) keys.nextElement();
   if ( theDate.after(startDate) &&
        theDate.before(endDate) )
     System.out.println( theDate.toLocaleString() +
                          " - " +
                          vals.nextElement());

   else
        vals.nextElement();
}
System.out.println("---End of Reminders---");

// put up a text menu
boolean done = false;

while (!done)
{
        System.out.println("\n<<< Reminder Menu >>>\n");
        System.out.println("   1) add Reminder.");
        System.out.println("   2) list Reminders.");
        System.out.println("   3) exit.\n");
        System.out.print("Enter Choice : ");
        System.out.flush();
        String choiceStr=null;
        try {
          choiceStr = dis.readLine();
        } catch (Exception e)
          {
                System.out.println("IO Error");
                System.exit(1);
          }
        int choice = 0;
        if (choiceStr.length() > 0)
```

```
                        choice = Integer.parseInt(choiceStr);

            switch (choice) {
                case 1:
                        Record aRec = Record.getRecord();

                        if (aRec != null)
                        {
                           // add the Record to the hashTable
                           reminders.put(aRec.getDate(),
                                        aRec.getInfo());
                        }
                        else
                        {
                           System.out.println("Unable to get a Reminder.");
                        }
                        break;
                case 2:
                        // Enumerate the hashTable
                        Enumeration k,v;
                        k = reminders.keys();
                        v = reminders.elements();

                        for ( ; k.hasMoreElements(); )
            System.out.println(((Date)k.nextElement()).toLocaleString() +
                                        " - " +
                                        v.nextElement());
                        break;
                case 3:
                        done = true;
                        break;
                default:
                        System.out.println("Invalid Choice: " +
                                        choiceStr);
            }
    }

try {
  // dump hash table to file
  FileOutputStream fos = new FileOutputStream("Reminder.data");
  PrintStream ps = new PrintStream(fos);
  Enumeration k,v;
```

```
        k = reminders.keys();
        v = reminders.elements();

        for ( ; k.hasMoreElements(); )
            ps.println(((Date)k.nextElement()).toLocaleString() +
                          "-" +
                          v.nextElement());
        fos.close();
    } catch (Exception e)
      {
            System.out.println("IO error on reminder.data");
            System.exit(1);
      }

    }
}
```

A run of Source 4.17 produces:

```
C:\java\bin>java Reminder
Now is : 11/17/95 03:28:30
---Reminders for today---
11/17/95 09:00:00 - Meeting with boss.
11/17/95 06:00:00 - Wake up and answer email before work.
---End of Reminders---

<<< Reminder Menu >>>

    1) add Reminder.
    2) list Reminders.
    3) exit.

Enter Choice : 1
Enter Reminder Date as (MM/DD/YY HH:MM) : 11/18/95 10:30
Enter reminder: Programmer's code walk-through.

<<< Reminder Menu >>>

    1) add Reminder.
    2) list Reminders.
    3) exit.

Enter Choice : 2
```

```
11/18/95 10:30:00 - Programmer's code walk-through.
11/17/95 09:00:00 - Meeting with boss.
11/17/95 06:00:00 - Wake up and answer email before work.

<<< Reminder Menu >>>

    1) add Reminder.
    2) list Reminders.
    3) exit.

Enter Choice : 3
```

io Package

A robust implementation of input and output classes and methods that combines the best of the C standard library and the C++ standard library.

Input Streams. Classes and facilities to retrieve and manipulate input from a variety of sources.

- InputStream. An abstract class that represents an input stream of bytes. All input streams extend this class.
- ByteArrayInputStream. This class extends InputStream. The class implements a byte buffer that can be used as an input stream—very useful for reading persistent objects. See Source 4.21 in the database package below for a demonstration of this class.
- FilterInputStream. This class extends InputStream, and allows multiple input streams to be chained together. This concept will be very familiar to UNIX users who often insert filters between an input and output stream using pipes. Source 4.18 demonstrates the use of a FilterInputStream to strip comments from a Java source file. The program optionally lets you save the comments to a separate file.

SOURCE 4.18

```
import java.io.FilterInputStream;
import java.io.FileInputStream;
import java.io.FileNotFoundException;
import java.io.FileOutputStream;
import java.io.PrintStream;
```

```java
import java.io.InputStream;
import java.io.PushbackInputStream;
import java.io.IOException;
import java.util.Stack;
import java.lang.Character;

class CommentFilter extends FilterInputStream {
        private boolean OutputComments=false;
        private FileOutputStream fos;
        private PrintStream ps;
        private static char currentChar=0, lastChar=0, nextChar=0;
        private static boolean inLineComment=false;
        private static boolean inMultiLineComment=false;

        // just strip comments
        CommentFilter(InputStream src)
        {
                super(src);
                PushbackInputStream pis = new PushbackInputStream(src);
                in = pis;
        }

        /* open a potential output stream for comments
           if output flag is set */
        CommentFilter(InputStream src, String outFileName)
        {
                super(src);
                PushbackInputStream pis = new PushbackInputStream(src);
                in = pis;
                OutputComments = true;

                try {
                        fos = new FileOutputStream(outFileName);
                        ps = new PrintStream(fos);
                } catch (IOException e)
                  {
                        System.out.println("IO Error on " + outFileName);
                        System.exit(1);
                  }
                  catch (Exception e)
                  {
                        System.out.println("Unable to filter input");
```

```
                            System.exit(1);
                }
}

public int read()
{
        int input=0;
        boolean peekAhead = false;

        try {
            input = super.read();
            if (input == -1)
                return -1;
            currentChar = (char) input;
        } catch (IOException ioe) { return -1; }

        if (currentChar == '/' && !inLineComment &&
            !inMultiLineComment)
        {
            // peek ahead
            try {
                input = super.read();
                if (input == -1)
                        return -1;
              nextChar = (char) input;
              peekAhead = true;
            } catch (IOException ioe) { return -1; }

            if (nextChar != '/' && nextChar != '*')
            {
                // push it back on the stream for next read
                try {
                  ((PushbackInputStream)in).unread(nextChar);
                } catch (IOException ioe) { return -1; }
            }
        }

        if (currentChar == '/' && nextChar == '*')
        {
                if (!inLineComment)
                    inMultiLineComment = true;
        }
```

```
else if (currentChar == '/' && nextChar == '/')
{
        if (!inMultiLineComment)
            inLineComment = true;
}


if (inLineComment || inMultiLineComment)
{
   while (inLineComment || inMultiLineComment)
   {
        if (OutputComments)
        {
                ps.print(currentChar);
                if (peekAhead)
                {
                        ps.print(nextChar);
                        peekAhead = false;
                }
                ps.flush();
        }

        // check if comment is over
        if (inMultiLineComment && lastChar == '*' &&
            currentChar == '/')
        {
                inMultiLineComment = false;
                if (OutputComments)
                {
                        ps.print('\n');
                        ps.flush();
                }
        }

        if (inLineComment &&
            (currentChar == 10 || currentChar == 13))
        {
                if (OutputComments)
                {
                        ps.print('\n');
                        ps.flush();
                }
```

```
                                inLineComment = false;
                                lastChar = currentChar;
                                return currentChar;
                        }

                        lastChar = currentChar;

                        // get next character
                        try {
                            input = super.read();
                            if (input == -1)
                                return -1;
                          currentChar = (char) input;
                        } catch (IOException ioe) { return -1; }
                    }
                }
                else
                        return currentChar;

                return currentChar;
        }

    public void finalize()
    {
        try {
            fos.close();
        } catch (Exception e) { }
    }
}

class runCommentFilter {
        public static void main(String args[])
        {
                // Get command line argument
                if (args.length < 1)
                {
                        System.out.println("USAGE: java runCommentFilter fileToRead
                                [-output commentFile]");
                        System.out.println("  -output flag is optional.");
                        System.exit(1);
                }
```

```
String fileName = null;
String commentFileName = null;
boolean captureComments = false;
for (int i=0; i < args.length; i++)
{
        if (args[i].equals("-output"))
        {
                if (args.length > i + 1)
                {
                        commentFileName = new String(args[i+1]);
                        i++;
                        captureComments = true;
                }
                else
                {
                   System.out.println("No output file specified.");
                        System.exit(1);
                }
        }
        else
                fileName = new String(args[i]);
}

System.out.println("fileName is " + fileName);

FileInputStream fis=null;
// open the input file
try {
    fis = new FileInputStream(fileName);
} catch (FileNotFoundException fnf)
  {
        System.out.println("Unable to open " + fileName);
        System.exit(1);
  }

if (captureComments)
        System.out.println("Comment File is " + commentFileName);

CommentFilter cf=null;
if (captureComments)
        cf = new CommentFilter(fis, commentFileName);
else
```

```
                  cf = new CommentFilter(fis);

    int in=0;
    while ( (in = cf.read()) != -1)
    {
            System.out.print((char)in);
            System.out.flush();
    }

    try {
      fis.close();
    } catch (Exception e) { }
  }
}
```

A run of Source 4.18 produces:

```
// Copyright (c) 1995 by Michael C. Daconta
// check if file exists
// philosophy & credits
// define DB
// select DB
// add record
// view records
// close DB
// exit
```

- PushbackInputStream. This class extends InputStream. This is an input stream with a 1-byte push back buffer. Source 4.18 uses the PushbackInputStream to allow a 1-character peek ahead in the input stream when checking for comments.
- StringBufferInputStream. This class extends InputStream. It allows a StringBuffer to be used as an input stream.
- DataInput. An interface to read all Java primitive types in a machine-independent way.
- DataInputStream. This class extends FilterInputStream. This is one of the most commonly used streams in Java programs. It allows the reading of Java primitive types (i.e., integer, floats, strings) in a machine-independent way. Almost every program in this book that accepts input uses DataInputStream.
- BufferedInputStream. This class extends FilterInputStream. It implements a byte buffer to improve the performance of reads.

This is similar to the C standard library fread( ) versus the non-buffered UNIX read( ).

- LineNumberInputStream. This class extends FilterInputStream. This is an input stream that keeps track of the line number. This class is very useful for debugging source code. Source 4.19 demonstrates a source code listing utility that comes with many compilers. The LineNumFilter in Source 4.19 creates a source code listing that includes the line number. For the majority of debugging this utility is sufficient to isolate the error. In fact, this simple utility was used throughout this book instead of using the Java debugger (jdb).

SOURCE 4.19

```java
import java.io.FileInputStream;
import java.io.FileOutputStream;
import java.io.InputStream;
import java.io.LineNumberInputStream;
import java.io.IOException;
import java.io.PrintStream;
import java.io.FileNotFoundException;

class LineNumFilter extends LineNumberInputStream {
        private static String lineNumber=null;
        private static int StrPos=0;
        private char currentChar;

        LineNumFilter(InputStream src)
        {
                super(src);
                lineNumber = new String((getLineNumber()+1) + " ");
        }

        public int read()
        {
                int input=0;

                if (lineNumber != null && lineNumber.length() > 0
                    && StrPos < lineNumber.length())
                {
                        currentChar = lineNumber.charAt(StrPos++);
```

```
                        if (StrPos == lineNumber.length())
                        {
                                // dumped line number - reset
                                StrPos = 0;
                                lineNumber = null;
                        }
                }
                else
                {
                    try {
                        input = super.read();
                    } catch (IOException ioe) { return -1; }

                        if (input == -1)
                                return input;
                        currentChar = (char) input;
                        if (currentChar == '\n')
                        {
                            // set up lineNumber
                            lineNumber =
                                new String((getLineNumber()+1) + " ");
                        }
                }

                return currentChar;
        }
}


class runLineNumFilter {
        public static void main(String args[])
        {
                if (args.length < 1)
                {
                        System.out.println("USAGE: java runLineNumFilter fileToRead
                            [-output lineFile]");
                        System.out.println(" -output flag is optional.");
                        System.exit(1);
                }

                String fileName = null;
                String lineFileName = null;
                boolean captureLines = false;
```

```java
for (int i=0; i < args.length; i++)
{
        if (args[i].equals("-output"))
        {
                if (args.length > i + 1)
                {
                        lineFileName = new String(args[i+1]);
                        i++;
                        captureLines = true;
                }
                else
                {
                        System.out.println("No output file specified.");
                        System.exit(1);
                }
        }
        else
                fileName = new String(args[i]);
}

System.out.println("fileName is " + fileName);

FileInputStream fis=null;
// open the input file
try {
    fis = new FileInputStream(fileName);
} catch (FileNotFoundException fnf)
  {
        System.out.println("Unable to open " + fileName);
        System.exit(1);
  }

if (captureLines)
        System.out.println("Line File is " + lineFileName);

LineNumFilter lf = new LineNumFilter(fis);
FileOutputStream fos = null;
PrintStream ps = null;

if (captureLines)
{
    try {
```

```
                    fos = new FileOutputStream(lineFileName);
                    ps = new PrintStream(fos);
            } catch (IOException e)
            {
                System.out.println("IO Error on " + lineFileName);
                System.exit(1);
            }
            catch (Exception e)
            {
                System.out.println("Unable to filter input");
                System.exit(1);
            }

        }

        int in=0;
        while ( (in = lf.read()) != -1)
        {
                if (captureLines)
                {
                        ps.print((char)in);
                        ps.flush();
                }
                else
                {
                        System.out.print((char)in);
                        System.out.flush();
                }
        }

        try {
          fis.close();
          fos.close();
        } catch (Exception e) { }
    }
}
```

A run of Source 4.19 produces:

```
1 class Aobj {
2        int inum;
3        Aobj(int inNum) { inum = inNum; }
```

```
4          int getNum() { return inum; }
5 }
6
7 class Bobj {
8          float fnum;
9          Bobj(float inNum) { fnum = inNum; }
10          float getNum() { return fnum; }
11 }
12
13 class tstObject {
14          public static void main(String args[])
15          {
16                  Aobj a1 = new Aobj(10);
17                  Aobj a2 = new Aobj(20);
18                  Bobj b1 = new Bobj((float)5.0);
19
20                  if (a1.equals(a2))
21                          System.out.println("a1 equals a2");
22
23                  if (a1.equals(b1))
24                          System.out.println("a1 equals b1");
25                  else
26                          System.out.println("a1 does NOT equal b1");
27
28                  Aobj a3 = (Aobj) a1.clone();
29                  System.out.println("a1 is               : " + a1.toString());
30                  System.out.println("a3 is an a1 clone: " + a3.toString());
31          }
32 }
33
```

It is very important to understand that the LineNumFilter, like all FilterInputStreams, must have the ability to be used the same as any input stream. In fact, you are placing your filter between an input and output. This is demonstrated in the above program when we use the LineNumFilter in the same manner we read from an input stream with this code:

```
while ( (in = lf.read()) != -1)
```

In the case of our LineNumFilter, we are actually inserting extra characters into the stream (the string version of the line number). Understanding the above source will allow you to create all sorts of interesting filters. Have fun!

- SequenceInputStream. This class extends InputStream. It converts a sequence of input streams into a single input stream.
- PipedInputStream. This class extends InputStream. This is an input stream that must be connected to a pipedOutputStream before use. This is useful for communication between threads.
- StreamTokenizer. A class used to transform a stream of bytes into a stream of tokens. This class has numerous methods to define the lexical analysis of tokens. This class is extremely useful for creating parsers.

Output Streams. This category provides numerous streams for outputting data in a variety of formats and to a variety of sinks.

- OutputStream. An abstract class that represents an output stream of bytes. All output streams extend this class.
- FilterOutputStream. This class extends OutputStream. This is an abstract filter for an output stream. This allows you to chain together output streams with each filter potentially modifying the stream.
- DataOutput. An interface for outputting all the Java primitive types in a machine-independent way.
- DataOutputStream. This class extends FilterOutputStream and implements the DataOutput interface. This stream allows you to output all the primitive types in a machine-independent way. This is useful especially when combined with DataInputStream. This will let you write data to a file, network, or any other sink in a machine-independent manner. Since all major software and hardware vendors have thrown their support behind Java, this will open up a new era in sharing data between software applications! Source 4.21 demonstrates the use of DataOutputStream.
- BufferedOutputStream. This class extends FilterOutputStream. This class implements a byte buffer to improve the performance of writes. This is similar to the fwrite( ) function in the C standard library as compared to the unbuffered write( ) function in UNIX.
- PrintStream. This class extends FilterOutputStream. This is by far the most common output stream used in almost every Java program. The System's out data member is a PrintStream. You have seen the call System.out.println( ) hundreds of times in this book already.
- ByteArrayOutputStream. This class extends OutputStream. This class allows the use of a byte buffer as an output stream. This is

very useful for creating persistent objects that can be accessed using ByteArrayInputStream. In fact, I demonstrate a flexible database package that does just this. Specifically, Source 4.21 demonstrates the use of this class.

- PipedOutputStream. This class extends OutputStream. It is an output stream that must be connected to a PipedInputStream. This is useful for interthread communication.

Files. These classes allow streams to be connected to file objects, read from, and written to.

- File. A class that represents a file on the host system. There are numerous methods to get the file path, check if the file exists, check if it is a directory, list the files in the directory, and many more. This is very useful class. Source 4.20 demonstrates the use of the File class. This class is even more exciting when you think of the cross-platform utilities you could create. I expect to see some very interesting shells produced using the file and system utilities that will run on all major operating systems.
- FileInputStream. This class extends InputStream, and allows a file to be an input stream. It is very useful in conjunction with DataInputStream. Source 4.24 demonstrates the use of FileInput-Stream.
- FileOutputStream. This class extends OutputStream and allows a file to be an output stream. Very useful, especially in conjunction with DataOutputStream and PrintStream. Source 4.22 demonstrates the use of FileOutputStream.
- RandomAccessFile. This class implements both the DataOutput and DataInput interfaces. It gives you the ability to create a random access file equivalent to the C binary file type. It allows seeking to, reading, and writing to any position in the file, and is similar to the C standard library fseek( ), fwrite( ), and fread( ) functions. The only crucial difference is that the Java RandomAccessFile is in a machine-independent format. The database application below uses a RandomAccessFile as a platform-independent database to store variable-length user-definable records. Specifically, see Source 4.25 for a demonstration of using RandomAccessFile.

A Database Package, Application, and Persistent Objects. I have always disliked snippets of code in technical books. I would rather see a short working program than a snippet. I also would like to see non-trivial examples instead of trivial, throwaway ones. In order to really demonstrate the power of the Java io package, I ported a freeware program that I had coded in C to Java. The code below consists of a database application and a database package that the application uses. I will describe the design and functioning of each module of the package and application. While porting the code, I realized the need for persistent objects and devised an interface to accomplish them. I hope you will find this code useful from the learning standpoint as well as to experiment with and add capabilities to. I hereby give you the right to use this code on a royalty-free basis as long as you clearly cite the source in your resulting program. Now let's examine the design and functionality of the application in detail.

Let's begin by examining all the files in the application and the database package. This will give us the big picture. There is only one file for the application, called EZDB.java. EZDB stands for Easy Database. This program is a simple, command-line driven database program that lets you define databases with any number of fields (string, float, or integer). Once a database is defined and the definition stored in a schema file, you are able to add records to the database and view records in the database. At the end of this section, I will discuss how to extend the capabilities of this application.

Before we discuss the four Java files that make up the database package, you need to understand the general idea of what the package considers a database. A database consists of a schema file that describes all the fields in a database record, a data file that stores all the variable length records, and one or more index files that store indexes into the data file. Therefore, our definition of a database consists of three or more files. Each file has a specific purpose and is necessary to implement a variable-length record, flexible database system that can create numerous different databases, each with a different record format. Of course, there is much room for improvement of this application in terms of user interface, capabilities (modify, delete, search), and performance, but the following code will give you a good starting point. The four files in the database package are:

- Schema.java. The code to define a database, generate and parse a schema file.
- DB.java. A class that represents a container for all the parts of a database (schema, data file, and index files). In the original C program, there was no "wrapper" structure that limited the program to only opening a single database at a time. All the pieces were managed separately. The DB class is an improvement on this concept, and will allow multiple databases to be opened simultaneously. I leave this modification to the EZDB program for you as an exercise.

- dbHeader.java. This is the class that represents all the relevant information in a database. This header information also keeps track of the current state of a database. The database header is also stored in the data file of the database. The header is always the first record in the index file.
- dbFiles.java. This class performs all the actual writing and reading to and from the database. The current implementation only uses a single index file. However, for large databases, index files sorted on a particular field value are necessary.

We will describe the classes and key methods (excluding intuitive ones like constructors) of each Java file:

- Source 4.20 is the EZDB application.

    Classes: none

    Key methods:

1. public static void main( ). This method presents a menu to the user and dispatches to the appropriate function based on the user's choice. The options are define a DB, select a DB, add a Record, view Records, and close a DB.
2. dbHeader select_db( ). This method prompts the user for a database name to select. It checks if a schema file exists for the database (created by choosing the define a DB option). If so, it creates a dbHeader object by calling the dbHeader constructor and returns the object.

SOURCE 4.20

```
// Copyright (c) 1995 by Michael C. Daconta
import java.io.RandomAccessFile;
import java.io.DataInputStream;
import java.io.IOException;
import java.io.File;
import database.Schema;
import database.dbHeader;
import database.DB;
import java.util.Vector;

class EZDB {
        static DataInputStream dis = new DataInputStream(System.in);
```

```
static dbHeader select_db()
{
        dbHeader outHeader=null;
        System.out.print("Enter the database name: ");
        System.out.flush();
        String buf=null;
        try {
                buf = dis.readLine();
        } catch (Exception e) { return null; }

        if (buf.length() > 0)
        {
                buf.replace(' ', '_');

                // check if file exists
                File afile = new File(buf + ".schema");
                if (afile.exists())
                        outHeader = new dbHeader(buf + ".schema");
                else
                        return null;
        }
        else
                System.out.println("Invalid db name.");

        System.out.println(buf + " selected...OK");
        return outHeader;
}

public static void main(String args[])
{
        boolean done = false;
        DB theDB = null;
        Schema DBschema = null;

        while (!done)
        {
                System.out.println(" ");
                System.out.println("<<<<<<<<<<<<<<<<<<<<<<<<>>>>>>>>>>>>>>>>>>>>>>>");
                System.out.println("<<<<<<<<<<<< EZ DB 1.02J >>>>>>>>>>>>>>");
                System.out.println("<<<<<<<<<<<<<<<<<<<<<<<<>>>>>>>>>>>>>>>>>>>>>>>");
                System.out.println(" ");
                System.out.println("        0) Philosophy & Credits");
```

```java
System.out.println("          1) Define DB");
System.out.println("          2) Select DB");
System.out.println("          3) Add Record");
System.out.println("          4) View Records");
System.out.println("          5) Close DB");
System.out.println("          6) Exit");
System.out.println(" ");
System.out.print("Enter choice : ");
System.out.flush();
String choiceStr=null;
try {
     choiceStr = dis.readLine();
} catch (IOException ioe)
  {
        System.out.println("Error reading choice.");
        System.exit(1);
  }

int choice = -1;
if (choiceStr.length() > 0)
        choice = Integer.parseInt(choiceStr);

switch (choice) {
        case 0:
 // philosophy & credits
 System.out.println(" ");
 System.out.println("<<<<<<<<<<< EZDB Philosophy >>>>>>>>>>");
 System.out.println("This program is based on the idea that");
 System.out.println("most people do not need an expensive, ");
 System.out.println("feature-packed database. What the common ");
 System.out.println("person needs is a simple, efficient ");
 System.out.println("database to help them keep track of the");
 System.out.println("people, places, and things in their");
 System.out.println("lives.  EZDB is a free solution. Enjoy!");
 System.out.println(" ");

 System.out.println("The Original EZDB was in C and had more");
 System.out.println("options (i.e. find, delete, modify...).");
 System.out.println("There was also a version with a GUI.");
 System.out.println("This is just a demonstration of the");
 System.out.println("concepts in Java.");
 System.out.println(" ");
```

```java
            System.out.println("Press Enter to continue: ");
      try { dis.readLine(); } catch (Exception e) { }
break;
            case 1: // define DB
                    DBschema = new Schema();
                    if (DBschema.buildSchema())
                    {
                            DBschema.outputSchema();
                            System.out.println("Schema stored as : " +
                                            DBschema.getFileName());
                    }
                    break;
            case 2: // select DB
                    if (theDB == null)
                    {
                       dbHeader aHeader = select_db();
                       if (aHeader != null)
                       {
                            theDB = new DB();
                            theDB.setHeader(aHeader);
                       }
                       else
                            System.out.println("DB does not exist.");
                    }
                    else
                       System.out.println("Close current DB first.
                          Choose Option 5.");
                    break;
            case 3: // add record
                    if (theDB != null)
                    {
                            System.out.println("Enter Record data...");
                            Vector recVals = theDB.createRecord();

                            if (!theDB.addRecord(recVals))
                                    System.out.println("Unable to add
                                        Record to DB.");
                            else
                                    System.out.println("Successfully
                                        added Record to DB.");
                    }
```

```
                    else
                            System.out.println("MUST selecte a DB.
                                Choose option 2.");
                    break;
            case 4: // view records
                    if (theDB != null)
                            theDB.viewRecords();
                    else
                            System.out.println("MUST selecte a DB.
                                Choose option 2.");

                    break;
            case 5: // close DB
                    if (theDB != null)
                    {
                            theDB.close();
                            theDB = null;
                    }
                    break;
            case 6: // exit
                    done = true;
                    if (theDB != null)
                            theDB.close();
                    break;
            default:
                    System.out.println("Choice must be between
                        0 and 10.");
            }
        }
    }
}
```

A run of Source 4.20 produces:

```
C:\java\bin>java EZDB


<<<<<<<<<<<<<<<<<<<<<<<>>>>>>>>>>>>>>>>>>>>
<<<<<<<<<<<< EZ DB 1.02J >>>>>>>>>>>>>>
<<<<<<<<<<<<<<<<<<<<<<<>>>>>>>>>>>>>>>>>>>>


        0) Philosophy & Credits
        1) Define DB
```

```
            2) Select DB
            3) Add Record
            4) View Records
            5) Close DB
            6) Exit

Enter choice : 1
Defining a database consists of two steps:
1) Name the database.
2) Describe the fields of the database.

Hit Return to continue, else type 99 to return to main menu.
Enter the database name: employee

To describe the fields in your database.
There are two pieces of information for each field.
1) The field name.  This is what you call the data,
   for example, an address database would have names
   like - name, street, city...
2) The data type.  This is what type of data the field
   holds.  There are currently only three (3) choices:
   string (text), number (whole numbers), decimal.

Enter the field name: name
Choose the field type:
1) String (text - alpha and numbers)
2) Long (whole numbers)
3) Double (decimals)
Enter choice:
...
<<<<<<<<<<<<<<<<<<<<<<<>>>>>>>>>>>>>>>>>>>>>>
<<<<<<<<<<< EZ DB 1.02J >>>>>>>>>>>>>>
<<<<<<<<<<<<<<<<<<<<<<<>>>>>>>>>>>>>>>>>>>>>>

            0) Philosophy & Credits
            1) Define DB
            2) Select DB
            3) Add Record
            4) View Records
            5) Close DB
            6) Exit

Enter choice : 3
```

```
Enter Record data...
name : Mike Daconta
department : Telemedecine
Salary : 100500.99
Database successfully initialized.
Successfully added Record to DB.


<<<<<<<<<<<<<<<<<<<<<>>>>>>>>>>>>>>>>>>>
<<<<<<<<<<<< EZ DB 1.02J >>>>>>>>>>>>>>>
<<<<<<<<<<<<<<<<<<<<<>>>>>>>>>>>>>>>>>>>


          0) Philosophy & Credits
          1) Define DB
          2) Select DB
          3) Add Record
          4) View Records
          5) Close DB
          6) Exit

Enter choice : 4
> 2 records in the DB.
name : Mike Daconta
department : Telemedecine
Salary : 100501
Hit Return to continue or 99 to return to main menu.

name : Samantha Daconta
department : training
Salary : 45000
Hit Return to continue or 99 to return to main menu.
```

- Source 4.21 is the DB class in the database package.
    Classes:
    1. DB. A representation of a database; has data members for a Schema class, a dbHeader class, a dbFiles class, and a recordCount.

    Key methods:
    1. public synchronized Vector createRecord( ). This method displays each fieldname in the database and prompts the user for the value. The string input by the user is converted to the proper field type as defined by the Schema and stored in the dbHeader class. The method returns the values in a Vector.

2. public synchronized void displayRecord(Vector RecVals). Displays the fieldnames and field values of the Vector passed in.

3. public synchronized byte[] RecValsToByteArray(Vector Rec-Vals). Converts the record Vector into an array of bytes. Uses ByteArrayOutputStream and DataOutputStream to do this. This is a very important method as well as the methodology used to create a persistent object in Java. The dbHeader class and idxRecord class implement the Persistent interface (Source 4.23). It would be smart to have every new class you create implement the Persistent interface (just as you should always implement the toString( ) method). The Persistent interface is described below.

4. public synchronized Vector ByteArrayToRecVals(byte bytes[]). This method uses ByteArrayInputStream and DataInputStream to translate a byte array into a database record. This method and its opposite are the key translation functions that go between a file representation of our record and its viewable (human readable) representation.

5. public void initDBfiles( ). This method either creates a new database or opens an existing one. It either creates the header (for an initialization) and stores it in the database or retrieves it from the existing database.

6. public void close( ). Writes the current dbHeader to the data file and closes all open files.

7. public boolean addRecord(Vector RecVals). This method adds the current Record to the database. To do this it converts the record to a byte array, calls initDBfiles( ) if this is the first write, then calls the dbFiles method writeBytes( ) to actually write the byte array to the appropriate files. It is important to understand how this routine will need to change when you implement record deletion. Since all record lengths and positions in the data file are stored in the master index file (which is what allows us to store records of variable length), the easiest way to delete a record is to just set its index record to some special deletion marker (i.e., a −99 in the length and position field). This deletion marker would cause you to skip the record during viewing or searching through the database. Before you write the deletion marker to the index file, you first record the record position and length in a Free List of space available to be reused. Then, before you add a record to the end of the database

(also known as growing the database), you check the Free List to see if there are any available "holes." This implementation of record deletion is left for you as an exercise.

8. public void viewRecords( ). This method sequences through all the records in the database. This is a good example of a class that should implement the Enumeration interface. See Source 5.2 for a demonstration of a List package implementing the Enumeration interface.

SOURCE 4.21

```
// Copyright (c) 1995 by Michael C. Daconta
package database;

import java.io.DataInputStream;
import java.io.DataOutputStream;
import java.io.IOException;
import java.io.OutputStream;
import java.io.InputStream;
import java.util.Vector;
import java.io.ByteArrayInputStream;
import java.io.ByteArrayOutputStream;

/* the single all-encompassing DB class
   will allow multiple DB's to be open simultaneously.
   This will be important when you scale up to a DB server. */

public class DB {
        static DataInputStream dis = new DataInputStream(System.in);
        protected Schema theSchema;
        protected dbHeader theHeader;
        protected dbFiles theFiles;
        protected long recordCount;

        public DB()
        {
                recordCount = 0;
        }

        public void setSchema(Schema inSchema)
        { theSchema = inSchema; }
```

```java
public void setHeader(dbHeader inHeader)
{
        theHeader = inHeader;
        recordCount = inHeader.getnum_db_entries();
}

public void setdbFiles(dbFiles inFiles)
{ theFiles = inFiles; }

public Schema getSchema() { return theSchema; }
public dbHeader getHeader() { return theHeader; }
public dbFiles getdbFiles() { return theFiles; }

public synchronized Vector createRecord()
{
        Vector fldTypes = theHeader.getfldTypes();
        Vector fldNames = theHeader.getfldNames();
        Vector RecVals = new Vector(3);

        for (int i=0; i < fldTypes.size(); i++)
        {
                System.out.print((String)fldNames.elementAt(i) +
                                                " : ");
                System.out.flush();
                String buf = null;
                try {
                    buf = dis.readLine();
                } catch (IOException ioe)
                  {
                    System.out.println(ioe.getMessage());
                    return null;
                  }

                try {
                    switch (((Integer)fldTypes.elementAt(i)).intValue()) {
                        case dbHeader.STRING_TYPE:
                                RecVals.addElement(new String(buf));
                                break;
                        case dbHeader.LONG_TYPE:
                                Long num = Long.valueOf(buf);
                                RecVals.addElement(num);
                                break;
```

```
                               case dbHeader.DOUBLE_TYPE:
                                        Double aDoub = Double.valueOf(buf);
                                        RecVals.addElement(aDoub);
                                        break;
                               default:
                                        System.out.println("Unknown Type!");
                                        return null;
                          }
                   } catch (Exception e)
                   {
                        System.out.println(e.getMessage());
                        return null;
                   }
            }
            return RecVals;
     }

public synchronized void displayRecord(Vector RecVals)
{
            Vector fldTypes = theHeader.getfldTypes();
            Vector fldNames = theHeader.getfldNames();

            for (int i=0; i < fldTypes.size(); i++)
            {
                    System.out.println((String)fldNames.elementAt(i) +
                                            " : " +
                                    RecVals.elementAt(i));
            }
}

public synchronized byte [] RecValsToByteArray(Vector RecVals)
{
      if (RecVals == null)
          return null;

      ByteArrayOutputStream bos;
      try {
          bos = new ByteArrayOutputStream();
          DataOutputStream dos = new DataOutputStream(bos);
          Vector fldTypes = theHeader.getfldTypes();

          for (int i=0; i < fldTypes.size(); i++)
```

```
        {
                switch (((Integer)fldTypes.elementAt(i)).intValue()) {
                    case dbHeader.STRING_TYPE:
                            dos.writeUTF((String)RecVals.elementAt(i));
                            break;
                    case dbHeader.LONG_TYPE:
                            dos.writeLong(((Long)RecVals.elementAt(i)).
                                longValue());
                            break;
                    case dbHeader.DOUBLE_TYPE:

            dos.writeDouble(((Double)RecVals.elementAt(i)).doubleValue());
                            break;
                    default:
                            System.out.println("Unknown Type!");
                            return null;
                }
        }

    } catch (Exception e)
      {
         System.out.println(e.getMessage());
         return null;
      }

   return bos.toByteArray();
}

public synchronized Vector ByteArrayToRecVals(byte bytes[])
{
    Vector RecVals = new Vector(3);
    ByteArrayInputStream bis = new ByteArrayInputStream(bytes);
    DataInputStream dis = new DataInputStream(bis);

    try {
        Vector fldTypes = theHeader.getfldTypes();

        for (int i=0; i < fldTypes.size(); i++)
        {
                switch (((Integer)fldTypes.elementAt(i)).intValue()) {
                    case dbHeader.STRING_TYPE:
                            RecVals.addElement(new String(dis.readUTF()));
```

```java
                                      break;
                      case dbHeader.LONG_TYPE:
                            RecVals.addElement(new Long(dis.readLong()));
                            break;
                                         case dbHeader.DOUBLE_TYPE:
                                               RecVals.addElement(new
                                                  Double(dis.readDouble()));
                                               break;
                                   default:
                      System.out.println("Unknown Type!");
                            return null;

                  }
          }

      } catch (Exception e)
        {
          System.out.println(e.getMessage());
          return null;
        }

    return RecVals;
}


// initialize (create or open) a Database
public void initDBfiles()
{
      theFiles = new dbFiles(theHeader.getdbname());

      if (theFiles.getdataFileLength() == 0)
      {
         // INIT the DB
         /* theHeader is stored in the data file but
            is ALWAYS the first record in the idx file. */
         byte headerBytes[] = theHeader.toByteArray();

         // write the header to the data file at 0 idxPos
         if (theFiles.writeBytes(headerBytes, 0, 0))
         {
             System.out.println("Database successfully initialized.");
         }
         else
         {
```

```java
                    System.out.println("Failed to initialize DB.");
                    System.exit(1);
            }
        }
        else
        {
            // OPEN DB and retrieve header
            byte headerBytes[] = theFiles.readBytes(0);

            if (headerBytes != null)
            {
                    theHeader = new dbHeader(headerBytes);
                    recordCount = theHeader.getnum_db_entries();
                    System.out.println("Database successfully opened.");
            }
            else
            {
                    System.out.println("Failed to open the DB.");
                    System.exit(1);
            }
        }
    }


public void close()
{
        if (theFiles != null)
        {
                /* write the current header out to
                   the data file. */
                theFiles.writeHeader(theHeader);
                theFiles.close();
        }
}


public boolean addRecord(Vector RecVals)
{
        // convert vector to bytes
        byte dataBytes[] = RecValsToByteArray(RecVals);
        if (dataBytes == null)
                return false;

        /* write the bytes to the dbfiles at the
```

```
                EOF  **** !!! modify after delete!!!!!!!!! */

        if (theFiles == null)
                initDBfiles();

        if (!theFiles.writeBytes(dataBytes,
                                theFiles.getdataFileLength(),
                                theFiles.getidxFileLength()))
            return false;

        recordCount++;
        theHeader.setnum_db_entries(recordCount);
        return true;
}

public void viewRecords()
{
        if (theFiles == null)
                initDBfiles();

        if (recordCount > 0)
        {
                boolean done = false;
                System.out.println("> " + recordCount +
                                " records in the DB.");
                // note first idxRec for header
                long idxPos = idxRecord.REC_LENGTH;
                for (int i=0; i < recordCount; i++)
                {
                        byte dataBytes[] = theFiles.readBytes(idxPos);
                        if (dataBytes != null)
                        {
                            // convert to vector
                            Vector RecVals = ByteArrayToRecVals(dataBytes);
                            displayRecord(RecVals);
                            System.out.println("Hit Return to continue or" +
                                        " 99 to return to main menu.");
                            String buf=null;
                            try {
                                    buf = dis.readLine();
                            } catch (Exception e) { }
                            if (buf != null && buf.equals("99"))
```

```
                                    break;
                  }
                  else
                  {
                       System.out.println("Error reading Database.");
                          break;
                  }

                  idxPos += idxRecord.REC_LENGTH;
            }
       }
       else
            System.out.println("No records in DB.");
     }


}
```

- Source 4.22 is the Schema class in the database package.
  Classes:
  1. Schema. A representation of a description of a database record.

  Key methods:
  1. public boolean buildSchema( ). This method guides the user through text prompts that define a database. This is done by naming the database, naming the fields in a database record and choosing the type for each field. This information is all stored in a String Vector.
  2. void outputSchema( ). This method dumps the information in the String Vector to a text file. The text file is named <dbname>.schema.

SOURCE 4.22

```
// Copyright (c) 1995 by Michael C. Daconta
package database;
import java.util.Vector;
import java.io.DataInputStream;
import java.io.FileOutputStream;
import java.io.PrintStream;
```

```java
public class Schema {
      protected Vector strings;
      protected String fileName;

      public Schema()
      {
            strings = null;
            fileName = null;
      }

      public String getFileName()
      {
            return fileName;
      }

      public boolean buildSchema()
      {
            DataInputStream dis = new DataInputStream(System.in);
            System.out.println("Defining a database consists of two steps:");
            System.out.println("1) Name the database.");
            System.out.println("2) Describe the fields of the database.");
            System.out.println(" ");
            System.out.println("Hit Return to continue, else type 99 to return to
                main menu.");
            String buf=null;
            try {
                  buf = dis.readLine();
            } catch (Exception e) { return false; }
            if (buf.equals("99"))
                  return false;

            // get the dbname
            System.out.print("Enter the database name: ");
            System.out.flush();
            try { buf = dis.readLine(); } catch (Exception e) { return false; }

            if (buf.length() == 0)
            {
                  System.out.println("Must have a database name to define a DB.");
                  return false;
            }
```

```java
buf.replace(' ', '_');
// store the filename
fileName = new String(buf + ".schema");

System.out.println(" ");
System.out.println("To describe the fields in your database.");
System.out.println("There are two pieces of information for each
    field.");
System.out.println("1) The field name.  This is what you call the
    data,");
System.out.println("   for example, an address database would have
    names");
System.out.println("   like - name, street, city...");
System.out.println("2) The data type.  This is what type of data the
    field");
System.out.println("   holds.  There are currently only three (3)
    choices:");
System.out.println("   string (text), number (whole numbers), decimal.");

boolean finished = false;
strings = new Vector(3);

while (!finished)
{
        String fldName=null, fldType=null;
        boolean good = false;
        while (!good)
        {
                System.out.println(" ");
                System.out.print("Enter the field name: ");
                System.out.flush();
                try {
                        fldName = dis.readLine();
                } catch (Exception e) { return false; }
                if (fldName.length() > 0)
                        good = true;
        }

        // replace any blanks in the string
        fldName.replace(' ', '_');

        good = false;
```

```
while (!good)
{
        System.out.println("Choose the field type:");
        System.out.println("1) String (text - alpha and
            numbers)");
        System.out.println("2) Long (whole numbers)");
        System.out.println("3) Double (decimals)");
        System.out.print("Enter choice: ");
        System.out.flush();
        String choiceStr;
        try {
                choiceStr = dis.readLine();
        } catch (Exception e) { return false; }
        int choice = Integer.parseInt(choiceStr);
        switch (choice) {
                case 1:
                        fldType = new String("String");
                        good = true;
                        break;
                case 2:
                        fldType = new String("Long");
                        good = true;
                        break;
                case 3:
                        fldType = new String("Double");
                        good = true;
                        break;
                default:
                        System.out.println("Not a valid option!");
        }
}

// add the field data
strings.addElement(new String(fldName + " " + fldType));

System.out.println("Hit Return to continue, else type 99 when
    done entering fields.");
try {
        buf = dis.readLine();
} catch (Exception e) { return false; }
if (buf.equals("99"))
```

```
                              finished = true;
            }


            return true;
    }


public void outputSchema()
{
    try {
        FileOutputStream fos = new FileOutputStream(fileName);
        PrintStream ps = new PrintStream(fos);

        for (int i=0; i < strings.size(); i++)
                ps.println(((String)strings.elementAt(i)));

        fos.close();
    } catch (Exception e)
      {
        System.out.println("Unable to store Schema in " + fileName);
        System.out.println("Re-Enter schema with different filename.");
        return;
      }
    }
}
```

- Source 4.23 is the Persistent interface. The Persistent interface has a single function toByteArray( ) that converts the object to a byte array that is ready for storage in a RandomAccessFile or possibly for transmission over a network. You can think of this interface as making an object "persistent ready." Although this seems like only half the interface, the second half is best implemented as a constructor function of the object. This would be a good enhancement to the interface concept. The only other way to accomplish this would be to allow a static function in the interface, which is also currently illegal. If static methods are allowed you could have a method like this:

```
public static Object fromByteArray( );
```

You could add this as a non-static method, but it then forces the user to declare a dummy object just to call this method. Again, the best solution is to just implement an object constructor that takes a byte array and instantiates the object from the byte array. The dbHeader class (Source 4.24) and idxRecord class (Source 4.25) demonstrate this.

SOURCE 4.23

```
package database;

// an interface to create a persistent object

public interface Persistent {

        // a method to translate the object into the Byte array
        public byte [] toByteArray( );

        /* the reverse method is best as one of the objects
           constructors. The only other way would be a static
           method but they are not currently allowed in interfaces. */
}
```

- Source 4.24 is the dbHeader class in the database package.
  Classes:

  1. class dbHeader. A representation of a database header that stores the schema description information, a record count, and a free list (the free list is not yet implemented). This is a persistent-ready object that implements the Persistent interface.

  Key methods:

  1. public dbHeader(String schemafile). This class constructor parses the schema text file and initializes the dbHeader class. It stores fldNames and fldTypes in Vectors. The fld-Names data member is a Vector of strings while fldTypes is a Vector of integers. You could remove fldTypes by using Run Time Type Info (RTTI) to determine the value type. This is left to you as an exercise.

  2. public dbHeader(byte bytes[]). This method is part of the implementation of Persistent (although not yet explicitly), and initializes a dbHeader object from a byte array. This is used to initialize a dbHeader object from an existing database.

3. public byte [] toByteArray( ). This method must be implemented for this class to implement the Persistent interface. This method uses ByteArrayOutputStream and DataOutputStream to convert the dbHeader object to a byte array for persistent storage.

SOURCE 4.24

```
// Copyright (c) 1995 by Michael C. Daconta
package database;

import java.util.Vector;
import java.io.ByteArrayOutputStream;
import java.io.DataOutputStream;
import java.io.ByteArrayInputStream;
import java.io.DataInputStream;
import java.io.FileInputStream;
import java.util.StringTokenizer;

public class dbHeader implements Persistent {
        public static final int STRING_TYPE = 1;
        public static final int LONG_TYPE = 2;
        public static final int DOUBLE_TYPE = 3;

        protected String dbname;
        protected int numFields;
        protected Vector fldTypes; // ints
        protected Vector fldNames; // Strings
        protected long free_list_rec;
        protected long free_list_length;
        protected long num_fl_entries;
        protected long num_db_entries;

        // accessors
        public String getdbname() { return dbname; }
        public int getnumFields() { return numFields; }
        public Vector getfldTypes() { return fldTypes; }
        public Vector getfldNames() { return fldNames; }
        public long getfree_list_rec() { return free_list_rec; }
        public long getfree_list_length() { return free_list_length; }
        public long getnum_fl_entries() { return num_fl_entries; }
```

```
    public long getnum_db_entries() { return num_db_entries; }

    // mutators
    public void setfree_list_rec(long inRec)
    { free_list_rec = inRec; }
    public void setfree_list_length(long inLength)
    { free_list_length = inLength; }
    public void setnum_fl_entries(long inNum)
    { num_fl_entries = inNum; }
    public void setnum_db_entries(long inNum)
    { num_db_entries = inNum; }

    static int translateType(String inStr)
    {
            if (inStr.equals("String"))
                    return 1;
            else if (inStr.equals("Long"))
                    return 2;
            else if (inStr.equals("Double"))
                    return 3;
            else
                    return -1;
    }

    public dbHeader(String schemaFile)
    {
        // get dbname from schemafile name
        int dot = schemaFile.indexOf('.');
        dbname = schemaFile.substring(0,dot);

        fldTypes = new Vector(3);
        fldNames = new Vector(3);

        // parse the schema file and create the header
        try {
            FileInputStream fis = new FileInputStream(schemaFile);
            DataInputStream dis = new DataInputStream(fis);

            int fldCount=0;
            // each line with 2 tokens is a field
            String Line;
```

```
            while ( (Line = dis.readLine()) != null)
            {
                    StringTokenizer theToks = new StringTokenizer(Line," ");
                    if (theToks.countTokens() == 2)
                    {
                            fldCount++;
                            String fldName = theToks.nextToken();
                            String fldTypeStr = theToks.nextToken();
                            int fldType = translateType(fldTypeStr);

                            // store in Vectors
                            fldTypes.addElement(new Integer(fldType));
                            fldNames.addElement(new String(fldName));
                    }
            }

        numFields = fldCount;
        free_list_rec = 0;
        free_list_length = 0;
        num_fl_entries = 0;
        num_db_entries = 0;

    } catch (Exception e)
      {
        System.out.println(e.getMessage());
      }
}

public dbHeader(byte bytes[])
{
        // translate a byte array into a header
        ByteArrayInputStream bis = new ByteArrayInputStream(bytes);
        DataInputStream dis = new DataInputStream(bis);

        try {
                dbname = dis.readUTF();
                numFields = dis.readInt();
                fldTypes = new Vector(3);
                fldNames = new Vector(3);

                for (int i=0; i < numFields; i++)
                        fldTypes.addElement(new Integer(dis.readInt()));
```

```java
                        for (int i=0; i < numFields; i++)
                                fldNames.addElement(new String(dis.readUTF()));

                        free_list_rec = dis.readLong();
                        free_list_length = dis.readLong();
                        num_fl_entries = dis.readLong();
                        num_db_entries = dis.readLong();
                } catch (Exception e)
                  {
                        System.out.println("Could not translate header.");
                        System.out.println(e.getMessage());
                        return;
                  }
        }


public byte [] toByteArray()
{
        ByteArrayOutputStream bos = new ByteArrayOutputStream();
        DataOutputStream dos = new DataOutputStream(bos);

        try {
                dos.writeUTF(dbname);
                dos.writeInt(numFields);

                for (int i=0; i < numFields; i++)
                 dos.writeInt(((Integer)fldTypes.elementAt(i)).intValue());

                for (int i=0; i < numFields; i++)
                        dos.writeUTF((String)fldNames.elementAt(i));

                dos.writeLong(free_list_rec);
                dos.writeLong(free_list_length);
                dos.writeLong(num_fl_entries);
                dos.writeLong(num_db_entries);
        } catch (Exception e)
          {
                System.out.println(e.getMessage());
                return null;
          }

        return bos.toByteArray();
}
}
```

- Source 4.25 is the dbFiles class in the database package.

  Classes:

  1. idxRecord. A representation of an index record that implements the Persistent interface.

  2. dbFiles. A representation of the physical file objects necessary to implement our database. This class uses RandomAccessFile for the data and index files.

  Key methods:

  1. public boolean writeBytes(byte dataBytes[], long newDataPos, long newIdxPos). This function writes the bytes of the record (or persistent-ready object) to the file. It also creates and stores the persistent-ready idxRecord.

  2. public byte [] readBytes(long newIdxPos). Given the position in the master index file, this method retrieves the persistent index record, and using that, then retrieves the bytes from the data file that make up the database record.

  3. public void writeHeader(dbHeader inHeader). First makes the dbHeader class persistent-ready and then stores it in the data file. If it has grown too big for the "slot" it started at the method relocates it.

SOURCE 4.25

```
// Copyright (c) 1995 by Michael C. Daconta
package database;

import java.io.File;
import java.io.RandomAccessFile;
import java.io.IOException;
import java.io.ByteArrayInputStream;
import java.io.ByteArrayOutputStream;
import java.io.DataInputStream;
import java.io.DataOutputStream;

class idxRecord {
        public static final int REC_LENGTH = 16; // 16 bytes
        protected long recPos;
        protected long recLength;

        public idxRecord(long inPos, long inLength)
```

```
        {
                recPos = inPos;
                recLength = inLength;
        }

        // accessors
        public long getrecPos() { return recPos; }
        public long getrecLength() { return recLength; }

        public idxRecord(byte bytes[])
        {
                // translate a byte array into a header
                ByteArrayInputStream bis = new ByteArrayInputStream(bytes);
                DataInputStream dis = new DataInputStream(bis);

                try {
                        recPos = dis.readLong();
                        recLength = dis.readLong();
                } catch (Exception e)
                  {
                        System.out.println(e.getMessage());
                        return;
                  }
        }

        public byte [] toByteArray()
        {
                ByteArrayOutputStream bos = new ByteArrayOutputStream();
                DataOutputStream dos = new DataOutputStream(bos);

                try {
                        dos.writeLong(recPos);
                        dos.writeLong(recLength);
                } catch (Exception e)
                  {
                        System.out.println(e.getMessage());
                        return null;
                  }

                return bos.toByteArray();
        }
}
```

```java
public class dbFiles {
      protected RandomAccessFile dataFile;
      protected RandomAccessFile idxFile;
      protected long dataPos;
      protected long idxPos;

      // accessors
      public long getdataPos() { return dataPos; }
      public long getidxPos() { return idxPos; }

      public long getdataFileLength()
      {
            long outLen = -1;
            try {
                outLen = dataFile.length();
            } catch (IOException ioe)
              {
                    System.out.println("Cannot get length of data file.");
                    System.exit(1);
              }
            return outLen;
      }

      public long getidxFileLength()
      {
            long outLen = -1;
            try {
                outLen = idxFile.length();
            } catch (IOException ioe)
              {
                    System.out.println("Cannot get length of idx file.");
                    System.exit(1);
              }
            return outLen;
      }

      public dbFiles(String dbname)
      {
          try {
          // Create or Open the files
              dataFile = new RandomAccessFile(dbname + ".dat", "rw");
```

```java
            idxFile = new RandomAccessFile(dbname + ".idx", "rw");

            // set initial pos at end of files
            dataPos = dataFile.length();
            idxPos = idxFile.length();

        } catch (IOException ioe)
          {
            System.out.println("Cannot create the database files.");
            System.out.println(ioe.getMessage());
            System.exit(1);
          }
    }

    public boolean writeBytes(byte dataBytes[], long newDataPos, long newIdxPos)
    {
        try {
            // create an idxRecord
            idxRecord idxRec = new idxRecord(newDataPos, dataBytes.length);

            // write idxRecord to the idx File
            idxFile.seek(newIdxPos);

            // write the index record
            byte idxBytes[] = idxRec.toByteArray();
            idxFile.write(idxBytes,0,idxBytes.length);

            // write the data bytes to the data file
            dataFile.seek(newDataPos);
            dataFile.write(dataBytes,0,dataBytes.length);

            // store current pointers
            dataPos = dataFile.getFilePointer();
            idxPos = idxFile.getFilePointer();
        } catch (IOException e)
          {
            System.out.println("Unable to write record to DB.");
            System.out.println(e.getMessage());
            return false;
          }
        return true;
    }
```

```java
public byte [] readBytes(long newIdxPos)
{
    byte dataBytes[] = null;
    try {
        // read the idxRecord
        idxFile.seek(newIdxPos);

        // read the index record from the idx file
        byte idxBytes[] = new byte[idxRecord.REC_LENGTH];
        idxFile.read(idxBytes,0,idxBytes.length);

        // create the idxRecord
        idxRecord idxRec = new idxRecord(idxBytes);

        // read the data bytes from the data file
        dataBytes = new byte[(int)idxRec.getrecLength()];
        dataFile.seek(idxRec.getrecPos());
        dataFile.read(dataBytes,0,dataBytes.length);

        // store current pointers
        dataPos = dataFile.getFilePointer();
        idxPos = idxFile.getFilePointer();
    } catch (IOException e)
      {
        System.out.println("Unable to write record to DB.");
        System.out.println(e.getMessage());
      }

    return dataBytes;
}

public void close()
{
   try {
        dataFile.close();
        idxFile.close();
   } catch (Exception e) { }
}

public void writeHeader(dbHeader inHeader)
{
```

```
      byte headerBytes[] = inHeader.toByteArray();

      if (headerBytes == null)
      {
              System.out.println("Unable to write database header.");
              System.out.println("Database left in inconsistent state.");
              System.exit(1);
      }

      try {
         // read the idxRecord
         idxFile.seek(0);

         // read the index record from the idx file
         byte idxBytes[] = new byte[idxRecord.REC_LENGTH];
         idxFile.read(idxBytes,0,idxBytes.length);

         // create the idxRecord
         idxRecord idxRec = new idxRecord(idxBytes);

         // check if need to relocate the header
         if (headerBytes.length <= idxRec.getrecLength())
         {
                 this.writeBytes(headerBytes, idxRec.getrecPos(), 0);
         }
         else
         {
                 // relocate the record
                 long endOfData = this.getdataFileLength();
                 this.writeBytes(headerBytes, endOfData, 0);
         }
      } catch (IOException ioe)
        {
              System.out.println("Unable to write database header.");
              System.out.println("Database left in inconsistent state.");
              System.exit(1);
        }
      System.out.println("Successfully wrote header to DB.");
   }

}
```

Exceptions. The io package has defined exceptions unique to IO.

- IOException. This class extends Exception. A general I/O error like a disk read or disk write failure. For example, if a directory has the maximum number of files allowed in it (differs from OS to OS), this exception would be thrown if you attempted to create a new file in that directory.
- InterruptedIOException. This class extends IOException. An IO operation has been interrupted. This will be thrown if a low-priority thread is performing IO when a higher-priority thread interrupts it.
- FileNotFoundException. This class extends IOException. This class is thrown if you try to read a file that does not exist. You can avoid this by testing the exists( ) method in the File class. Source 4.20 demonstrates the use of the exists( ) method.
- EOFException. This class extends IOException. An End Of File was reached unexpectedly.
- UTFDataFormatException. This class extends IOException, and is thrown if a malformed UNICODE Text Format (UTF) string has been read from a DataInputStream.

net Package

This package provides networking classes and methods for both connecting to the internet (internetworking) and to other computers on a local network (networking).

Internetworking

- InetAddress. A class that represents an Internet address. It has methods to create and get Internet addresses. Source 4.26 demonstrates getting your host's internet address and the address of a remote host.

SOURCE 4.26

```
import java.net.InetAddress;
import java.net.UnknownHostException;

class tstInetAddress {
        public static void main(String args[])
```

```
{
        InetAddress myAddress=null;
        InetAddress Mystech=null;

        // get my machine's internet address
        try {
            myAddress = InetAddress.getLocalHost();
        } catch (UnknownHostException uhe)
          {
                System.out.println("Local host is unknown.");
                System.exit(1);
          }

    System.out.println(myAddress.toString());

        // get mystech's internet address
        try {
            Mystech = InetAddress.getByName("Mystech.com");
        } catch (UnknownHostException uhe)
          {
                System.out.println(uhe.toString());
                System.out.println("Mystech.com not known.");
                System.out.println("Ensure TCP/IP connection to
                    internet is up.");
                System.exit(1);
          }

    System.out.println(Mystech.toString());
    }
}
```

A run of Source 4.26 produces:

```
C:\java\bin>java tstInetAddress
Pdaconta.primenet.com/198.68.41.96
Mystech.com/198.3.157.1
```

- **URL.** This class is a representation of a Uniform Resource Locator (URL). This class allows you to create a URL by defining fields, create a URL by parsing a URL string, compare URLs, connect to a URL, getContent( ) of a URL object, and get a URLStreamHandler. Source 4.27 demonstrates creating and using a URL object.

- URLConnection. This is an abstract class that represents an active connection to a URL. This class allows a connection to be created, to guessContentType from the file extension, to getContent( ) of the object, to get an InputStream from the object or an OutputStream to the object. Source 4.27 demonstrates creating an input stream to a URL and receiving the content of that URL and writing that content to a file.

SOURCE 4.27

```java
import java.net.URL;
import java.net.MalformedURLException;
import java.io.InputStream;
import java.io.FileInputStream;
import java.io.DataInputStream;
import java.io.FileOutputStream;
import java.io.IOException;

class tstURL {
        public static void main(String args[])
        {
                if (args.length < 2)
                {
                        System.out.println(
                                "USAGE: java tstURL URL_string output_file_name");
                        System.exit(1);
                }

                String urlString = new String(args[0]);
                String fileName = new String(args[1]);

                URL theURL = null;
                try {
                        theURL = new URL(urlString);
                } catch (MalformedURLException mue)
                  {
                        System.out.println(mue.toString());
                        System.exit(1);
                  }

                try {
                  byte buf[] = new byte[1000];
```

```
        InputStream input = theURL.openStream();
        FileOutputStream fout = new FileOutputStream(fileName);
        int ch;
        int count = 0;
        while (true)
        {
            int n = input.read(buf, 0, 1000);
            if (n == -1) break;
            fout.write(buf, 0, n);
            count += n;
            System.out.print(".");
            System.out.flush();
        }

        fout.close();
        input.close();
    } catch (IOException ioe)
    {
            ioe.printStackTrace();
            System.exit(1);
    }
  }
}
```

A run of this program with the command line " java tstURL http://mystech.com urlout1.tst" produces the file urlout1.tst with the following contents (truncated here):

```
<HEAD>
<TITLE> Mystech Associate's Home Page </TITLE>
<BODY>
<CENTER>
<IMG SRC="http://mystech.com/logo.gif">
<P>
<H1>Welcome to Mystech Associates!</H1>
<HR></CENTER>

<H2>Learn more about us:</H2>
<DD> <font size=+2> <A HREF="http://mystech.com/philosophy.
html">Mystech - Meeting the User's Needs</font> </A>
```

```
<HR>

<H2>Corporate Announcements</H2>
<UL>

<li><STRONG>DIOSS</STRONG>  The DIOSS Beta Testing is complete! Thanks
to all who helped us. You can now <A HREF="http://www.in-
tech.com/">order DIOSS</A> and access some demonstrations and other
information.<br><p>

<li><STRONG>Resident Author</STRONG> Mike Daconta from our Sierra
Vista office  has published two programming books,
<UL>
<LI> <A HREF="http://www.wiley.com:80/compbooks/m7.html">C Pointers
and Dynamic Memory Management</A> U-0-471-56152-5  1993  368pp  paper
$39.95
<li> <A HREF="http://www.wiley.com:80/compbooks/m8.html">C++ Pointers
and Dynamic Memory Management</A> U-0-471-04998-0  1995  464pp
Book/Disk Pak  $39.95
</UL>
Both are available for review (and ordering) at <A
HREF="http://www.wiley.com">www.wiley.com</A><p>
...
```

- URLStreamHandler. An abstract class for a URL stream handler; should be subclassed to create stream handlers for specific protocols.
- ContentHandler. An abstract class to getContent( ) from a URL and create the object of the appropriate type.
- ContentHandlerFactory. An interface to create a ContentHandler for the specific mime content type.

Networking. Sockets are a very common method of network programming. They have been implemented on UNIX operating systems for many years. The beauty of socket programming is that it is very similar to reading and writing from and to a file.

- ServerSocket. A class that allows you to continually listen to a port and accept multiple connections from socket clients. Using threads, you could spawn off a thread for each incoming socket connection. Source 4.28 is a simple example that accepts and processes a single connection.

SOURCE 4.28

```
import java.net.ServerSocket;
import java.net.Socket;
import java.io.InputStream;
import java.io.DataInputStream;

class socketReader {
       public static void main(String args[])
       {
           if (args.length < 1)
           {
               System.out.println("USAGE: java socketReader port");
               System.exit(1);
           }

           String portStr = new String(args[0]);

           try {
               int port = Integer.parseInt(portStr);

               // create the server socket
               ServerSocket readServer = new ServerSocket(port);
               System.out.println("Server Socket created to " + port);
               System.out.println("Awaiting a connection...");

               // wait for a connection
               Socket connection = readServer.accept();
               System.out.println("Connection accepted.");

               // set up the streams
               InputStream inStream = connection.getInputStream();
               DataInputStream dis = new DataInputStream(inStream);

               // while input does not equal 'exit' output to socket
               boolean done = false;
               while (!done)
               {
                       String line = dis.readLine();
                       if (!line.startsWith("~READER_STOP~"))
                       {
                               System.out.println(line);
```

```
                    }
                else
                        done = true;
            }

        // close the server
        readServer.close();
    } catch (Exception e)
        {
        e.printStackTrace();
        System.exit(1);
        }
      }
}
```

A run of Source 4.28 produces:

```
C:\java\bin>java socketReader 100
Server Socket created to 100
Awaiting a connection...
Connection accepted.
Hello socket.
Java is a great technology that has been endorsed
by all the major vendors.
Goodbye socket.
```

- Socket. A class that represents a socket client. Methods in this class allow you to create a socket, get an output stream or an input stream to the socket, and close the socket. Source 4.29 demonstrates a socket client that can connect to a socket, accept input (similar to chat), and write it out to the socket. The program was run in conjunction with the socketReader above.

SOURCE 4.29

```
import java.net.Socket;
import java.io.OutputStream;
import java.io.DataInputStream;
import java.io.PrintStream;

class socketWriter {
```

```java
public static void main(String args[])
{
    if (args.length < 2)
    {
        System.out.println("USAGE: java socketWriter hostname port");
        System.exit(1);
    }

    String host = new String(args[0]);
    String portStr = new String(args[1]);

    try {
        int port = Integer.parseInt(portStr);

        // create the socket
        Socket outSock = new Socket(host,port);
        System.out.println("Socket created to " + host);

        // set up the streams
        OutputStream outStream = outSock.getOutputStream();
        PrintStream ps = new PrintStream(outStream);
        DataInputStream dis = new DataInputStream(System.in);

        // while input does not equal 'exit' output to socket
        boolean done = false;
        System.out.println("Type sentences to send. Type 'exit' to quit.");
        while (!done)
        {
            String line = dis.readLine();
            if (!line.startsWith("exit"))
            {
                ps.println(line);
            }
            else
            {
                // stop reader
                ps.println("~READER_STOP~");
                done = true;
            }
        }

        // close the socket
```

```
        outSock.close();
    } catch (Exception e)
     {
     e.printStackTrace();
     System.exit(1);
     }
   }
 }
```

A run of Source 4.29 produces:

```
C:\java\bin>java socketWriter Pdaconta.primenet.com 100
Socket created to Pdaconta.primenet.com
Type sentences to send. Type 'exit' to quit.
Hello socket.
Java is a great technology that has been endorsed
by all the major vendors.
Goodbye socket.
exit
```

- SocketImpl. An abstract class that lets you define your own socket implementation for different security policies or firewalls.
- SocketImplFactory. An interface that creates socket implementations for various security policies.

Exceptions. The net package defines exceptions unique to networking.

- ProtocolException. This class extends IOException. It is thrown if a socket connect gets a protocol error.
- SocketException. This class extends IOException. It is thrown if an error occurs while attempting to use a socket.
- UnknownHostException. This class extends IOException. The internet address requested by a network client could not be resolved.
- UnknownServiceException. This class extends IOException. An unknown service exception has occurred. For example, it is thrown if a server you are connected to cannot perform the type of service that you have requested.
- MalformedURLException. This class extends IOException. It is thrown if a URL string could not be parsed to create a URL class.

CHAPTER 5

Language Features Not in C or C++

If I have seen further than other men, it is because I have stood on the shoulders of giants.

—Sir Isaac Newton

OBJECTIVE

This chapter describes characteristics of Java that are not part of the C or C++ programming languages. It also explores the influence of other object-oriented languages on Java.

The evolution of a programming language follows the same process of natural selection as does biological evolution. In his magnificent science fiction series, *Dune*, Frank Herbert explored the potentiality of humanity through an order of women, called the Bene Gesserit, who attempted to create a perfect human through the careful control of breeding in order to magnify certain traits and suppress others. This analytical selection (called the analytical knife by Robert Persig) of beneficial characteristics that should survive and flourish over other characteristics is analogous to the language designer playing Bene Gesserit. The developers of Java began with a pared down C/C++ base stock and then grafted characteristics from other object-oriented languages into their creation. This is genetic engineering of the second degree. In Java, you will find influences of Ada, Objective-C, Small-talk, and Eiffel. We will examine these new Java features in light of their presence in other languages.

5.1   PACKAGES

The Ada language was developed for the Department of Defense (DoD) in the late 1970s with the ANSI standard published in January 1983. Also, a new object-oriented version called Ada 95 has been released this year. The Ada language was named in honor of Augusta Ada Byron, the Countess of Lovelace (1815–1852). Ada was the assistant and patron of Charles Babbage and worked on his mechanical analytical engine, which is generally thought of as the first mechanical computer. Because of her work with Charles Babbage, Ada is considered the world's first programmer.

Although Ada has not been widely adopted outside of DoD circles, it has proven itself to be a robust and reliable procedural language with many language features that object-oriented languages have just begun to exploit. Some of those features are: packages (similar to both Java classes and Java packages), private types (similar to the private access specifier), exceptions, generics (similar to C++ templates), and tasks (similar to threads). The Ada 95 standard has added such facilities as single inheritance, constructors, destructors, and improved generics and tasking. Unfortunately, since Ada was derived from Pascal, C and C++ programmers often feel the syntax is wordy and clunky. Also, like C++, it is a procedural language with object-oriented additions and not a pure object-oriented language like Java.

Compared to Java, Ada packages have more similarity to a class than to a Java package. Ada packages are primarily used for data hiding by placing a wall around a group of declarations and only permitting access to those that you intend to be visible. The Ada package comes in two parts: the specification, which describes the interface to the package user, and the body, which gives the hidden implementation. Another example of Ada packages being analogous to modern classes is that Ada private types are private to the whole package and not to any type.

In Java, a package is primarily used for managing namespaces; however, Java does allow a default "friendliness" among all classes inside a package. So the Java package is actually a blend of C++ namespace declaration and an Ada package. A Java package can be thought of as a container for related classes and interfaces. You have seen this in Chapter 4; the Java standard library was divided into packages.

Sources 5.1 through 5.6 demonstrate both aspects of a Java package. This is done by implementing a new package called List. The List package also implements two interfaces (discussed in the next section): the Enumeration interface and a new interface called the Traverse interface. We will examine each source of the list package to understand its purpose and functionality.

Source 5.1 is a simple program to demonstrate how to use the list package. Notice how the import statements are of the form <package>.<class>. That form of the import statement imports the specific class. In order to import ALL the classes in a package you use the following import statement:

```
import List.*;
```

The program also demonstrates how class data members by default are friendly within a package but not accessible (unless declared public) to any class outside the package.

SOURCE 5.1

```
import List.ListHead;
import List.singleLink;

class tstList {
        public static void main(String args[])
        {
                ListHead myList = new ListHead();

                myList.addElement(new Integer(10));
                myList.addElement(new Integer(20));
                myList.addElement(new Integer(30));

                myList.printAll();

                myList.showFriendly();

                // illegal - System.out.println(myList.head);
        }
}
```

A run of Source 5.1 produces:

```
C:\java\bin>java tstList
Calling singleLink Link
```

```
Calling singleLink Link
Node #0 : 10
Node #1 : 20
Node #2 : 30
Inside the package,
a class can access another class's
 variables, unless they are private.
node1.next.data is : 200
```

Source 5.2 is the ListHead class in the List package. This is the "list manager" class and the only class a program needs to import to get the functionality of a list.

- Classes:
  1. ListHead. This class manages a list of ListNodes (see ListNode class in Source 5.3). Data members of the class are a pointer to the head and tail of the list, a node count, and a few variables used to keep track of the current position and direction of the Enumeration (see Chapter 4) and Traverse (see Source 5.8) interface.

- Key Methods:
  1. public ListHead(boolean isDoubly). A class constructor that allows you to construct either a doubly linked or singly linked list. The benefit of a doubly linked list is that it allows list traversal in both directions (forward and backward). The way this list class can manage either type of node is that both the singleLink class and the doubleLink class are derived from an abstract parent class called ListNode.

  2. public addElement(Object data). This method allows you to store ANY Java object in the linked list. It is similar to the addElement method in the Vector container (see Source 1.7). This method creates a new ListNode and attaches it to the list. The "attaching" processing is considerably easier and faster by maintaining a tail pointer (remember by pointer we mean an uninstantiated ListNode object) to the end of the list. The tail pointer makes it unnecessary to traverse the list.

  3. public int size( ). This method returns the number of elements in the list; also identical to the Vector class.

The rest of the methods in the class implement the Enumeration and Traverse interfaces. The code is self-explanatory.

SOURCE 5.2

```
package List;
import java.util.Enumeration;
import java.util.NoSuchElementException;

public class ListHead implements Enumeration, Traverse {
        boolean doubly;
        ListNode head;
        ListNode tail;
        int count;

        // to implement Enumeration
        int current;
        ListNode curNode;

        // to implement Traverse
        boolean forward;

        public ListHead()
        {
                head = tail = null;
                count = current = 0;
                doubly = false;
                curNode = null;
                forward = true;
        }

        public ListHead(boolean isDoubly)
        {
                head = tail = null;
                count = 0;
                doubly = isDoubly;
                curNode = null;
                forward = true;
        }

        public void addElement(Object data)
        {
                ListNode inNode;
```

```
        if (doubly)
                inNode = new doubleLink(data);
        else
                inNode = new singleLink(data);

        if (head == null)
        {
                head = tail = inNode;
        }
        else
        {
                ListNode tmp = tail;
                tail = inNode;
                inNode.Link(tmp);
        }
        count++;
}

public synchronized Object removeFirst ()
{
        if (head != null)
        {
                ListNode tmp = head;
                if (tail == head)
                        tail = head.next();
                head = head.next();
                count--;
                return tmp.data;
        }
        return null;
}
public int size() { return count; }

public boolean hasMoreElements()
{
        if (count > 0 && current < count)
                return true;
        else
                return false;
}

public Object nextElement()
```

```
{
        if (count > 0 && current == 0)
        {
                curNode = head;
        }
        else if (current > 0 && current < count)
        {
                if (forward)
                        curNode = curNode.next();
        }
        else
                throw new NoSuchElementException();

        if (forward)
                current++;
        forward = true;
        return curNode.data;
}

public void printAll()
{
        ListNode traverse = head;

        for (int i=0; i < count; i++)
        {
                System.out.println("Node #" + i + " : "
                                        + traverse.data);
                traverse = traverse.next();
        }
}

public void showFriendly()
{
        singleLink node1 = new singleLink(new Integer(100));
        singleLink node2 = new singleLink(new Integer(200));

        node1.next = node2;
        System.out.println("Inside the package, ");
        System.out.println("a class can access another classes ");
        System.out.println(" variables, unless they are private.");
        System.out.println("node1.next.data is : " + node1.next.data);
}
```

```
// the Traverse interface...

// am I at the beginning? returns false for an empty list
public boolean atStart()
{
        if (count > 0 && current <= 0)
        {
                forward = true; // only possible direction
                return true;
        }
        else
                return false;
}

// am I at the end?
public boolean atEnd()
{
        if (count > 0 && current == count)
        {
                forward = false; // only possible direction
                return true;
        }
        else
                return false;
}

// access the next list element
public Object next()
{
        if (count > 0 && current == 0)
        {
                curNode = head;
        }
        else if (current > 0 && current < count)
        {
                if (forward)
                        curNode = curNode.next();
        }
        else
                throw new NoSuchElementException();
```

```
        if (forward)  // handle direction change
                current++;
        forward = true;
        return curNode.data;
}


// access the previous list element
public Object prev() throws illegalListOpException
{
        if (doubly)
        {
                if (count > 0 && current == count)
                {
                        curNode = tail;
                }
                else if (count > 0 && current > 0)
                {
                  if (forward == false)  // moving backward
                  {
                     try {
                        curNode = curNode.prev();
                     } catch (Exception e) { }
                  }
                }
                else if (count == 0 || current == 0)
                {
                        throw new illegalListOpException(
                                "Prev() invalid for empty list.");
                }
                else
                        throw new illegalListOpException("Prev() invalid.");
        }
        else
        {
                // undefined for singly linked lists
                throw new illegalListOpException(
                                "Prev() invalid for singly linked list.");
        }

        if (!forward)  // handle direction change
                current--;
        forward = false;
```

```
                return curNode.data;
        }


// jump to the head of the list
public Object start()
{
        if (count > 0)
        {
                current = 0;
                curNode = head;
                forward = true;
        }
        else
                throw new NoSuchElementException();
        return curNode.data;
}


// jump to the last element of the list
public Object end()
{
        if (count > 0)
        {
                current = count - 1;
                curNode = tail;
                forward = false;
        }
        else
                throw new NoSuchElementException();
        return curNode.data;
}

}
```

Source 5.3 is the abstract ListNode class in the List package. This is the abstract parent of the singleLink and doubleLink classes. Notice the abstract classes that BOTH children must implement. The Link( ) class is the key class that actually "links" or "connects" this node to the list. For a complete list implementation, this class needs two other abstract methods: a delete( ) method and an insert( ) method. These are left for you as an exercise.

SOURCE 5.3

```
package List;

public abstract class ListNode {
        Object data;

        public ListNode()
        {
                data = null;
        }

        public ListNode(Object inData)
        {
                data = inData;
        }

        abstract void Link(Object prev);
        abstract ListNode next();
        abstract ListNode prev() throws illegalListOpException;
}
```

Source 5.4 is the singleLink class in the List package. This class extends ListNode. This class is a representation of a node in a singly linked list. The key feature of a singly linked list is a single connection to the list in the form of a next pointer. Notice the use of the this pointer in the Link( ) method. The Link method is passed in a "pointer" to the previous node in the list. It then makes the previous node's next pointer point to "this" node. This package also defines a generic List exception called an illegalListOpException. This exception is thrown if an attempt is made to call the prev( ) method for a singly linked list.

SOURCE 5.4

```
package List;

public class singleLink extends ListNode {
        singleLink next; // link

        singleLink()
```

```
                              {
                                      data = null;
                                      next = null;
                              }

                              singleLink(Object theData)
                              {
                                      super(theData);
                                      next = null;
                              }

                              void Link(Object prev)
                              {
                                      System.out.println("Calling singleLink Link");
                                      ((singleLink)prev).next = this;
                              }

                              ListNode next()
                              {
                                      return this.next;
                              }

                              ListNode prev() throws illegalListOpException
                              {
                                      throw (
                                       new illegalListOpException("No prev() in singly" +
                                                                  " linked lists."));

                              }
                      }
```

Source 5.5 is the doubleLink class in the List package. This class extends ListNode. The defining feature of a doubly linked list is two connections to each node—a connection to the previous node and a connection to the next node. Again, examine the Link( ) method to see how we use the this pointer to make the connections.

SOURCE 5.5

```
package List;
```

```java
public class doubleLink extends ListNode {
        doubleLink prev;
        doubleLink next;

        doubleLink()
        {
                data = null;
                prev = next = null;
        }

        doubleLink(Object theData)
        {
                super(theData);
                next = null;
        }

        void Link(Object prev)
        {
                System.out.println("Calling double link");
                ((doubleLink)prev).next = this;
                this.prev = (doubleLink)prev;
        }

        ListNode next()
        {
                return this.next;
        }

        ListNode prev() throws illegalListOpException
        {
                return this.prev;
        }
}
```

Source 5.6 is the illegalListOpException in the list package. This class extends Exception. The exception represents an illegal list operation—for example, an attempt to get a previous node in a singly linked list. This exception could also be thrown for an attempt to delete a node from an empty list or delete a node when the current node points to the end of the list.

SOURCE 5.6

```
package List;

import java.lang.Exception;

public class illegalListOpException extends Exception {

        illegalListOpException(String msg)
        {
                super(msg);
        }
}
```

Although we have used interfaces in our list package, they have not yet been formally introduced; however, you should have a feeling that they are an obviously useful feature since we have already discussed them several times to include the Persistent interface, the Enumeration interface, and the Traverse interface. The next section explains them in detail.

5.2   INTERFACES

Objective-C is a superset of the C programming language developed by Brad Cox, formerly of the Stepstone Corporation. Objective-C has received a considerable amount of success due to its adoption by Steve Jobs, the founder of NeXT Computer, Inc., for the development of the object-oriented NeXTStep operating system. On April 4, 1995, NeXT Computer, Inc. acquired all the rights and trademark for the Objective-C language. It is important to note that many of the goals of Objective-C are identical to the goals of Java. In fact, Brad Cox produced a white paper and software (called TaskMaster) to extend Objective-C to include exception handling and lightweight multi-tasking (threads). There is currently not a standard implementation of Objective-C; however, NeXT now plans to lead the standardization effort.

One of NeXT's extensions to Objective-C is protocols. Protocols were added to specifically address some of the benefits of multiple inheritance without the complexity or implementation problems of multiple inheritance. Protocols allow you to group related methods into a high-level behavior that numerous classes can implement. Here is a simple protocol definition for archiving objects:

```
@protocol Archiving
- (int) readInt: (Stream *) stream;
- (void) writeInt: (Stream *) stream;
@end
```

In Java the archiving interface would look like this:

```
public interface Archiving {
     int readInt(InputStream stream);
     int writeInt(OutputStream stream);
}
```

Now we can discuss Java interfaces in detail. There are two ways to view interfaces. The first is as a set of methods that describe a high-level behavior. As an example, DataInput describes methods that perform data input in a machine-independent manner. Second, an interface is an abstract class that can point to any class that implements the interface. This means that an interface provides the same benefits with multiple classes that virtual functions provide to a singly inherited class hierarchy. The more you work with interfaces, the more you will understand their power and elegance.

Source 5.7 demonstrates the List package using the Enumeration interface. Remember the two methods of the Enumeration interface are hasMoreElements( ) and nextElement( ).

SOURCE 5.7

```
import List.ListHead;
import List.doubleLink;

class tstEnumeration {
     public static void main(String args[])
     {
            ListHead myList = new ListHead(true);

            myList.addElement(new Integer(10));
            myList.addElement(new Integer(20));
            myList.addElement(new Integer(30));

            while (myList.hasMoreElements())
```

```
                              System.out.println(((Integer)myList.
                                 nextElement()));

        }
    }
```

A run of Source 5.7 produces:

```
C:\java\bin>java tstEnumeration
Calling double link
Calling double link
10
20
30
```

Source 5.8 is the definition of the Traverse interface. Let's for a moment think about the benefits for creating this interface. The action we are describing is sequencing through a set of elements. However, if that was all, our requirement would be satisfied by the Enumeration interface. Our List container is different in that it allows both forward and backward list traversal. Secondly, with the head and tail pointer we can rapidly jump to the start or end of the list. Therefore, we can see how the Enumeration interface is not complete enough for what we want to accomplish. Therefore, we needed a new interface. In fact, it would be wise to modify the Vector class to also implement the Traverse interface. The Traverse interface consists of six functions: two testing functions (atStart and atEnd) and four traversal functions: (next, prev, start, and end).

SOURCE 5.8

```
package List;

/* Traverse is an interface that is an abstraction for
   free-flow viewing of a connected list of objects.
   By free-flow viewing, I mean six operations:
   atStart(), atEnd(), next(), prev(), start() , end() */

public interface Traverse {

        // check if at the start of list
```

```
                    public boolean atStart();

                    // check if at the end of list
                    public boolean atEnd();

                    // access the next list element
                    public Object next();

                    // access the previous list element
                    public Object prev() throws illegalListOpException;

                    // jump to the head of the list and return it
                    public Object start();

                    // jump to the end of the list and return it
                    public Object end();

        }
```

Source 5.9 demonstrates the use of the Traverse class with our List package. It clearly demonstrates some of the unique capabilities of the interface.

SOURCE 5.9

```
// tests the Traverse interface
import List.ListHead;
import List.doubleLink;
import List.illegalListOpException;

class tstTraverse {
        public static void main(String args[])
        {
                ListHead myList = new ListHead(true);

                myList.addElement(new Integer(100));
                myList.addElement(new Integer(200));
                myList.addElement(new Integer(300));
                myList.addElement(new Integer(400));
                myList.addElement(new Integer(500));
                myList.addElement(new Integer(600));
```

```
System.out.println("List size: " + myList.size());

System.out.println("Forward...");
while (!myList.atEnd())
        System.out.println(((Integer)myList.next()));

System.out.println("Backward...");
while (!myList.atStart())
{
    try {
        System.out.println(((Integer)myList.prev()));
    } catch (illegalListOpException iloe)
      {
        System.out.println(iloe.toString());
        System.exit(1);
      }
}

System.out.println("Go forward three nodes.");
for (int i=0; i < 3; i++)
        if (!myList.atEnd())
                System.out.println((Integer)myList.next());

System.out.println("Go Back three nodes.");
for (int i=0; i < 3; i++)
{
        if (!myList.atStart())
        {
            try {
                System.out.println(((Integer)myList.prev()));
            } catch (illegalListOpException iloe)
              {
                System.out.println(iloe.toString());
                System.exit(1);
              }
        }
}

System.out.println("Jump to Start...");
System.out.println((Integer)myList.start());

System.out.println("Jump to End...");
```

```
            System.out.println((Integer)myList.end());
       }
   }
```

A run of source 5.9 produces:

```
C:\java\bin>java tstTraverse
Calling double link
Calling double link
Calling double link
Calling double link
Calling double link
List size: 6
Forward...
100
200
300
400
500
600
Backward...
600
500
400
300
200
100
Go forward three nodes.
100
200
300
Go Back three nodes.
300
200
100
Jump to Start...
100
Jump to End...
600
```

Source 5.10 demonstrates using an interface as a type similar to an abstract class. As an abstract class, you cannot instantiate it directly. Instead assign it or instantiate a class that implements the interface. In the example below we declare a variable t of type Traverse that we assign myList to. This is legal since the ListHead class implements the Traverse interface.

SOURCE 5.10

```
import List.ListHead;
import List.Traverse;

class tstTravers2 {
        public static void main(String args[])
        {
                ListHead myList = new ListHead(true);

                myList.addElement(new Integer(100));
                myList.addElement(new Integer(200));
                myList.addElement(new Integer(300));
                myList.addElement(new Integer(400));
                myList.addElement(new Integer(500));
                myList.addElement(new Integer(600));

                Traverse t = myList;
                while (!t.atEnd())
                {
                        System.out.println((Integer)t.next());
                }
        }
}
```

A run of Source 5.10 produces:

```
C:\java\bin>java tstTravers2
Calling double link
Calling double link
Calling double link
Calling double link
Calling double link
100
200
300
```

400
500
600

Although not demonstrated above, interfaces can even have variables. This should reaffirm your understanding of an interface as an abstract class. When an interface has a variable that variable is final, public, and static by default. Methods in an interface are public and abstract by default.

5.3 MULTI-THREADING

Multi-threading is the ability of a single process to spawn multiple, simultaneous execution paths. As discussed previously, multi-threading is similar to multi-processing; however, with multi-threading all execution contexts share the same memory. This makes sharing data between threads simpler than sharing data between processes. See Sources 5.11 and 5.12 for a demonstration of Threads sharing classes.

The benefits of multi-threading are most apparent in graphical user interfaces and in applets. You do not want the user to be forced to wait on an applet (when running a browser) or a GUI function when he or she has decided to quit the application. Threads provide this asynchronous execution. Two other areas that benefit greatly from multi-threading are servers and simulations. A multi-threaded server can spawn a new thread for each incoming client request and is therefore always ready for a new connection. Also, a multi-threaded server will never make a high priority client service wait for a low priority one as a nonthreaded server would do. Simulations benefit by threading because they often model autonomous, interacting entities. A threaded simulation is demonstrated later in this chapter.

As stated earlier, multi-threading has been part of the Ada language, via the task construct, since its inception. In fact, in Ada 95 a form of synchronization has been added called a "protected type." Of course, in Ada a task is merely a procedure as a lightweight process, whereas in Java a Thread is a class that implements the Runnable interface. Being a class, a Java thread can have an unlimited number of methods. In the next section we will examine the Java implementation of threads in detail.

Thread Characteristics

Threads in Java have five characteristics that define their behavior. We will discuss each characteristic individually.

- Thread Body. This is the sequence of instructions for the thread to perform. This is defined by a run( ) method. There are two ways for you to supply a run( ) method to a thread.
  1. Extending the Thread class and overriding the run( ) method in Thread.

  2. Creating a Thread with a Runnable class as its target. A class can implement the Runnable interface and then be passed to a Thread constructor. The Runnable interface is simply implementing the run( ) method.

- Thread State. A thread can be in one of four states: new, runnable, nonrunnable, or dead. The thread's methods and the Java runtime control which state a thread is in. A thread's state also determines what methods are legal to run. For example, you cannot stop( ) a thread that is not running. If you attempt to run a method incompatible with the thread's state, an IllegalThreadStateException will be thrown.

  1. new Thread( ). When a constructor is called, the thread is created but is not yet run( ). Therefore, the thread is in the new state. In the new state the only legal methods are start( ) and stop( ).

  2. start( ). This method switches the thread into the runnable state and the Java run time will schedule the thread to run by invoking its run( ) method.

  3. stop( ). This method switches a thread's state to the dead state. A thread will also move to the dead state naturally when it reaches the end of its run( ) method.

  4. destroy( ). Stops a thread without any cleanup; ignores the thread state.

  5. suspend( ). Causes a thread to move to the nonrunnable state. The target thread will stay in the nonrunnable state until resume( ) is called.

  6. resume( ). Causes a thread to return to being runnable. See suspend( ).

  7. sleep(long millis). Causes a thread to be nonrunnable for a specific number of milliseconds.

  8. wait( ). This is a method of Object. A thread can call the wait( ) method of an object that it is waiting on to change state. If it calls wait, it moves itself into a nonrunnable status. The only way the thread can then become runnable is when a synchronized method in the object has changed state and calls notify( ).

9. yield( ). Only called when a thread is runnable and executing. Does not change the thread's state but instead allows other threads of the same priority to be executed.

- Thread Priority. Every thread has a priority. When threads are created, they are given the priority of their parent (if one exists, else a normal priority of 5). A thread's priority can be between 1 and 10, and determines how it will be scheduled. The scheduler follows a simple rule: At any given time the thread with the highest priority will be running. When a thread is running, it will not be preempted by a thread with the same priority. The Java run time does not time slice between threads of the same priority; instead, a thread may yield its execution to another thread of the same priority. A low priority thread will be interrupted when a higher priority thread becomes runnable.

1. setPriority(int newPriority). Sets the priority of this thread.

2. int getPriority( ). Gets the priority of this thread.

- Daemon Threads. This denotes that a thread is a "server" thread. A server thread is a thread that services client requests (by invoking one of the servers methods). Calling a server a "daemon" is based on UNIX tradition where these background server processes were considered mysterious and hidden things that could often cause you trouble (just like a "demon"). The Java run time treats daemon threads differently than normal threads. The run time will not exit until all normal threads have terminated. Not so with daemon threads. Since daemons are service providers (servers), if there are only daemon threads running, then the run time can exit. This makes sense because there are no more clients running for the daemon to provide a service to.

1. setDaemon( ). Sets a flag that denotes this thread as a daemon thread.

2. isDaemon( ). Returns true if this thread is a daemon else returns false.

- Thread Groups. For large programs that spawn many threads, Java allows you to group similar threads and manage them as a group. A ThreadGroup is a class distinct from the Thread class. A ThreadGroup is a group of threads or other thread groups. A thread does have the ability to access information about its ThreadGroup and the other threads in its group. The ThreadGroup has methods to manipulate the group as a whole like setDaemon( ), setMaxPriority( ), stop( ), suspend( ), remove( ), and others.

Now that you understand the major characteristics of threads, let's examine a non-trivial program that uses threads.

A Multi-threaded Bank Simulation

Source 5.11 is a time-stepped simulation of the queueing problems that a bank faces in handling customers. The purpose of the simulation is simply to determine how many tellers would be necessary to adequately handle a typical busy day at the bank. The program uses threads to represent the autonomous actions of all the major simulation entities: the customers and tellers. Let's now discuss the major classes and methods in the simulation while highlighting the use of threads.

The class simData is a simple class to get the number of seconds to run the simulation and the number of tellers to put on duty.

The class simRun extends Thread. The run( ) method of the thread executes the simulation. The simulation first kicks off the teller threads, then the clock thread. The clock thread is an endless loop that updates simulation time every second. This simulates time compression where one second simulates one minute of the day. You should notice that the clock class does not extend Thread. Instead it implements the Runnable interface. Examine how the simRun class creates the Thread for this "runnable" target. The rest of the simulation revolves around time-stepping through the day and generating customers based on a customer-probability function. The important thing to understand is that the major parts of the simulation are being executed asynchronously and autonomously by the customer and teller threads. In a non-threaded synchronous program the simRun loop would control everything. The occurrence of many simultaneous autonomous activities is much closer to real life.

The class customer extends thread. The customer thread simulates a customer entering the bank, spending a few minutes filling out forms or thinking about what he or she needs to do, and then waiting in line to perform a specific activity. The activity to perform is a subclass of an abstract action class. Executing the activity takes a certain number of minutes for the teller.

The teller class extends Thread. The teller thread checks if there are any customers waiting. If so, the teller calls a customer over (retrieves from the list), and assists the customer with his or her banking activity. The teller is busy for however many minutes the customer's action takes. The teller thread simulates being busy by sleeping the appropriate number of simulated minutes.

SOURCE 5.11

```
import java.lang.Thread;
import java.io.DataInputStream;
import java.io.IOException;
import java.lang.Runnable;
import java.util.Random;
import List.ListHead;

class simData {
        int numTellers;
        int secondsToRun;

        simData() throws Exception
        {
                String secStr=null;
                String numStr=null;

                System.out.println(" ");
                System.out.print("Enter number of tellers on duty: ");
                System.out.flush();
                try {
                        numStr = bankSim.dis.readLine();
                } catch (IOException ioe)
                  {
                        System.out.println(ioe.toString());
                        System.exit(1);
                  }

                if (numStr != null && numStr.length() > 0)
                        numTellers = Integer.parseInt(numStr);
                else
                        throw new Exception("Invalid number of tellers.");

                System.out.println("Time is compressed for this Sim.");
                System.out.println("One second equals one minute.");
                System.out.print("Enter number of seconds to run Sim: ");
                System.out.flush();
                try {
                        secStr = bankSim.dis.readLine();
                } catch (IOException ioe)
```

```
                    {
                            System.out.println(ioe.toString());
                            System.exit(1);
                    }

                if (secStr != null && secStr.length() > 0)
                        secondsToRun = Integer.parseInt(secStr);
                else
                        throw new Exception("Invalid number of Seconds.");

        }

        int getnumTellers()
        { return numTellers; }

        int getsecondsToRun()
        { return secondsToRun; }

}

// thread for running the sim
class simRun extends Thread {
        public long simTime;
        public boolean quitting_time;
        Thread clockThread;
        public Random dice;
        simData sData;
        simStats sStats;
        ListHead bankLine;

        static int customerProbability(long minute_in_day)
        {
                /* uses a Parabola mapped to an 8-hour day.
                   x-axis is minutes.
                   y-axis is probability. */

                return (int) - ( ( (minute_in_day - 240) *
                                    (minute_in_day - 240) ) -
                                   (3 * 240 * 98) ) /
                                   (3 * 240);
        }
```

```
simRun(simData theData, simStats theStats)
{
        simTime = 0;
        quitting_time = false;
        dice = new Random();
        sData = theData;
        sStats = theStats;
        bankLine = new ListHead();
}

public void run()
{
        int duration = sData.getsecondsToRun();

        // generate tellers
        int numTellers = sData.getnumTellers();

        // update stats
        sStats.numTellers = numTellers;
        sStats.simDuration = duration;

        for (int i=0; i < numTellers; i++)
        {
                teller aTeller = new teller(bankLine, this, sStats);
                aTeller.start();
        }

        // kick off clock thread
        clock aClock = new clock(this);
        clockThread = new Thread(aClock);

        // set clock priority as the highest in group
        clockThread.setPriority(6);
        clockThread.start();

        // sleep a sec
        try { sleep(1000); } catch (Exception e) { }

        while (!quitting_time)
        {
                // generate customers based on function
                int probability = customerProbability(simTime);
```

```
                     //System.out.println("Probability: " + probability);

                     // roll dice
                     int roll = dice.nextInt() % 100;
                     if (roll < 0) roll = -roll;

                     if (roll <= probability)
                     {
                              System.out.println("A customer just walked in...");

                              // update stats
                              sStats.totalNumCustomers += 1;

                              // generate customer thread
                              customer aCustomer = new customer(bankLine);
                              aCustomer.start();
                     }

                     // update line size stats
                     if (bankLine.size() > sStats.maxLineSize)
                              sStats.maxLineSize = bankLine.size();

                     try {
                              sleep(1000);
                     } catch (Exception e) { }


                     if (simTime >= duration)
                              quitting_time = true;
              }
              System.out.println("Simulation complete.");
         }
}

// clock thread
class clock implements Runnable {
       simRun theRun;

       clock(simRun aRun) { theRun = aRun; }

       public void run()
```

```
        {
            while (!theRun.quitting_time)
            {
                try {
                        Thread.sleep(1000);
                        theRun.simTime++;
                        if (theRun.simTime % 10 == 0)
                            System.out.println("CLOCK: " +
                                                    theRun.simTime);
                } catch (Exception e) { }
            }
        }
}


// abstract action class
abstract class Action {
        abstract int execute();
}

class open_account extends Action {
        int execute()
        {
                System.out.println("open an account...");
                return 5;
        }
}

class close_account extends Action {
        int execute()
        {
                System.out.println("close an account...");
                return 3;
        }
}

class rob_bank extends Action {
        int execute()
        {
                System.out.println("rob the bank...");
                return 20;
        }
}
```

```
class deposit_check extends Action {
      int execute()
      {
               System.out.println("deposit a check...");
               return 4;
      }
}

class cash_check extends Action {
      int execute()
      {
               System.out.println("cash a check...");
               return 7;
      }
}


/* Thread per customer.
   The concept of each entity in a Simulation being a
   separate thread has great potential for creating
   Autonomous, Polymorphous Entities (APE).  This would be a
   large breakthrough for the modeling of computer
   generated forces (cgf) and human intelligence collection. */
class customer extends Thread implements Cloneable {
      public static int customerCount = 0;
      private int Id;
      ListHead bankLine;
      Action myAction=null;

      customer()
      {
               customerCount++;
               Id = customerCount;
      }

      customer(ListHead theLine)
      {
               customerCount++;
               Id = customerCount;
               bankLine = theLine;
      }
```

```
Action getmyAction()
{ return myAction; }

int getId()
{ return Id; }

public Object clone()
{
   try {
       Object result = super.clone();
       return result;
   } catch (Exception e) { return null; }
}

public void run()
{
       /* be busy a random number of sim minutes before
          entering the bank line. */
       Random dice = new Random();
       int busy = dice.nextInt() % 10;
       if (busy < 0) busy = -busy;

       try { sleep(busy * 1000); } catch (Exception e) { }

       /* after this "thinking" the customer knows
          what they came to do. */
       int decide = dice.nextInt() % 5;
       if (decide < 0) decide = -decide;

       switch (decide) {
              case 0:
                      myAction = new open_account();
                      break;
              case 1:
                      myAction = new close_account();
                      break;
              case 2:
                      myAction = new rob_bank();
                      break;
              case 3:
                      myAction = new deposit_check();
                      break;
```

```
                        case 4:
                                myAction = new cash_check();
                                break;
                        default:
                                myAction = new open_account();
                                System.out.println("Unknown action.");
                }

                // now wait on line
                customer newCustomer = (customer) this.clone();
                bankLine.addElement(newCustomer);
                System.out.println("Customer #" + Id +
                                   " is now waiting on line.");

                // sleep a little to allow println
                try { sleep(2000); } catch (Exception e) { }
        }
}

// Thread for teller
class teller extends Thread {
        public static int tellerCount = 0;
        private int Id;
        ListHead theLine;
        simRun sRun;
        simStats sStats;

        teller(ListHead aLine, simRun aRun, simStats inStats)
        {
                tellerCount++;
                Id = tellerCount;
                theLine = aLine;
                sRun = aRun;
                sStats = inStats;
        }

        public void run()
        {
                // pause a second to allow menu println to finish
                try { sleep(1000); } catch (Exception e) { }

                // if free, pops a customer and serves the customer
```

```
                boolean stillWaiting = false;
                while (!sRun.quitting_time)
                {
                        if (theLine.size() > 0)
                        {
                                stillWaiting = false;
                                customer currentCustomer = (customer)
                                        theLine.removeFirst();
                                System.out.print("Teller #" +
                                                Id + " is helping " +
                                                "Customer #" +
                                                currentCustomer.getId() +
                                                " to ");

                                System.out.flush();
                                int helping =
                                        (currentCustomer.getmyAction()).execute();

                                // update the stats
                                sStats.totalCustomersServed += 1;

                                try {
                                        sleep(helping * 1000);
                                } catch (Exception e) { }
                        }
                        else
                        {
                            if (!stillWaiting)
                                System.out.println("Teller #" + Id +
                                                " is waiting to help someone.");
                            stillWaiting = true;
                        }

                        try { sleep(2000); } catch (Exception e) { }
                }
        }
}

class simStats {
        public int numTellers;
        public int simDuration;
        public int totalNumCustomers;
```

```
        public int totalCustomersServed;
        public int maxLineSize;
        // exercise: maxCustomerWait, maxTellerWait

        simStats()
        {
                numTellers = 0;
                simDuration = 0;
                totalNumCustomers = 0;
                totalCustomersServed = 0;
                maxLineSize = 0;
        }

        void printStats()
        {
                System.out.println(" ");
                System.out.println("<<<<< SIM STATISTICS >>>>>");
                System.out.println("# Tellers            : " + numTellers);
                System.out.println("# minutes simulated  : " + simDuration);
                System.out.println("Tot customers entered: " + totalNumCustomers);
                System.out.println("Tot customers served : " +
                        totalCustomersServed);
                System.out.println("Maximum line size    : " + maxLineSize);
        }
}

class bankSim {
        static DataInputStream dis = new DataInputStream(System.in);

        public static void main(String args[])
        {
            boolean done = false;
            simData sData = null;
            simRun sRun = null;
            simStats sStats = new simStats();
            while (!done)
            {
                System.out.println(" ");
                System.out.println("<<<<<< Bank Sim >>>>>>");
                System.out.println("  1) Enter Simulation Data.");
                System.out.println("  2) Run Simulation.");
                System.out.println("  3) Stop Simulation.");
```

```
System.out.println("    4) Print Simulation Stats.");
System.out.println("    5) Exit.");
System.out.println(" ");
System.out.print("Enter choice: ");
System.out.flush();
String choiceStr=null;
try {
        choiceStr = dis.readLine();
} catch (IOException ioe)
  {
        System.out.println(ioe.toString());
        System.exit(1);
  }

if (choiceStr != null && choiceStr.length() > 0)
{
        int choice = Integer.parseInt(choiceStr);
        switch (choice) {
                case 1: try {
                            sData = new simData();
                        } catch (Exception e)
                            {
                                System.out.println(e.toString());
                                sData = null;
                            }
                        break;
                case 2:
                        if (sData != null)
                        {
                                sRun = new simRun(sData,sStats);
                                sRun.start();
                                System.out.println("Sim started.");
                        }
                        else
                            System.out.println("Must enter sim data
                                first.");
                        break;
                case 3:
                        if (sRun != null)
                        {
                                System.out.print("Stopping...");
                                sRun.quitting_time = true;
```

```
                                      try {
                                              Thread.sleep(1000);
                                      } catch (Exception e) { }
                                      System.out.println("Done.");
                                      sRun.stop();
                                      System.out.println("Sim stopped.");
                                  }
                                  else
                                     System.out.println("Sim must be running to
                                        stop.");
                                  break;
                          case 4:
                                  sStats.printStats();
                                  break;
                          case 5:
                                  done = true;
                                  break;
                          default:
                                  System.out.println("Invalid choice");
                      }
                  }
              else
                      System.out.println("Invalid choice.");
          }
      System.exit(1);
    }
}
```

A run of Source 5.11 produces:

```
C:\java\bin>java bankSim

<<<<<< Bank Sim >>>>>>
    1) Enter Simulation Data.
    2) Run Simulation.
    3) Stop Simulation.
    4) Print Simulation Stats.
    5) Exit.

Enter choice: 1
```

```
Enter number of tellers on duty: 3
Time is compressed for this Sim.
One second equals one minute.
Enter number of seconds to run Sim: 120

<<<<<< Bank Sim >>>>>>
    1) Enter Simulation Data.
    2) Run Simulation.
    3) Stop Simulation.
    4) Print Simulation Stats.
    5) Exit.

Enter choice: 2
Sim started.

<<<<<< Bank Sim >>>>>>
    1) Enter Simulation Data.
    2) Run Simulation.
    3) Stop Simulation.
    4) Print Simulation Stats.
    5) Exit.

Enter choice: Teller #2 is waiting to help someone.
Teller #3 is waiting to help someone.
Teller #1 is waiting to help someone.
A customer just walked in...
A customer just walked in...
Customer #1 is now waiting on line.
Teller #3 is helping Customer #1 to
CLOCK: 10
Customer #2 is now waiting on line.
Teller #1 is helping Customer #2 to cash a check...
close an account...
Teller #1 is waiting to help someone.
A customer just walked in...
Teller #3 is waiting to help someone.
CLOCK: 20
A customer just walked in...
A customer just walked in...
A customer just walked in...
Customer #4 is now waiting on line.
Teller #3 is helping Customer #4 to deposit a check...
```

```
Customer #3 is now waiting on line.
A customer just walked in...
Customer #6 is now waiting on line.
Teller #2 is helping Customer #3 to rob the bank...
Teller #1 is helping Customer #6 to rob the bank...
A customer just walked in...
...
Teller #3 is helping Customer #28 to cash a check...
A customer just walked in...
Customer #54 is now waiting on line.
Customer #58 is now waiting on line.
CLOCK: 120
Simulation complete.
Customer #57 is now waiting on line.
Customer #59 is now waiting on line.
4

<<<<< SIM STATISTICS >>>>>
# Tellers            : 3
# minutes simulated  : 120
Tot customers entered: 59
Tot customers served : 27
Maximum line size    : 29

<<<<<< Bank Sim >>>>>>
    1) Enter Simulation Data.
    2) Run Simulation.
    3) Stop Simulation.
    4) Print Simulation Stats.
    5) Exit.

Enter choice: 5
```

Examining the statistics of the simulation run, you can tell that our three tellers were extremely overworked that day. This is a very busy bank in a big city. Obviously, an important criterion for the accuracy of this simulation is how you determine when a customer enters the bank. I chose to map a simple curve to our 8-hour day and then determine the probability of a customer entering the bank to our position on the curve. The formula for the parabola mapped to our 8-hour day is:

$$y = \frac{((x - 240)^2 - (3 \cdot 240 \cdot 98))}{3 \cdot 240}$$

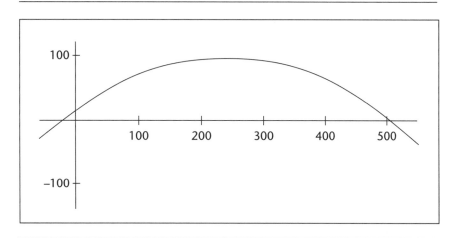

FIGURE 5.1   Parabola graph.

Figure 5.1 is a graph of the same curve.

I recommend experimenting with this simulation by modifying the customer probability (I recommend lowering it), adding new actions for the customer to perform, and allowing the bank manager to increase staff at peak bank periods. Also, it is important to determine the maximum number of minutes a customer had to wait on line. Another possible enhancement would be to determine the number of minutes a teller sat idle. These are left to you as an exercise.

Now we need to discuss how threads can share data in a controlled fashion.

Sharing Data between Threads

As stated above, all threads share the same memory space and therefore have access to objects created in other threads and the main process. When you share data among threads it is necessary to insure that the shared variables are not updated by two threads simultaneously. To prevent that, the synchronized keyword insures that multiple threads will NOT run ANY synchronized method in a class concurrently. This is accomplished by the Java runtime placing a software "lock" on the object that only allows one thread access at a time. Source 5.12 demonstrates threads sharing an object that uses synchronized methods. The object that uses synchronized methods is the Stack class.

SOURCE 5.12

```java
import java.lang.Thread;
import java.lang.Exception;
import java.lang.Integer;
import java.util.Stack;
import java.util.Random;

class Producer extends Thread {
        int Rest, qty, myNumber;
        Stack theStorage;
        static int ProducerCount = 0;

        Producer(int millisRest, int numberToProduce, Stack aStack)
        {
                Rest = millisRest;
                qty = numberToProduce;
                ProducerCount++;
                myNumber = ProducerCount;
                theStorage = aStack;
        }

        public void run()
        {
                int i=qty;

                while (i > 0)
                {
                        System.out.println("Producer: " + myNumber +
                                            " created and stored a product.");
                        Integer anInt = new Integer(myNumber);
                        theStorage.push(anInt);
                        try { sleep(Rest); } catch (Exception e) { }
                        i--;
                }
        }
}

class Consumer extends Thread {
        static int ConsumerCount = 0;
        int myNumber, delay, count;
        Stack theStorage;
```

```
        Consumer(int millisToConsume, int numberToConsume, Stack aStack)
        {
                delay = millisToConsume;
                count = numberToConsume;
                theStorage = aStack;
                ConsumerCount++;
                myNumber = ConsumerCount;
        }

        public void run()
        {
                int i=count;
                while (i > 0)
                {
                        System.out.println("Store holds " + theStorage.size() +
                                            " products.");
                        if (theStorage.size() > 0)
                        {
                                Object o = theStorage.pop();
                                System.out.println("Consumer: " + myNumber +
                                                    " consumed a product.");
                                try { sleep(delay); } catch (Exception e) { }
                        }
                        else
                        {
                                System.out.println("Consumer: " + myNumber +
                                                    " could NOT get any product!");
                                break;
                        }
                        i--;
                }
        }
}

class tstSynch {
        public static void main(String args[])
        {
                if (args.length < 2)
                {
                        System.out.println("Usage: java tstSynch #producers
                                #consumers");
                        System.exit(1);
```

```
        }

        int producers = Integer.parseInt(args[0]);
        int consumers = Integer.parseInt(args[1]);

        // create the stack
        Stack theStore = new Stack();

        Random dice = new Random();

        for (int i=0; i < producers; i++)
        {
                int produceCount = dice.nextInt() % 5;
                if (produceCount < 0) produceCount = -produceCount;
                int millis = dice.nextInt() % 500;
                if (millis < 0) millis = -millis;
                System.out.println("ProduceCount " + produceCount);
                Producer p = new Producer(millis, produceCount, theStore);
                p.start();
        }

        try { Thread.sleep(200); } catch (Exception e) { }

        for (int i=0; i < consumers; i++)
        {
                int hunger = dice.nextInt() % 5;
                if (hunger < 0) hunger = -hunger;
                int timeToEat = dice.nextInt() % 500;
                if (timeToEat < 0) timeToEat = -timeToEat;
                System.out.println("hunger: " + hunger);
                Consumer c = new Consumer(timeToEat, hunger, theStore);
                c.start();
        }

        try { Thread.sleep(2000); } catch (Exception e) { }

        System.out.println("Active threads: " + Thread.activeCount());
    }
}
```

Here is a run of Source 5.12.

```
C:\java\bin>java tstSynch 2 2
ProduceCount 4
ProduceCount 2
Producer: 2 created and stored a product.
Producer: 1 created and stored a product.
Producer: 2 created and stored a product.
Producer: 1 created and stored a product.
hunger: 0
hunger: 2
Store holds 4 products.
Consumer: 2 consumed a product.
Producer: 1 created and stored a product.
Store holds 4 products.
Consumer: 2 consumed a product.
Producer: 1 created and stored a product.
Active threads: 1
```

The Producer and Consumer threads share the same Stack object. The synchronized methods in the Stack object insure that only one thread accesses the Stack object at a time. It also allows threads to wait for a certain condition in the object (like the Consumer waiting for the Producer to put a product on the shelf). As an experiment, you should modify the above program to make a Consumer wait for a product if the Stack is empty. This is left for you as an exercise.

PART 2

Programming in Java and JavaScript

CHAPTER 6

Abstract Window Toolkit

One of the cornerstones of the Macintosh philosophy is that people should tell computers what to do and not the other way around.

—Stephen Chernicoff, *Macintosh Revealed*

OBJECTIVE

This chapter enables the reader to understand the implementation of the Abstract Window Toolkit, how to use all the major GUI elements in the AWT, and last, to see a complete example of a GUI for a previous text-based application.

In 1984, the Apple Macintosh changed the face of computing by evangelizing the benefits of graphical user interfaces (GUI) to the masses. In the following years, the Massachusetts Institute of Technology created X Windows for UNIX platforms and Microsoft created MS Windows for Intel-compatible PCs. The graphical user interfaces on these three platform groups have evolved and improved over the years. The Macintosh GUI has been enhanced in small and large ways, most recently by pioneering video and virtual reality on every mac with Quicktime and QuickTime VR. The various UNIX vendors have agreed upon and transitioned to a single GUI standard called the Common Desktop Environment (CDE). Microsoft has now caught up to the other two camps with its latest release of Windows, Windows 95. The success and market demand for graphical user interfaces are simply a validation of a common sense principle: "A picture is worth a thousand words." There are many forms of information that can be processed faster in a graphical fashion. Secondly, many GUI elements can be manipulated via a mouse, which eliminates the need for advanced typing skills to use the computer. Therefore, combining the mouse with the elements of a graphical user interface brings us closer to the computer becoming an "information appliance." The introduction of sub-$500 internet appliances that run Java applications could increase this trend as well as truly bringing computing to the masses. Most homeowners do not need a $3000 Pentium to store their cooking recipes or to send email to Grandma Whitaker in Florida.

The abstract window toolkit (AWT) is a platform-independent interface that allows development of a GUI that runs on all major platforms. In the following sections we will describe how the AWT performs this cross-platform feat and then demonstrate all the major AWT functionality.

6.1   UNDERSTANDING THE IMPLEMENTATION OF THE AWT

In all cross-platform products the product developer must choose between one of two strategies: a common look and feel or common functionality with a platform-unique look and feel. The first strategy of a common look and feel is much harder to implement; however, you gain the advantage of customers knowing how to work the application no matter which platform they are on. In essence, this is the strategy of the Common Desktop Environment. It is important to note, however, that CDE is possible because the various UNIX flavors are all very similar and all use X Windows as the GUI backbone. Some Microsoft applications also follow this common look and feel approach. The problem with the common look and feel approach is that it tends to stifle new innovation on a single platform that has not yet migrated (and may never) to all supported platforms.

The AWT uses the "common functionality/specific implementation" approach. The idea is very object-oriented in that the functionality is the superclass (high level abstraction) and each platform's specific look and feel is a subclass. This allows applications to take advantage of a platform's unique GUI and make Java applications look and feel just like other native applications. It also encourages innovation by allowing third parties to develop variations of GUI components.

The practice of modifying and replacing portions of the GUI is widespread in the Macintosh and UNIX domains. For example, there are many superb alternate window managers for UNIX like the GNU window manager (GWM) and virtual window managers like FVWM. On the Macintosh, you can find virtual desktop replacements, Copland style folders and windows, and 3D buttons. Now let's examine the specifics behind how the AWT supports this common functionality/platform-unique look and feel.

The Java AWT uses three concepts to implement common functionality/platform-unique look and feel: abstract objects, toolkits, and peers. Every GUI element supported by the AWT will have a class. Objects of that class can be instantiated. For example, a Button object can be instantiated from the Button class even though there is no physical display of a button. There is no physical display of a button because the Button class in the AWT does not represent a specific look and feel. The specific look and feel would be a "Solaris button" or a "Macintosh button" or an "MS Windows button." The AWT GUI objects are platform-independent abstractions of a GUI. Just as Java byte-codes are platform-independent assembly language instructions for a virtual machine, AWT objects are platform-independent GUI elements for a virtual operating system display. The toolkit is the platform-specific implementation of all the GUI elements supported by the AWT. Each toolkit implements the platform-specific GUI elements by creating a GUI "peer." A peer is an individual platform-specific GUI element. Since every AWT GUI object is derived from the generic AWT object called a Component, every Component will have a peer. Of course, the peer implements the platform specific behavior of the AWT component. The peer is added to the generic AWT object when the object is added to a container that has a peer. Let's examine some code that demonstrates toolkits and peers.

Source 6.1 demonstrates accessing the default toolkit and printing toolkit platform and hardware specific properties.

SOURCE 6.1

```
import java.awt.Toolkit;
import java.awt.Dimension;

class tstToolkit {
        public static void main(String args[])
        {
                Toolkit defTk = Toolkit.getDefaultToolkit();
```

```
                          String name = System.getProperty("awt.toolkit");
                          System.out.println("Toolkit name: " + name);

                          Dimension screen = defTk.getScreenSize();
                          System.out.println("Screen Dimension       : " +
                                              screen.toString());
                          System.out.println("Screen Resolution (dpi): " +
                                              defTk.getScreenResolution());
                          System.out.println("Font List.");
                          String fonts[] = defTk.getFontList();
                          for (int i=0; i < fonts.length; i++)
                                  System.out.println(i + ") " + fonts[i]);

                          System.exit(0);
                  }
          }
```

A run of Source 6.1 produces:

```
C:\java\bin>java tstToolkit
Toolkit name: sun.awt.win32.MToolkit
Screen Dimension       : java.awt.Dimension[width=640,height=480]
Screen Resolution (dpi): 96
Font List.
0) Dialog
1) Helvetica
2) TimesRoman
3) Courier
4) Symbol
```

Source 6.2 demonstrates the separate creation of an AWT object from its peer.

SOURCE 6.2

```
import java.awt.Button;
import java.awt.peer.ComponentPeer;
import java.awt.Frame;

class tstPeer {
        public static void main(String args[])
        {
```

```
Button myButton = new Button("my Button");
ComponentPeer buttonPeer = myButton.getPeer();

if (buttonPeer == null)
{
        System.out.println("Button peer not yet created.");
        System.out.println("Button is: " + myButton.toString());
}
else
{
        System.out.println("Button Peer is Created!");
        System.out.println(buttonPeer.toString());
}

Frame myFrame = new Frame("my Frame");
myFrame.add("Center", myButton);
myFrame.pack();
myFrame.show();  // Here is where peer will be created.

buttonPeer = myButton.getPeer();
if (buttonPeer == null)
{
        System.out.println("Button peer not yet created.");
        System.out.println("Button is: " + myButton.toString());
}
else
{
        System.out.println("Button Peer is Created!");
        System.out.println(buttonPeer.toString());
}

ComponentPeer framePeer = myFrame.getPeer();
System.out.println("Frame Peer is also created.");
System.out.println(framePeer.toString());
    }
}
```

A run of Source 6.2 produces both text output (below) and the window in Figure 6.1.

```
C:\java\bin>java tstPeer
Button peer not yet created.
```

FIGURE 6.1   A button peer.

```
Button is: java.awt.Button[0,0,0x0,invalid,label=my Button]
Button Peer is Created!
sun.awt.win32.MButtonPeer[java.awt.Button[0,0,67x24,label=my Button]]
Frame Peer is also created.
sun.awt.win32.MFramePeer[java.awt.Frame[8,46,104x22,layout=java.awt.BorderLayout
,resizable,title= my Frame]]
```

Source 6.1 demonstrates two points well:

1. **The fact that peers are separate from the AWT object.** An AWT object contains a peer. Of course, this relationship was not implemented using inheritance; instead, it was implemented using the idea of containment.

2. **When the peer is created.** The peer is not created until there is a physical screen representation (i.e., associated with the show( ) method). In the example above, the button peer is not created until the Frame (a type of window) is created and shown. Now that you understand toolkits and peers we can explore all the elements supported by the Java AWT. You can also feel confident that the AWT will constantly be evolving and improving!

6.2   MAJOR ELEMENTS OF THE AWT

I have divided the AWT into five major areas:

1. **Components.** The basic elements of every GUI. This is implemented with an abstract Component class and then subclasses that implement specific GUI components. For X Window programmers, an AWT component is analogous to an X Window widget.

2. **Events.** A user action that is translated into an Event data structure (stores type of action, where it occurred, etc.) and sent to the Java interpreter from the operating system. The Java Event class only takes the common set of events from all the supported platforms. Events are dispatched to GUI components when the event pertains to that component. You handle Events in a Java AWT program by overriding the handleEvent( ) method or one of the specific "event" functions in the Component class.

3. **Containers.** Components that store other components. The most common container is the window. A Panel is another very common Java AWT container that serves the purpose of grouping components inside your window.
4. **Layout.** A methodology for arranging components in a container. A layout determines where the component will be drawn.
5. **Painting and Updating.** Although the prefabricated components are useful, you will quickly find it necessary to do custom drawing in your applications. The Java AWT provides paint( ), repaint( ), and update( ) methods to allow you to do just that.

Now let's discuss each of these elements in detail as well as demonstrate each with source code.

Components

GUI Components are the objects that instantly come to mind when people think of what makes up a graphical user interface. Components are buttons, menus, lists, check boxes, and so on. A GUI could be defined as simply a collection of Components arranged in a visually appealing manner.

In Java the Component class is the central element of the AWT. Figure 6.2 depicts the Component hierarchy in the AWT.

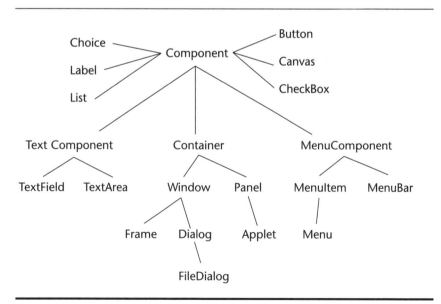

FIGURE 6.2   The Component hierarchy.

Although graphical user interfaces often scare novice programmers, creating AWT Components is as simple as instantiating any Java class. As in using any class in the Java standard library, you simply know the constructor arguments and instantiate the object using the new operator and the appropriate constructor. The appendix contains the entire Java API. Source 6.3 demonstrates the instantiation and display of the majority of AWT Components.

SOURCE 6.3

```java
import java.awt.Frame;
import java.awt.Button;
import java.awt.Label;
import java.awt.Checkbox;
import java.awt.List;
import java.awt.FlowLayout;
import java.awt.BorderLayout;
import java.awt.Panel;
import java.awt.Choice;
import java.awt.Canvas;
import java.awt.Color;
import java.awt.Event;
import java.awt.TextArea;
import java.awt.TextField;
import java.awt.Scrollbar;

class componentHolder extends Frame {
        componentHolder()
        {
                super("AWT Basic Components");
                setLayout(new BorderLayout());

                Panel topP = new Panel();
                topP.setLayout(new FlowLayout(FlowLayout.LEFT));
                topP.add(new Button("my Button"));
                topP.add(new Label("my Label"));
                topP.add(new Checkbox("my CheckBox"));
                add("North", topP);

                Panel midP = new Panel();
                midP.setLayout(new FlowLayout(FlowLayout.LEFT));
                List l = null;
```

```
            midP.add(l = new List(5,true));
            l.addItem("listItem1");
            l.addItem("listItem2");
            l.addItem("listItem3");
            Choice c = null;
            midP.add(c = new Choice());
            c.addItem("choiceItem1");
            c.addItem("choiceItem2");
            c.addItem("choiceItem3");
            Canvas can;
            midP.add(can = new Canvas());
            can.setBackground(Color.white);
            add("Center", midP);

            Panel botP = new Panel();
            botP.setLayout(new FlowLayout(FlowLayout.LEFT));
            botP.add(new TextField("my text field."));
            botP.add(new TextArea("my text Area."));
            botP.add(new Scrollbar(Scrollbar.VERTICAL));
            add("South", botP);

            pack();
            show();
        }

        public boolean handleEvent(Event evt)
        {
            switch (evt.id) {
                case Event.WINDOW_DESTROY:
                    System.exit(0);
            }
            return false;
        }
    }

class tstComponents {
        public static void main(String args[])
        {
            new componentHolder();
        }
    }
```

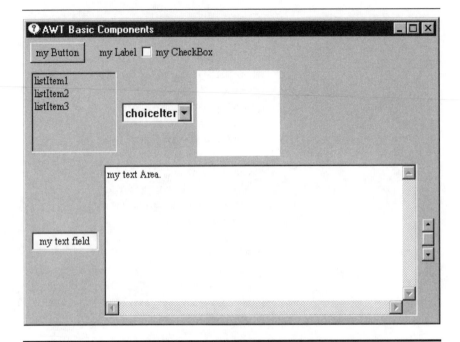

FIGURE 6.3   The AWT Components.

A run of Source 6.3 produces the output shown in Figure 6.3.

The purpose of Source 6.3 is to demonstrate the creation of Components; however, there are other constructs required to display them. The creation of Components is the most trivial part of the above application. For example, the creation of the button is the call to

```
new Button("my Button");
```

The supporting constructs are the Frame, Panel, and FlowLayout classes. Frame and Panels are containers, while FlowLayout is a layout manager. These will all be discussed in the sections to follow. For now just understand the simplicity of creating components. The rest will follow.

Events

Programming graphical user interfaces introduced a new style of programming called "event-driven" programming. Although the terminology differs between X Windows, MS Windows, and the Mac OS, the methodology for event-driven programming is the same. Event-driven programming describes a new paradigm for the control flow of a program. In the event-driven paradigm, your program becomes a set of event handlers that are invoked by a user-triggered event (button press, menu selection or key press, etc.). On the Macintosh and MS Windows, the application programmer actually writes the small function to retrieve and dispatch events. This main function is the infamous "event loop" (although MS Windows calls events messages). In X Windows and the Java AWT, the event loop is hidden from you. In X Windows the application programmer registers function pointers to event handling routines (called callbacks) and then calls a function called XtAppMainLoop( ). In the Java AWT events are retrieved and dispatched by the Java runtime. Your Java application receives the dispatched events via two methods:

1. Overriding the handleEvent( ) routine for a component. This is useful for receiving all events sent to the component.
2. Overriding one of the specific event handler functions defined in the Component class. The functions are: mouseDown( ), mouseDrag( ), mouseUp( ), mouseMove( ), mouseEnter( ), mouseExit( ), keyDown( ), action( ), gotFocus( ), and lostFocus( ).

Source 6.4 demonstrates receiving events by overriding the handleEvent( ) function of a Frame (type of window).

SOURCE 6.4

```
import java.awt.Frame;
import java.awt.MenuBar;
import java.awt.Menu;
import java.awt.MenuItem;
import java.awt.Event;
import java.util.Vector;
import java.awt.CheckboxMenuItem;
import java.io.FileOutputStream;
import java.io.IOException;
import java.io.PrintStream;
import java.awt.Panel;

class eventWindow extends Frame {
        private boolean capture;
```

```java
private boolean print;
private Vector evtVector;

eventWindow()
{
        super("Event Tester");
        capture = print = false;
        evtVector = new Vector(100);

        MenuBar mBar = new MenuBar();
        setMenuBar(mBar);
        Menu fileMenu = new Menu("File");
        mBar.add(fileMenu);
        fileMenu.add(new CheckboxMenuItem("Capture Events"));
        fileMenu.add(new CheckboxMenuItem("Print Events"));
        fileMenu.add(new MenuItem("Dump Events To File"));
        fileMenu.add(new MenuItem("Exit"));
        Panel p = new Panel();
        add("Center", p);
        move(100,100);
        resize(200,200);
        show();
}

public boolean handleEvent(Event evt)
{
        switch (evt.id) {
                case Event.ACTION_EVENT:
                        if (print)
                            System.out.println("ACTION_EVENT");
                        if ("Exit".equals(evt.arg))
                        {
                                System.exit(0);
                        }
                        else if ("Capture Events".equals(evt.arg))
                        {
                                capture = !capture;
                        }
                        else if ("Print Events".equals(evt.arg))
                        {
                                print = !print;
                        }
```

```
                    else if ("Dump Events To File".equals(evt.arg))
                    {
                            if (evtVector.size() > 0)
                            {
                                try {
                                    FileOutputStream fos = new
                                        FileOutputStream("Event.txt");
                                    PrintStream ps = new
                                        PrintStream(fos);
                                    for (int i=0; i < evtVector.size();
                                        i++)
                                            ps.println(((Event)evtVector.
                                                elementAt(i)).toString());
                                    fos.close();
                                } catch (IOException ioe)
                                {
                                    System.out.println(ioe.toString());
                                    System.out.println("Unable to dump
                                        to file.");
                                }
                            }
                            else
                            {
                                System.out.println("event vector is
                                    empty.");
                            }
                    }
                break;
        case Event.WINDOW_DESTROY:
                if (print)
                    System.out.println("WINDOW_DESTROY");
                break;
        case Event.WINDOW_EXPOSE:
                if (print)
                    System.out.println("WINOW_EXPOSE");
                break;
        case Event.WINDOW_ICONIFY:
                if (print)
                    System.out.println("WINDOW_ICONIFY");
                break;
        case Event.WINDOW_DEICONIFY:
                if (print)
```

```java
                          System.out.println("WINDOW_DEICONIFY");
            break;
case Event.WINDOW_MOVED:
            if (print)
                System.out.println("WINDOW_MOVED");
            break;
case Event.KEY_PRESS:
            if (print)
                System.out.println("KEY_PRESS");
            break;
case Event.KEY_RELEASE:
            if (print)
                System.out.println("KEY_RELEASE");
            break;
case Event.KEY_ACTION:
            if (print)
                System.out.println("KEY_ACTION");
            break;
case Event.KEY_ACTION_RELEASE:
            if (print)
                System.out.println("KEY_ACTION_RELEASE");
            break;
case Event.MOUSE_DOWN:
            if (print)
                System.out.println("MOUSE_DOWN");
            break;
case Event.MOUSE_UP:
            if (print)
                System.out.println("MOUSE_UP");
            break;
case Event.MOUSE_MOVE:
            if (print)
            {
                System.out.print(" (" + evt.x + "," +
                                         evt.y + ")");
                System.out.flush();
            }
            break;
case Event.MOUSE_ENTER:
            if (print)
                System.out.println("MOUSE_ENTER");
            break;
```

```
            case Event.MOUSE_EXIT:
                    if (print)
                        System.out.println("MOUSE_EXIT");
                    break;
            case Event.MOUSE_DRAG:
                    if (print)
                        System.out.println("MOUSE_DRAG");
                    break;
            case Event.SCROLL_LINE_UP:
                    if (print)
                        System.out.println("SCROLL_LINE_UP");
                    break;
            case Event.SCROLL_LINE_DOWN:
                    if (print)
                        System.out.println("SCROLL_LINE_DOWN");
                    break;
            case Event.SCROLL_PAGE_UP:
                    if (print)
                        System.out.println("SCROLL_PAGE_UP");
                    break;
            case Event.SCROLL_ABSOLUTE:
                    if (print)
                        System.out.println("SCROLL_ABSOLUTE");
                    break;
            case Event.LIST_SELECT:
                    if (print)
                        System.out.println("LIST_SELECT");
                    break;
            case Event.LIST_DESELECT:
                    if (print)
                        System.out.println("LIST_DESELECT");
                    break;
            case Event.LOAD_FILE:
                    if (print)
                        System.out.println("LOAD_FILE");
                    break;
            case Event.SAVE_FILE:
                    if (print)
                        System.out.println("SAVE_FILE");
                    break;
            case Event.GOT_FOCUS:
                    if (print)
```

```
                                    System.out.println("GOT_FOCUS");
                            break;
                    case Event.LOST_FOCUS:
                            if (print)
                                    System.out.println("LOST_FOCUS");
                            break;
                    default:
                            System.out.println("*** Unknown Event ***");
                            System.out.println(evt.toString());
            }
            if (capture)
            {
                    Event newEvt = new Event(evt.target, evt.when,
                                             evt.id, evt.x, evt.y,
                                             evt.key, evt.modifiers,
                                             evt.arg);
                    evtVector.addElement(newEvt);
            }
            return true;
        }
}

class tstEvents {
        public static void main(String args[])
        {
                new eventWindow();
        }
}
```

A run of Source 6.4 produces three outputs: output to the screen, output to a file, and a window (Figure 6.4). Here is the output to the screen:

```
C:\java\bin>java tstEvents
MOUSE_ENTER
 (16,24) (15,24) (7,6)MOUSE_EXIT
ACTION_EVENT
MOUSE_ENTER
 (10,5)GOT_FOCUS
 (10,5)MOUSE_DOWN
```

FIGURE 6.4   The Event Tester GUI.

```
MOUSE_DRAG
MOUSE_UP
 (10,5)MOUSE_DOWN
MOUSE_DRAG
MOUSE_DRAG
MOUSE_DRAG
MOUSE_DRAG
MOUSE_DRAG
MOUSE_DRAG
MOUSE_DRAG
MOUSE_DRAG
MOUSE_DRAG
MOUSE_UP
 (17,12) (16,12)MOUSE_EXIT
LOST_FOCUS
MOUSE_ENTER
 (106,1) (106,2) (106,3) (105,4) (104,5)GOT_FOCUS
 (104,5)MOUSE_DOWN
MOUSE_DRAG
MOUSE_UP
 (104,5)KEY_PRESS
KEY_RELEASE
KEY_PRESS
```

```
            KEY_RELEASE
            KEY_PRESS
            KEY_RELEASE
            KEY_PRESS
            KEY_RELEASE
             (105,5) (111,5) (119,5) (127,5) (137,4)MOUSE_EXIT
            WINDOW_DESTROY
            ACTION_EVENT
            MOUSE_ENTER
             (16,42) (15,41) (14,33) (13,25) (13,17) (13,9) (13,7)MOUSE_EXIT
            ACTION_EVENT
```

Here is a small sample of the output to the file:

```
java.awt.Event[id=1001,x=0,y=0,target=java.awt.CheckboxMenuItem[label=Capture
        Events,state=true],arg=Capture Events]
java.awt.Event[id=504,x=22,y=7,target=java.awt.Panel[0,0,196x177,layout=java.awt.
        FlowLayout]]
java.awt.Event[id=503,x=22,y=7,target=java.awt.Panel[0,0,196x177,layout=java.awt.
        FlowLayout]]
java.awt.Event[id=503,x=23,y=7,target=java.awt.Panel[0,0,196x177,layout=java.awt.
        FlowLayout]]
...
java.awt.Event[id=503,x=122,y=36,target=java.awt.Panel[0,0,196x177,layout=java.awt.
        FlowLayout]]
java.awt.Event[id=503,x=122,y=37,target=java.awt.Panel[0,0,196x177,layout=java.awt.
        FlowLayout]]
java.awt.Event[id=501,x=122,y=37,target=java.awt.Panel[0,0,196x177,layout=java.awt.
        FlowLayout]]
java.awt.Event[id=506,x=122,y=37,target=java.awt.Panel[0,0,196x177,layout=java.awt.
        FlowLayout]]
java.awt.Event[id=502,x=122,y=37,target=java.awt.Panel[0,0,196x177,layout=java.awt.
        FlowLayout]]
java.awt.Event[id=503,x=122,y=37,target=java.awt.Panel[0,0,196x177,layout=java.awt.
        FlowLayout]]
java.awt.Event[id=501,x=122,y=37,control,target=java.awt.Panel[0,0,196x177,layout=java.awt.
        FlowLayout]]
java.awt.Event[id=506,x=122,y=37,target=java.awt.Panel[0,0,196x177,layout=java.awt.
        FlowLayout]]
java.awt.Event[id=502,x=122,y=37,target=java.awt.Panel[0,0,196x177,layout=java.awt.
        FlowLayout]]
java.awt.Event[id=501,x=108,y=41,target=java.awt.Panel[0,0,196x177,layout=java.awt.
        FlowLayout]]
```

```
java.awt.Event[id=506,x=108,y=41,target=java.awt.Panel[0,0,196x177,layout=java.awt.
      FlowLayout]]
java.awt.Event[id=502,x=108,y=41,target=java.awt.Panel[0,0,196x177,layout=java.awt.
      FlowLayout]]
java.awt.Event[id=503,x=108,y=41,target=java.awt.Panel[0,0,196x177,layout=java.awt.
      FlowLayout]]
java.awt.Event[id=401,x=108,y=41,key=97,target=java.awt.Panel[0,0,196x177,layout=java.awt.
      FlowLayout]]
java.awt.Event[id=402,x=108,y=41,key=97,target=java.awt.Panel[0,0,196x177,layout=java.awt.
      FlowLayout]]
java.awt.Event[id=401,x=108,y=41,key=111,target=java.awt.Panel[0,0,196x177,layout=java.awt.
      FlowLayout]]
java.awt.Event[id=402,x=108,y=41,key=111,target=java.awt.Panel[0,0,196x177,layout=java.awt.
      FlowLayout]]
...
java.awt.Event[id=503,x=169,y=5,target=java.awt.Panel[0,0,196x177,layout=java.awt.
      FlowLayout]]
java.awt.Event[id=505,x=179,y=-
      42,target=java.awt.Panel[0,0,196x177,layout=java.awt.FlowLayout]]
java.awt.Event[id=201,x=0,y=0,target=eventWindow[108,165,196x177,layout=java.awt.
      BorderLayout,
      resizable,title= Event Tester]]
java.awt.Event[id=1001,x=0,y=0,target=java.awt.CheckboxMenuItem[label=Print
      Events,state=true],arg=Print Events]
java.awt.Event[id=504,x=19,y=23,target=java.awt.Panel[0,0,196x177,layout=java.awt.
      FlowLayout]]
java.awt.Event[id=505,x=19,y=-
      1,target=java.awt.Panel[0,0,196x177,layout=java.awt.FlowLayout]]
```

The key points to note about Source 6.4 are:

1. You will notice that I use a separate import statement for each class used. This is different than many of the AWT examples that just say:

```
import java.awt.*;
```

which imports all the classes in the AWT package. I list them separately on purpose. The benefit of listing them separately is that it is a simple extra step that helps you memorize the AWT classes (and all the other classes for that matter) more quickly. Once you have memorized the classes then you can go ahead and use the easy method.

2. The Frame component (discussed in detail in the next section) is solely used in order to have a component to receive events. I could have used any of the container classes.
3. The ACTION_EVENT is used to receive menu selections and button selections.
4. All the events that Java can dispatch are in the switch expression; however, many will never be sent to this Frame component because they are component specific. Examples of these are the LIST_SELECT event and the SCROLL_LINE_UP event.

Now that we understand components and events, we can move on to those components that hold other components: Containers.

Containers

A container is a component that stores other components and arranges them inside the container according to a Layout manager. The general screen representation of a container is a rectangle, therefore components are arranged within the container rectangle. There are two types of containers: windows and panels. A window can be thought of as a standalone container that is the primary viewport of your application. A window is a communication conduit between your application and the user. If you think of your application as a black box, then a window is the link between your application and the outside world. A panel is a section of a window. Panels allow windows to be divided into subsections that may have a different Layout manager for each subsection (Source 6.3 used panels and the next section covers panels and layouts in detail). An applet is a panel that is displayed inside the browser's window (see Chapter 7 for an explanation and demonstration of applets).

There are several types of windows and each has a different purpose. Source 6.5 demonstrates the following four window types:

- **Window.** A top-level window with no borders and no menu bar. Ideal for implementing pop-up menus.
- **Frame.** A top-level window with a border that can contain a menu bar. The border can have a title of the frame.
- **Dialog.** A window with a border that is normally a subwindow within an application that is used to get input from the user. There are two types of dialogs depending upon the necessity of the information required from the user or being conveyed to the user. If information from the user is absolutely necessary for the program to continue and the user cannot do anything else before providing

this information, you are putting the program (and user) into a certain "mode" of operation. To do this with the AWT you specify the dialog as a "modal dialog." A modal dialog will capture all input of the application. This means that the user must respond to the dialog. In general, you should not put the user into such modes, but let the user have as much freedom of choice as possible. An example of a modal dialog is the print dialog that most operating systems put up before allowing a print operation. The user is forced to either enter the information in the dialog or cancel the operation. The user cannot do anything else when the print dialog is present. If you want the user to enter information but can also allow the user to perform other actions in the application, you create a "modeless dialog." This is done by setting Modal to false in the AWT dialog constructor. An example of a "modeless dialog" would be the Find dialog where the user enters information to search for. The user is not put into a "mode" and therefore can leave the find dialog up while performing other actions in the application.

- **FileDialog.** A special purpose dialog that is used to save a file to disk or open a file from disk. It presents the user with a listing of all the files in the current directory and allows the user to navigate up and down the directory hierarchy before deciding where to place the file (or get the file from). Once the user has chosen a directory, the dialog also allows the user to enter the filename.

SOURCE 6.5

```
import java.awt.Frame;
import java.awt.MenuBar;
import java.awt.Menu;
import java.awt.MenuItem;
import java.awt.Window;
import java.awt.Dialog;
import java.awt.FileDialog;
import java.awt.Event;

class topLevel extends Frame {
        topLevel()
        {
                super("AWT Windows");
```

```java
        MenuBar mb = new MenuBar();
        setMenuBar(mb);

        Menu fileMenu = new Menu("File");
        mb.add(fileMenu);
        fileMenu.add(new MenuItem("Frame"));
        fileMenu.add(new MenuItem("Window"));
        fileMenu.add(new MenuItem("Modeless Dialog"));
        fileMenu.add(new MenuItem("Modal Dialog"));
        fileMenu.add(new MenuItem("FileDialog"));
        fileMenu.add(new MenuItem("Exit"));
        move(100,100);
        resize(200,200);
        show();
}

public boolean handleEvent(Event evt)
{
        switch (evt.id)
        {
                case Event.ACTION_EVENT:
                        if ("Exit".equals(evt.arg))
                        {
                                System.exit(0);
                        }
                        else if ("Frame".equals(evt.arg))
                        {
                                new bareFrame();
                                return true;
                        }
                        else if ("Window".equals(evt.arg))
                        {
                                new bareWindow(this);
                                return true;
                        }
                        else if ("Modeless Dialog".equals(evt.arg))
                        {
                                new bareDialog(this,false,"Modeless
                                    Dialog");
                                return true;
                        }
                        else if ("Modal Dialog".equals(evt.arg))
```

```
                        {
                                new bareDialog(this,true,"Modal Dialog");
                                return true;
                        }
                        else if ("FileDialog".equals(evt.arg))
                        {
                                new bareFileDialog(this);
                                return true;
                        }
                        break;
                case Event.WINDOW_DESTROY:
                        System.exit(0);
                        break;
                default:
                        return false;
                }
                return false;
        }
}

class bareFrame extends Frame {
        bareFrame()
        {
                super("A Frame");
                move(110,150);
                resize(150,150);
                show();
        }

        public boolean handleEvent(Event evt)
        {
                switch (evt.id)
                {
                        case Event.WINDOW_DESTROY:
                                dispose();
                                break;
                        default:
                                return false;
                }
                return false;
        }
}
```

```java
class bareWindow extends Window {
        bareWindow(Frame parent)
        {
                super(parent);
                move(110,150);
                resize(150,150);
                show();
        }

        public boolean handleEvent(Event evt)
        {
                switch (evt.id)
                {
                        case Event.MOUSE_DOWN:
                                dispose();
                                break;
                        case Event.WINDOW_DESTROY:
                                dispose();
                                break;
                        default:
                                return false;
                }
                return false;
        }
}

class bareDialog extends Dialog {
        bareDialog(Frame parent, boolean modal, String title)
        {
                super(parent,modal);
                setTitle(title);
                move(110,150);
                resize(200,150);
                show();
        }

        public boolean handleEvent(Event evt)
        {
                switch (evt.id)
                {
                        case Event.WINDOW_DESTROY:
```

```
                                        dispose();
                                        break;
                        default:
                                return false;
                }
                return false;
        }
}

class bareFileDialog extends FileDialog {
        bareFileDialog(Frame parent)
        {
                super(parent,"A File Dialog");
                move(110,150);
                show();
        }

        public boolean handleEvent(Event evt)
        {
                switch (evt.id)
                {
                        case Event.WINDOW_DESTROY:
                                dispose();
                                break;
                        case Event.ACTION_EVENT:
                                if ("Cancel".equals(evt.arg))
                                        dispose();
                                break;
                        default:
                                return false;
                }
                return false;
        }
}

class tstWindows {
        public static void main(String args[])
        {
                new topLevel();
        }
}
```

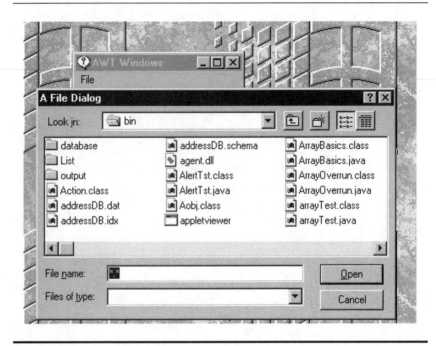

FIGURE 6.5   A File Dialog.

A run of Source 6.5 produces the output shown in Figure 6.5.

Figure 6.5 displays the AWT file dialog. Now that we understand the different types of containers available to our programs, we can move on to how components are arranged within these containers. That brings us to the AWT Layout managers.

Layout

Layouts are especially important in AWT programming because AWT graphical user interfaces must run on a variety of platforms and operating systems. This causes problems for simple X and Y arrangement of components because components are different sizes on different operating systems. Therefore, it is best to use one of the predefined layout managers provided in the AWT. We will first discuss the relationship between Containers and Layout managers and then cover all the predefined classes that implement the LayoutManager interface.

Containers and the LayoutManager Interface. A LayoutManager is an interface that describes the methods a class must implement in order to layout a container. By "laying out" a container, we mean a class that uses a specific methodology for arranging components within a container's rectangle (specified by its Dimension). Every container must have a LayoutManager. The default Layout manager is the BorderLayout (discussed in the next section). Containers have the following methods that are specific to Laying out components:

1. public setLayout(LayoutManager mgr). This method sets the LayoutManager class for the container. You can set the LayoutManager to one of the predefined LayoutManagers as described in the next section or one of your own LayoutManagers. You can also set the LayoutManager to null and lay out the components yourself by using the reshape( ) method in the component class. Setting the Layout manager to null is not recommended because it makes the look of your GUI only correct for your system. Your GUI may look horrible on another operating system or hardware configuration.

2. public LayoutManager getLayout( ). This method returns the current LayoutManager.

3. public synchronized Component add(String name, Component comp). This method adds a component to BOTH the container and the LayoutManager. This is in contrast to the functionality of add( ), which is discussed next. In order for a component to be displayed, a location must be placed on the container and a width and height. This is the job of the LayoutManager. It is possible to do this manually using reshape( ), but this is NOT RECOMMENDED. Not only does laying out components manually not account for platform component differences, your components will also not be relaid out automatically if the window gets resized. The re-laying out of components as a function of Container size is another function of a Layout manager. This is accomplished using the valid flag in each component. A component is considered invalid if it has not been laid out. Once a component is shown via the show( ) method it is again invalidated. The component is invalidated so that it will get relaid out if the window size changes.

4. public synchronized Component add(Component comp). This method ONLY adds a component to the container and NOT to the Layout manager. Your components will not be displayed if added in this fashion unless you call reshape( ) for each component. Source 6.6 demonstrates using reshape( ) to manually place components. By examining the result in Figure 6.6 it should be obvious that you should either create a new LayoutManager that handles all sizing and resizing properly or use one of the pre-defined LayoutManager classes.

SOURCE 6.6

```
import java.awt.Frame;
import java.awt.Button;

class tstValidate {
        public static void main(String args[])
        {
                Button button1 = new Button("button One");
                Button button2 = new Button("button Two");
                Button button3 = new Button("button Three");

                Frame myFrame = new Frame("Validate tester");
                myFrame.add(button1); // add to container, NOT layout mgr
                myFrame.add(button2);
                myFrame.add(button3);

                // manually layout
                button1.reshape(5,5,50,20);
                button1.validate();
                button2.reshape(20,30,50,20);
                button2.validate();
                button3.reshape(40,55,50,20);
                button3.validate();

                myFrame.move(100,100);
                myFrame.resize(200,200);
                myFrame.show();
        }
}
```

A run of Source 6.6 produces the output shown in Figure 6.6.

Now that you understand the relationship between Layout managers and Containers, let's examine the predefined Layout managers in the AWT.

Predefined AWT Classes That Implement LayoutManager.
Source 6.7 demonstrates the use of five classes that implement LayoutManager.

- BorderLayout. A Layout that represents a wall of components that surrounds a center component; implemented by only having five components labeled one of "North," "South," "East," "West,"

FIGURE 6.6   A manual Layout.

and "Center." You can also specify a horizontal and vertical gap (in pixels) between components.

- FlowLayout. A Layout that represents components in a row. Implemented by placing components on a line from left to right. If there are too many components to fit on a single line, a new line will be created. You can also specify a horizontal and vertical gap between lines.
- GridLayout. A Layout that represents a simple grid with a component per cell. Implemented by specifying the number of rows and columns in your grid. All cells are equally sized. Components are placed in each cell by filling rows first.
- GridBagLayout. A Layout that represents a very flexible grid. Implemented by a rectangular grid of cells where a component can be placed in any cell AND a component may occupy one or more cells. This is more complicated than the other layouts but is much more powerful and flexible. We demonstrate this Layout in Source 6.7 and then discuss it in detail.
- CardLayout. A Layout that represents a stack of cards. Implemented by only displaying a single component at a time and allowing you to flip through components.

SOURCE 6.7

```
import java.awt.Frame;
import java.awt.Button;
```

```java
import java.awt.MenuBar;
import java.awt.MenuItem;
import java.awt.Menu;
import java.awt.FlowLayout;
import java.awt.GridLayout;
import java.awt.BorderLayout;
import java.awt.GridBagLayout;
import java.awt.GridBagConstraints;
import java.awt.CardLayout;
import java.awt.Panel;
import java.awt.Event;

class layoutWindow extends Frame {
        Button buttons[];
        CardLayout cl;

        layoutWindow()
        {
                super("Layout Tester");

                buttons = new Button[5];
                buttons[0] = new Button("One");
                buttons[1] = new Button("Two");
                buttons[2] = new Button("Three");
                buttons[3] = new Button("Four");
                buttons[4] = new Button("Five");

                // start with border Layout
                setLayout(new BorderLayout());
                add("North",buttons[0]);
                add("Center",buttons[1]);
                add("South",buttons[2]);
                add("West",buttons[3]);
                add("East",buttons[4]);

                // add the MenuBar
                MenuBar mBar = new MenuBar();
                setMenuBar(mBar);
                Menu fileMenu = new Menu("File");
                mBar.add(fileMenu);
                Menu layoutMenu = new Menu("Layouts");
                mBar.add(layoutMenu);
```

```
        fileMenu.add(new MenuItem("Exit"));

        layoutMenu.add(new MenuItem("BorderLayout"));
        layoutMenu.add(new MenuItem("FlowLayout"));
        layoutMenu.add(new MenuItem("GridLayout"));
        layoutMenu.add(new MenuItem("GridBagLayout"));
        layoutMenu.add(new MenuItem("CardLayout"));

        resize(300,300);
        move(50,50);
        show();
}


public boolean action(Event evt, Object obj)
{
        if (evt.target instanceof MenuItem)
        {
                String label = (String) obj;
                if (label.equals("Exit"))
                {
                        dispose();
                        System.exit(0);
                }
                else if (label.equals("BorderLayout"))
                {
                        removeAll();
                        setLayout(new BorderLayout());
                        add("North",buttons[0]);
                        add("Center",buttons[1]);
                        add("South",buttons[2]);
                        add("West",buttons[3]);
                        add("East",buttons[4]);
                        layout();
                        repaint();
                }
                else if (label.equals("FlowLayout"))
                {
                        removeAll();
                        setLayout(new FlowLayout(FlowLayout.LEFT));
                        add(buttons[0]);
                        add(buttons[1]);
```

```
                add(buttons[2]);
                add(buttons[3]);
                add(buttons[4]);
                layout();
                repaint();
        }
        else if (label.equals("GridLayout"))
        {
                removeAll();
                setLayout(new GridLayout(0,2));
                add(buttons[0]);
                add(buttons[1]);
                add(buttons[2]);
                add(buttons[3]);
                add(buttons[4]);
                layout();
                repaint();
        }
        else if (label.equals("GridBagLayout"))
        {
                removeAll();
                GridBagLayout gbl = new GridBagLayout();
                setLayout(gbl);

                GridBagConstraints c[] = new GridBagConstraints[5];
                for (int i=0; i < 5; i++)
                        c[i] = new GridBagConstraints();

                c[0].gridwidth = 1;
                c[0].gridheight = 1;
                c[0].gridx = 0;
                c[0].gridy = 0;
                gbl.setConstraints(buttons[0],c[0]);
                add("One",buttons[0]);

                c[1].gridwidth = 1;
                c[1].gridheight = 1;
                c[1].gridx = 1;
                c[1].gridy = 1;
                gbl.setConstraints(buttons[1],c[1]);
                add("Two",buttons[1]);
```

```
                c[2].gridwidth = 1;
                c[2].gridheight = 1;
                c[2].gridx = 2;
                c[2].gridy = 2;
                gbl.setConstraints(buttons[2],c[2]);
                add("Three",buttons[2]);

                c[3].gridwidth = 1;
                c[3].gridheight = 1;
                c[3].gridx = 3;
                c[3].gridy = 3;
                gbl.setConstraints(buttons[3],c[3]);
                add("Four",buttons[3]);

                c[4].gridwidth = 1;
                c[4].gridheight = 1;
                c[4].gridx = 4;
                c[4].gridy = 4;
                gbl.setConstraints(buttons[4],c[4]);
                add("Five",buttons[4]);
                layout();
                repaint();
        }
        else if (label.equals("CardLayout"))
        {
                removeAll();
                cl = new CardLayout();
                setLayout(cl);
                Panel p[] = new Panel[5];
                for (int i=0; i < 5; i++)
                {
                        p[i] = new Panel();
                        p[i].setLayout(new BorderLayout());
                }

                p[0].add("Center",buttons[0]);
                p[0].add("South", new Button("Next"));
                p[1].add("Center",buttons[1]);
                p[1].add("South", new Button("Next"));
                p[2].add("Center",buttons[2]);
                p[2].add("South", new Button("Next"));
                p[3].add("Center",buttons[3]);
```

```
                                        p[3].add("South", new Button("Next"));
                                        p[4].add("Center",buttons[4]);
                                        p[4].add("South", new Button("No More"));

                                        add("One",p[0]);
                                        add("Two",p[1]);
                                        add("Three",p[2]);
                                        add("Four",p[3]);
                                        add("Five",p[4]);
                                        cl.first(this);
                                        layout();
                                        repaint();
                                }
                        }
                        else if (evt.target instanceof Button)
                        {
                                String label = (String)obj;
                                if (label.equals("Next"))
                                {
                                        // card Layout - next card
                                        cl.next(this);
                                }
                        }
                        return false;
                }
        }
}

class tstLayout {
        public static void main(String args[])
        {
                new layoutWindow();
        }
}
```

A run of Source 6.7 produces five different layouts as depicted in Figures 6.7 through 6.11.

From the above descriptions and code you should have a good idea of how to lay out components using the predefined Layout managers. The GridBagLayout deserves special attention because it is both more complex and more powerful. The next section examines it in detail.

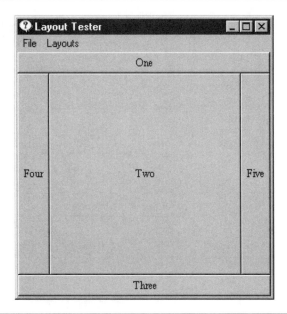

FIGURE 6.7   The BorderLayout.

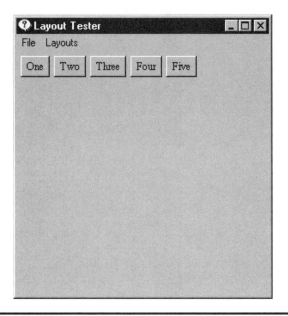

FIGURE 6.8   The FlowLayout.

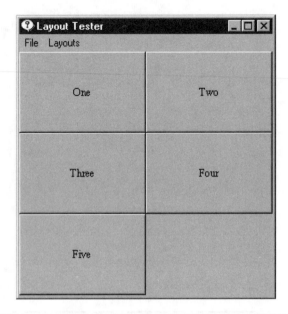

FIGURE 6.9   The GridLayout.

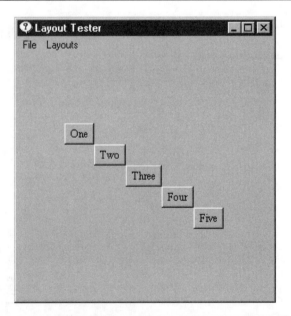

FIGURE 6.10   The GridBagLayout.

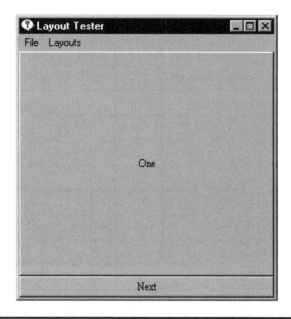

FIGURE 6.11   The CardLayout.

The GridBagLayout Up Close. My first experiences with the Grid-
BagLayout class were not good ones. The little documentation available did not make sense, the GridConstraint variables did not make
sense, and components would not be placed where I thought they
would. I first thought that a GridBag was a grid of grids where you
specified a separate grid for each component. This impression was
formed because of the fact that you specified a gridheight and gridwidth for each component. This did not seem very elegant or simple to
me. It seemed to violate the principle of simplicity that Java espoused.

Through a very fruitful email exchange with Stephen Uhler of Sun
Microsystems and some more experimentation, I now understand the
GridBagLayout and see its power and elegance. The first thing to clear
up is that a GridBag is NOT a grid of grids. It is a single grid that lets
you place components anywhere in the grid. You specify where to place
the component in the grid by modifying the gridx and gridy variables
of the constraints for each component.

Second, a component does not have to occupy a single cell as is the
case with the simple GridLayout. A component may occupy one or
more cells as specified by the gridheight and gridwidth variables of the
constraints for each component. The variables gridheight and grid-

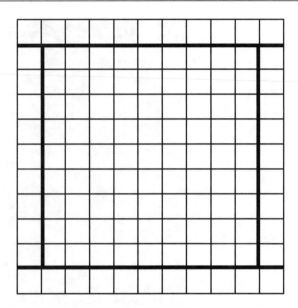

FIGURE 6.12 Design for the GridBagLayout test.

width specify the width and height of a subgrid within the single grid.
You could also think of this as the number of cells wide and number of
cells high occupied by the component. Once you have defined this display area for a component, you can also specify where the component
should be anchored in this display area if the display area is larger
than the component (the default is CENTER). Figure 6.12 shows how I
set up the GridBagLayout of Source 6.8. I wanted to use GridBagLayout in a similar fashion as a BorderLayout with the BIG exception that
the GridBagLayout would not make the buttons fill the entire window.
Source 6.8 demonstrates how to do this with the GridBagLayout.

SOURCE 6.8

```
import java.awt.Frame;
import java.awt.Button;
import java.awt.GridBagLayout;
import java.awt.GridBagConstraints;
```

```
class tstGridBag {
      public static void main(String args[])
      {
              Button theButtons[] = new Button[5];
              for (int i=0; i < 5; i++)
                      theButtons[i] = new Button("Button #" + (i+1));

              GridBagConstraints theConstraints[] = new GridBagConstraints[5];
              for (int i=0; i < 5; i++)
                      theConstraints[i] = new GridBagConstraints();

              // create the Frame
              Frame theFrame = new Frame("Grid Bag Tester");
              theFrame.resize(300,300);

              // set the layout of this container
              GridBagLayout gblayout = new GridBagLayout();
              theFrame.setLayout(gblayout);

              // set the constraints for each component and
              // add it to the container
              theConstraints[0].gridwidth = 11;
              theConstraints[0].gridheight = 1;
              theConstraints[0].gridx = 0;
              theConstraints[0].gridy = 0;
              theConstraints[0].weightx = 1.0;
              theConstraints[0].weighty = 1.0;
              theFrame.add("button one",theButtons[0]);
              gblayout.setConstraints(theButtons[0],theConstraints[0]);

              theConstraints[1].gridwidth = 1;
              theConstraints[1].gridheight = 9;
              theConstraints[1].gridx = 0;
              theConstraints[1].gridy = 1;
              theConstraints[1].weightx = 1.0;
              theConstraints[1].weighty = 1.0;
              theFrame.add("button two",theButtons[1]);
              gblayout.setConstraints(theButtons[1],theConstraints[1]);

              theConstraints[2].gridwidth = 9;
              theConstraints[2].gridheight = 9;
              theConstraints[2].gridx = 1;
```

```
theConstraints[2].gridy = 1;
theConstraints[2].weightx = 1.0;
theConstraints[2].weighty = 1.0;
theFrame.add("button three",theButtons[2]);
gblayout.setConstraints(theButtons[2],theConstraints[2]);

theConstraints[3].gridwidth = 1;
theConstraints[3].gridheight = 9;
theConstraints[3].gridx = 10;
theConstraints[3].gridy = 1;
theConstraints[3].weightx = 1.0;
theConstraints[3].weighty = 1.0;
theFrame.add("button four",theButtons[3]);
gblayout.setConstraints(theButtons[3],theConstraints[3]);

theConstraints[4].gridwidth = 11;
theConstraints[4].gridheight = 1;
theConstraints[4].gridx = 0;
theConstraints[4].gridy = 10;
theConstraints[4].weightx = 1.0;
theConstraints[4].weighty = 1.0;
theFrame.add("button five",theButtons[4]);
gblayout.setConstraints(theButtons[4],theConstraints[4]);

theFrame.move(50,50);
theFrame.show();
    }
}
```

A run of Source 6.8 produces Figure 6.13.

Now that we are comfortable with the GridBagLayout we can move on to another advanced GUI topic: painting and updating.

Painting and Updating

All graphical user interface systems have the concept of a graphics data structure to store context specific information about a drawing area. This drawing area could be the whole screen, a portion of the screen (like a single component), or even a printer. The benefit of this is that it allows you to divide the physical monitor into a potentially

FIGURE 6.13   The GridBagLayout test.

infinite number of drawing areas (a simple example would be a graphics context per window). Each graphics context (and consequentially, each drawing area) could have a different set of graphic characteristics like background color, default font, line size, and so on. On the Macintosh this graphics data structure is called the GrafPort (for Graphics Port). On MS Windows it is called the Device Context (DC). On X Windows, it is called GC (short for Graphics Context). Another way to think about the graphics context, devices, or ports is that they allow drawing to occur in a generic way without specifying where the drawing will occur. This makes it device-independent and allows such things as outputting to the printer by simply directing the draw routines at the printers graphics port (or device).

In Java, the graphics context is represented by the abstract Graphics class. Just as the toolkit and peer is instantiated when the show( ) method is called, the graphics context is also platform specific and instantiated at the same time. Source 6.9 demonstrates accessing and drawing into a graphics context.

SOURCE 6.9

```java
import java.awt.*;

class myPanel extends Panel {
      myPanel()
      {
              setBackground(Color.white);
      }

      void printGC()
      {
              Graphics GC = this.getGraphics();
              if (GC != null)
              {
                    System.out.println("A Graphics Context exists for this
                        component.");
                    System.out.println("The GC is : "
                            + GC.toString());
                    System.out.println("Would you like to draw something in
                        it?");
                    System.out.println("Sure, here's a circle for you.");
                    GC.setColor(Color.red);
                    GC.drawOval(25,25, 50,50);
              }
              else
                    System.out.println("No Graphics context for this" +
                                        " component.");
      }
}

      class tstGraphics {
      public static void main(String args[])
      {
              Frame myFrame = new Frame("Graphics Context test");
              myFrame.resize(100,100);
              myPanel aPanel = new myPanel();
              myFrame.add("Center",aPanel);
              myFrame.show(); // GC created
              aPanel.printGC();
      }
}
```

FIGURE 6.14　　Drawing to a graphics context.

A run of Source 6.9 produces both text output (below) and Figure 6.14.

```
C:\java\bin>java tstGraphics
A Graphics Context exists for this component.
The GC is : sun.awt.win32.Win32Graphics[0,0,1,1]
Would you like to draw something in it?
Sure, here's a circle for you.
```

One important thing to note about drawing into the graphics context like this is that if a window overlaps your window and you then click to bring your window again to the foreground, your window will not have your drawing in it. In our example, the red circle would be gone and you would just see a white background. The solution to this involves a special method called the paint( ) method that is automatically called whenever your component is exposed (made visible).

There are three critical "painting" methods in every component; it is very important to understand what they do and the relationship between them.

1. paint(Graphics g). The default method in a component does nothing. You override this method to paint the component. This method is called when the component is first shown (with a call to show( )) and then every time the window is re-exposed after having been covered by another window.
2. repaint( ). With no argument, this method calls the update method of the component as soon as possible. You can also specify a number of milliseconds to call update( ) within.
3. update(Graphics g). The default method repaints the background and then calls paint. The repainting of the background is what causes the infamous "animation flicker." This can be solved in two

ways: dirty rectangle animation and double buffered animation. You will find dirty rectangle animation satisfactory for most of your applications unless they involve heavy animation. You perform dirty rectangle animation by using the paint( ) method to paint the initial background and foreground of the scene, then override update( ) method to paint anything that changes in the scene. This means you override update( ) to erase the old and paint the new. This works fine for small changes in a scene. Source 6.10 demonstrates the successful use of this technique. For heavy animation you will want to switch to double buffered animation. This is a technique that mirrors the way animated movies work. The key is to create a full scene with background and foreground that is a slight change from the current background and foreground currently displayed. Then you copy this new scene over the old one in a single operation. This is done by overriding the update( ) method to call the paint( ) method but supplying the graphics context of an offscreen image. The paint( ) then does all of its painting of the current scene into the offscreen image. You then copy the offscreen image onto the current screen.

Source 6.10 demonstrates dirty rectangle animation.

SOURCE 6.10

```java
import java.awt.*;

class keyboardCanvas extends Canvas {
        private Rectangle board;
        private Rectangle keys[][];
        private Rectangle spaceBar;
        private int keySize;
        static String letters0[] = { "1", "2", "3", "4", "5", "6", "7", "8",
                                    "9", "0", "]", "}" };
        static String letters1[] = { "\"", "<", ">", "P", "Y", "F", "G", "C",
                                    "R", "L", "?", "+" };
        static String letters2[] = { "A", "O", "E", "U", "I", "D", "H", "T",
                                    "N", "S", "_" };
        static String letters3[] = { ":", "Q", "J", "K", "X", "B", "M", "W",
                                    "V", "Z" };


        public boolean pressed[][];
        public Point asciiPos[];
```

```
public boolean update;
public int updateRow, updateCol;

static String pos2String(int row, int col)
{
        String outstr=null;
        switch (row) {
                case 0:
                        outstr = letters0[col];
                        break;
                case 1:
                        outstr = letters1[col];
                        break;
                case 2:
                        outstr = letters2[col];
                        break;
                case 3:
                        outstr = letters3[col];
                        break;
        }
        return outstr;
}

keyboardCanvas(Container parent)
{
        Dimension psize = parent.size();

        // initialize variables
        update = false;

        // ascii position to dvorak key
        // start at ascii 33.
        asciiPos = new Point[96];
        asciiPos[0] = new Point(0,0); asciiPos[1] = new Point(1,0);
        asciiPos[2] = new Point(0,2); asciiPos[3] = new Point(0,3);
        asciiPos[4] = new Point(0,4); asciiPos[5] = new Point(0,6);
        asciiPos[6] = new Point(1,0); asciiPos[7] = new Point(0,8);
        asciiPos[8] = new Point(0,9); asciiPos[9] = new Point(0,7);
        asciiPos[10] = new Point(1,11); asciiPos[11] = new Point(1,1);
        asciiPos[12] = new Point(2,10); asciiPos[13] = new Point(1,2);
        asciiPos[14] = new Point(1,10); asciiPos[15] = new Point(0,9);
        asciiPos[16] = new Point(0,0); asciiPos[17] = new Point(0,1);
```

```
asciiPos[18] = new Point(0,2); asciiPos[19] = new Point(0,3);
asciiPos[20] = new Point(0,4); asciiPos[21] = new Point(0,5);
asciiPos[22] = new Point(0,6); asciiPos[23] = new Point(0,7);
asciiPos[24] = new Point(0,8); asciiPos[25] = new Point(3,0);
asciiPos[26] = new Point(3,0); asciiPos[27] = new Point(1,1);
asciiPos[28] = new Point(1,0); asciiPos[29] = new Point(1,2);
asciiPos[30] = new Point(1,10); asciiPos[31] = new Point(0,1);
asciiPos[32] = new Point(2,0); asciiPos[33] = new Point(3,5);
asciiPos[34] = new Point(1,7); asciiPos[35] = new Point(2,5);
asciiPos[36] = new Point(2,2); asciiPos[37] = new Point(1,5);
asciiPos[38] = new Point(1,6); asciiPos[39] = new Point(2,6);
asciiPos[40] = new Point(2,4); asciiPos[41] = new Point(3,2);
asciiPos[42] = new Point(3,3); asciiPos[43] = new Point(1,9);
asciiPos[44] = new Point(3,6); asciiPos[45] = new Point(2,8);
asciiPos[46] = new Point(2,1); asciiPos[47] = new Point(1,3);
asciiPos[48] = new Point(3,1); asciiPos[49] = new Point(1,8);
asciiPos[50] = new Point(2,9); asciiPos[51] = new Point(2,7);
asciiPos[52] = new Point(2,3); asciiPos[53] = new Point(3,8);
asciiPos[54] = new Point(3,7); asciiPos[55] = new Point(3,4);
asciiPos[56] = new Point(1,4); asciiPos[57] = new Point(3,9);
asciiPos[58] = new Point(0,10); asciiPos[59] = new Point(-1,-1);
asciiPos[60] = new Point(0,10); asciiPos[61] = new Point(-1,-1);
asciiPos[62] = new Point(2,10); asciiPos[63] = new Point(-1,-1);
asciiPos[64] = new Point(2,0); asciiPos[65] = new Point(3,5);
asciiPos[66] = new Point(1,7); asciiPos[67] = new Point(2,5);
asciiPos[68] = new Point(2,2); asciiPos[69] = new Point(1,5);
asciiPos[70] = new Point(1,6); asciiPos[71] = new Point(2,6);
asciiPos[72] = new Point(2,4); asciiPos[73] = new Point(3,2);
asciiPos[74] = new Point(3,3); asciiPos[75] = new Point(1,9);
asciiPos[76] = new Point(3,6); asciiPos[77] = new Point(2,8);
asciiPos[78] = new Point(2,1); asciiPos[79] = new Point(1,3);
asciiPos[80] = new Point(3,1); asciiPos[81] = new Point(1,8);
asciiPos[82] = new Point(2,9); asciiPos[83] = new Point(2,7);
asciiPos[84] = new Point(2,3); asciiPos[85] = new Point(3,8);
asciiPos[86] = new Point(3,7); asciiPos[87] = new Point(3,4);
asciiPos[88] = new Point(1,4); asciiPos[89] = new Point(3,9);
asciiPos[90] = new Point(0,11); asciiPos[91] = new Point(0,11);
asciiPos[92] = new Point(-1,-1); asciiPos[93] = new Point(-1,-1);

setBackground(Color.gray);
setForeground(Color.black);
int boardSize = psize.width/8 * 4;
```

```
                board = new Rectangle(psize.width/8 * 2,
                                  2,boardSize
                                  ,80);
            spaceBar = new Rectangle(psize.width/16 * 6,
                                     84, psize.width/16 * 4,
                                     10);

            keys = new Rectangle[4][];
            keys[0] = new Rectangle[12];
            keys[1] = new Rectangle[12];
            keys[2] = new Rectangle[11];
            keys[3] = new Rectangle[10];

            // pressed array
            pressed = new boolean[4][12];

            for (int i=0; i < 4; i++)
                    for (int j=0; j < pressed[i].length; j++)
                          pressed[i][j] = false;

            keySize = boardSize/14;
            int RowStart[] = new int[4];
            RowStart[0] = psize.width/8 * 2 + keySize;
            RowStart[1] = RowStart[0] + keySize/2;
            RowStart[2] = RowStart[1] + keySize/2;
            RowStart[3] = RowStart[2] + keySize/2;

            for (int i = 0; i < 4; i++)
                    for (int j=0; j < keys[i].length; j++)
                          keys[i][j] = new Rectangle(RowStart[i] + (j *
                              keySize),
                                            board.y + (20 * i),
                                            keySize, 20);

    }


public void paint(Graphics g)
{
    if (!update)
    {
        g.setColor(Color.black);
        g.drawRect(board.x-1,board.y-1,board.width+1,board.height+1);
```

```
g.setColor(Color.white);
g.fillRect(board.x,board.y,board.width, board.height);

// space bar
g.setColor(Color.black);
g.drawRect(spaceBar.x-1, spaceBar.y-1, spaceBar.width+1,
           spaceBar.height+1);
g.setColor(Color.lightGray);
g.fillRect(spaceBar.x, spaceBar.y, spaceBar.width,
           spaceBar.height);
g.setColor(Color.white);
g.fillRoundRect(spaceBar.x+1, spaceBar.y+1,
                spaceBar.width - 2,
                spaceBar.height - 4, 5, 5);


// key borders
g.setColor(Color.black);
g.drawLine(board.x, board.y+20, board.x + board.width,
           board.y+20);
// shorten for Return key
g.drawLine(board.x, board.y+40,
           board.x + (keySize * 13 + keySize/2),
           board.y+40);
g.drawLine(board.x, board.y+60, board.x + board.width,
           board.y+60);

// draw keys
for (int i = 0; i < 4; i++)
      for (int j=0; j < keys[i].length; j++)
      {
            g.setColor(Color.black);
            g.drawRect(keys[i][j].x,
                       keys[i][j].y,
                       keys[i][j].width,
                       keys[i][j].height);
            g.setColor(Color.lightGray);
            g.fillRect(keys[i][j].x+1,
                       keys[i][j].y+1,
                       keys[i][j].width-1,
                       keys[i][j].height-1);

            /* *** if key pressed change
```

```
                                    to yellow */
                    if (!pressed[i][j])
                      g.setColor(Color.white);
                    else
                      g.setColor(Color.yellow);

                    g.fillRoundRect(keys[i][j].x+2,
                                    keys[i][j].y+2,
                                    keys[i][j].width - 3,
                                    keys[i][j].height - 3, 2, 2);
                    // draw Letter
                    g.setColor(Color.black);
                    g.drawString(pos2String(i,j),
                                 keys[i][j].x + keySize/4,
                                 keys[i][j].y + (keys[i][j].height - 4));
            }
        }
    }


public void update(Graphics g)
{
                    g.setColor(Color.black);
                    g.drawRect(keys[updateRow][updateCol].x,
                               keys[updateRow][updateCol].y,
                               keys[updateRow][updateCol].width,
                               keys[updateRow][updateCol].height);
                    g.setColor(Color.lightGray);
                    g.fillRect(keys[updateRow][updateCol].x+1,
                               keys[updateRow][updateCol].y+1,
                               keys[updateRow][updateCol].width-1,
                               keys[updateRow][updateCol].height-1);

                    /* *** if key pressed change
                           to yellow */
                    if (!pressed[updateRow][updateCol])
                      g.setColor(Color.white);
                    else
                      g.setColor(Color.yellow);

                    g.fillRoundRect(keys[updateRow][updateCol].x+2,
                                    keys[updateRow][updateCol].y+2,
                                    keys[updateRow][updateCol].width - 3,
```

```
                                        keys[updateRow][updateCol].height -
                                            3, 2, 2);
                        // draw Letter
                        g.setColor(Color.black);
                        g.drawString(pos2String(updateRow,updateCol),
                                keys[updateRow][updateCol].x +
                                    keySize/4,
                                keys[updateRow][updateCol].y +
                                    (keys[updateRow][updateCol].
                                        height - 4));

        }

        public boolean handleEvent(Event evt)
        {
                return false; // pass everything on up
        }
}

class editPanel extends Panel {
        editPanel()
        {
                super();
        }

        public Insets insets()
        {
                return new Insets(3,3,3,3);
        }
}

class dvorakWindow extends Frame {
        private int defWidth, defHeight;

        keyboardCanvas keyboard;

        dvorakWindow()
        {
                super("Your First Dvorak Lesson");

                setLayout(new BorderLayout());
```

```java
        // get screen dimensions to size window
        Toolkit theToolkit = Toolkit.getDefaultToolkit();
        Dimension size = theToolkit.getScreenSize();
        defWidth = size.width/12 * 7;
        defHeight = size.height/12 * 5;

        MenuBar mBar = new MenuBar();
        setMenuBar(mBar);
        Menu fileMenu = new Menu("File");
        mBar.add(fileMenu);
        fileMenu.add(new MenuItem("Exit"));

        editPanel centerP = new editPanel();
        centerP.setLayout(new BorderLayout());
        centerP.setBackground(Color.gray);
        centerP.setForeground(Color.black);
        add("Center", centerP);

        // add a keyboardCanvas
        move(size.width/12,size.height/20);
        resize(defWidth, defHeight);

        centerP.add("North",
                new Label("The Dvorak Keyboard",Label.CENTER));

        // add keyboard to Panel
        keyboard = new keyboardCanvas(this);
        keyboard.resize(defWidth,defHeight);
        centerP.add("Center",keyboard);

        centerP.add("South",
                new Label("Type a key to see its dvorak counterpart.",
                        Label.CENTER));

        show();
}

public boolean handleEvent(Event evt)
{
        switch (evt.id) {
                case Event.ACTION_EVENT:
                        if ("Exit".equals(evt.arg))
```

```java
                    {
                            dispose();
                            System.exit(0);
                    }
            break;
case Event.WINDOW_DESTROY:
            dispose();
            System.exit(0);
            break;
case Event.KEY_PRESS:
            if (evt.key >= 33)
            {
                keyboard.update = true;
                Point keyPos = keyboard.asciiPos[evt.key - 33];
                if (keyPos.x != -1)
                {
                    keyboard.updateRow = keyPos.x;
                    keyboard.updateCol = keyPos.y;
                    keyboard.pressed[keyPos.x][keyPos.y] = true;
                    keyboard.repaint();
                }
            }
            return true;
case Event.KEY_RELEASE:
            if (evt.key >= 33)
            {
                keyboard.update = true;
                Point keyPos = keyboard.asciiPos[evt.key - 33];
                if (keyPos.x != -1)
                {
                    keyboard.updateRow = keyPos.x;
                    keyboard.updateCol = keyPos.y;
                    keyboard.pressed[keyPos.x][keyPos.y] = false;
                    keyboard.repaint();
                }
            }
            return true;
case Event.GOT_FOCUS:
            keyboard.update = false;
            keyboard.paint(keyboard.getGraphics());
            break;
default:
```

```
                              return false;
                   }
              return false; // pass to parent if not handled
         }
}

class miniDvorak {
      public static void main(String args[])
      {
              new dvorakWindow();
      }
}
```

A run of Source 6.10 produces Figure 6.15.

Now we have a complete understanding of all the major components of an AWT GUI. We are ready now to put it all together.

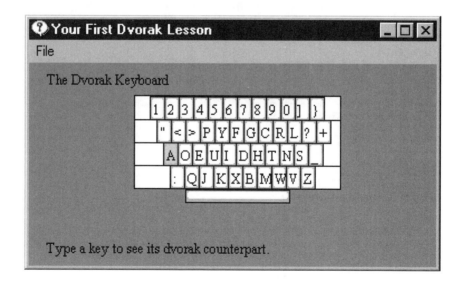

FIGURE 6.15   The Dvorak keyboard GUI.

6.3 A GRAPHICAL REMINDER APPLICATION

In Chapter 4, The Java Standard Library, we demonstrated the Hashtable and Date class by creating a text-based Reminder application. In this chapter, we will develop a graphical user interface for that program.

In designing the GUI for the application there were four key design goals:

- A top-level window would both display reminders and serve as the launch point for all other application features. I chose the AWT List class to display the reminders. This would make it simple to add and delete entries as well as it fit in well since we already translated the record into a String with the toString( ) method.
- All the functionality of the application would be as both menu commands and as buttons. This gives the user maximum flexibility.
- The Add function needed its own dialog. We need to make the entry of the Record as quick and easy as possible. To that end we include Choice boxes for month and year.
- Reuse of the Record class. We should reuse as much code as possible from the original text-based application. I was able to reuse the Record class without modification.

Source 6.11 implements the above design goals.

SOURCE 6.11

```
import java.util.Date;
import java.io.DataInputStream;
import java.util.StringTokenizer;
import java.io.File;
import java.io.FileInputStream;
import java.io.FileOutputStream;
import java.io.PrintStream;
import java.util.Vector;

import java.awt.*;

class AddDialog extends Dialog {
        TextField hourTF, minutesTF, dateTF;
        Choice month, years;
        TextField notice;
```

```
Vector theRecords;
List theList;

AddDialog(Vector records, List aList, Frame parent)
{
        super(parent, true);
        setTitle("Add an Event");

        theRecords = records;
        theList = aList;

        // two main panels
        Panel centerP = new Panel();
        centerP.setLayout(new BorderLayout());
        Panel bottomP = new Panel();
        bottomP.setLayout(new FlowLayout(FlowLayout.CENTER));

        add("Center", centerP);
        add("South", bottomP);

        // add two more panels to center Panel
        Panel northCenterPanel = new Panel();
        northCenterPanel.setLayout(new FlowLayout(FlowLayout.LEFT));
        Panel centerCenterPanel = new Panel();
        centerCenterPanel.setLayout(new BorderLayout());

        centerP.add("North",northCenterPanel);
        centerP.add("Center",centerCenterPanel);

        // now add components
        bottomP.add(new Button("Add"));
        bottomP.add(new Button("Clear"));
        bottomP.add(new Button("Done"));

        hourTF = new TextField(3);
        minutesTF = new TextField(3);
        dateTF = new TextField(3);
        month = new Choice();
        month.addItem("January   ");
        month.addItem("February  ");
        month.addItem("March     ");
        month.addItem("April     ");
```

```
        month.addItem("May       ");
        month.addItem("June      ");
        month.addItem("July      ");
        month.addItem("August    ");
        month.addItem("September ");
        month.addItem("October   ");
        month.addItem("November  ");
        month.addItem("December  ");

        years = new Choice();
        years.addItem("1995  ");
        years.addItem("1996  ");
        years.addItem("1997  ");
        years.addItem("1998  ");
        years.addItem("1999  ");
        years.addItem("2000  ");

        northCenterPanel.add(new Label("Event Date:"));
        northCenterPanel.add(new Label("HOUR:"));
        northCenterPanel.add(hourTF);
        northCenterPanel.add(new Label("MIN:"));
        northCenterPanel.add(minutesTF);
        northCenterPanel.add(new Label("DATE:"));
        northCenterPanel.add(dateTF);
        northCenterPanel.add(month);
        northCenterPanel.add(years);

        centerCenterPanel.add("North",new Label("Event Notice"));
        notice = new TextField(60);
        centerCenterPanel.add("Center",notice);

        move(50,80);
        pack();
        show();
}

public boolean handleEvent(Event evt)
{
        switch (evt.id) {
                case Event.ACTION_EVENT:
                        if ("Done".equals(evt.arg))
                        {
```

```
                dispose();
                return true;
        }
        else if ("Add".equals(evt.arg))
        {
                String hourStr=null, minStr=null;
                String dateStr=null, yearStr=null;
                hourStr = hourTF.getText();
                minStr = minutesTF.getText();
                dateStr = dateTF.getText();
                yearStr = years.getSelectedItem();
                yearStr = yearStr.trim();
                int mon = month.getSelectedIndex();
                int hour, min, date, year;
                try {
                        hour = Integer.parseInt(hourStr);
                        min = Integer.parseInt(minStr);
                        date = Integer.parseInt(dateStr);
                        year = Integer.parseInt(yearStr);
                        year -= 1900;
                } catch (Exception e)
                  {
                        e.printStackTrace();
                        return true;
                  }

                Date aDate = new Date(year,mon,date,
                                      hour,min,0);

                String msg = notice.getText();

                Record aRec = new Record(aDate,msg);

                // store in Vector
                theRecords.addElement(aRec);

                // add it to List
                theList.addItem(aRec.toString());

                return true; // handle locally
        }
        else if ("Clear".equals(evt.arg))
```

```
                        {
                                hourTF.setText("");
                                minutesTF.setText("");
                                dateTF.setText("");
                                notice.setText("");
                        }
                        break;
                case Event.WINDOW_DESTROY:
                        dispose();
                        return true;
                default:
                        return false;
                }
                return false;
        }
}

class ReminderWindow extends Frame {
        private Vector reminders;
        private int defWidth, defHeight;
        private List RecordList;
        private int currentCount;
        private Date now;
        private Date startDate;
        private Date endDate;

        ReminderWindow()
        {
                super("Memory Assistant");
                reminders = new Vector(3);
                RecordList = new List(12,true);
                DataInputStream dis = new DataInputStream(System.in);

                // get the current date
                now = new Date();
                startDate = (Date) new Date(now.getTime());
                startDate.setHours(0);
                startDate.setMinutes(0);
                endDate = (Date) new Date(now.getTime());
                endDate.setHours(23);
                endDate.setMinutes(59);
```

```java
// Check if a Reminder File exists
File dataFile = new File("Reminder.data");
if (dataFile.exists())
{
 try {
        FileInputStream fis = new FileInputStream("Reminder.data");
        DataInputStream dis2 = new DataInputStream(fis);
        String line = null;

        while ( (line = dis2.readLine()) != null)
        {
                Record theRec = Record.parseRecord(line);
                if (theRec != null)
                {
                        reminders.addElement(theRec);

                        // At startup post Today's reminders
                        Date theDate = (Date) theRec.getDate();
                        if ( theDate.after(startDate) &&
                            theDate.before(endDate) )
                        {
                                RecordList.addItem(theRec.toString());
                        }
                }
                else
                {
                        System.out.println("Unable to get a Reminder.");
                }
        }
        fis.close();
    } catch (Exception e)
    {
                System.out.println("Unable to process Reminder.dat");
                e.printStackTrace();
                System.exit(1);
    }
}

currentCount = reminders.size();

// get screen dimensions to size window
Toolkit theToolkit = Toolkit.getDefaultToolkit();
```

```java
        Dimension size = theToolkit.getScreenSize();
        defWidth = size.width/12 * 8;
        defHeight = size.height/12 * 10;

        // add MenuBar
        MenuBar mBar = new MenuBar();
        setMenuBar(mBar);
        Menu fileMenu = new Menu("File");
        mBar.add(fileMenu);
        Menu RecordMenu = new Menu("Record");
        mBar.add(RecordMenu);

        fileMenu.add(new MenuItem("Exit"));

        RecordMenu.add(new MenuItem("Add"));
        RecordMenu.add(new MenuItem("Delete"));
        RecordMenu.add(new MenuItem("Today"));
        RecordMenu.add(new MenuItem("All"));

        Panel centerP = new Panel();
        centerP.setLayout(new BorderLayout());

        Panel bottomP = new Panel();
        bottomP.setLayout(new FlowLayout(FlowLayout.LEFT));

        add("Center",centerP);
        add("South", bottomP);

        centerP.add("Center",RecordList);

        bottomP.add(new Label("Now: " + now.toLocaleString()
                              + "  "));
        bottomP.add(new Button("Today"));
        bottomP.add(new Button("All"));
        bottomP.add(new Button("Add"));
        bottomP.add(new Button("Delete"));
        bottomP.add(new Button("Exit"));

        move(size.width/12,size.height/20);
        resize(defWidth, defHeight);
        show();
    }
```

```
public boolean handleEvent(Event evt)
{
        switch (evt.id) {
                case Event.ACTION_EVENT:
                        if ("Exit".equals(evt.arg))
                        {
                          dispose();
                          try {
                                  // dump hash table to file
                                  FileOutputStream fos = new FileOutputStream
                                      ("Reminder.data");
                                  PrintStream ps = new PrintStream(fos);

                                  for (int i=0; i < reminders.size(); i++)
                                          ps.println(((Record)reminders.
                                              elementAt(i)).toString());

                                  fos.close();
                          } catch (Exception e)
                            {
                                  System.out.println("IO error on
                                      reminder.data");
                                  System.exit(1);
                            }
                                  System.exit(0);
                        }
                        else if ("Add".equals(evt.arg))
                        {
                                  // Add dialog
                                  new AddDialog(reminders,
                                              RecordList, this);
                        }
                        else if ("Delete".equals(evt.arg))
                        {
                                  String items[] = RecordList.
                                      getSelectedItems();
                                  for (int i=0; i < items.length; i++)
                                  {
                                          Record theRecord =
                                              Record.parseRecord
                                              (items[i]);
```

```java
                        // delete from Vector
                        for (int j=0; j < reminders.size(); j++)
                        {
                                if (((theRecord.getDate()).equals(
                                    ((Record) reminders.elementAt
                                        (j)).getDate())) &&
                                    ((theRecord.getInfo()).equals(
                                    ((Record) reminders.elementAt
                                        (j)).getInfo())))
                                {
                                    // match
                                    reminders.removeElementAt(j);
                                    break;
                                }
                        }


                        // get the selected items
                        int idx[] = RecordList.getSelectedIndexes();
                        for (int i=0; i < idx.length; i++)
                        {
                                if (i == 0)
                                        RecordList.delItem(idx[i]);
                                else
                                {
                                        int newIdx = idx[i] - i;
                                        RecordList.delItem(newIdx);
                                }
                        }


                }
                else if ("Today".equals(evt.arg))
                {
                        RecordList.delItems(0,RecordList.countItems()-1);

                        for (int i=0; i < reminders.size(); i++)
                        {
                                Date theDate =
                                        ((Record)reminders.elementAt
                                                (i)).getDate();
                                if ( theDate.after(startDate) &&
                                    theDate.before(endDate) )
```

```
                                        {
                                              RecordList.addItem(
                                                 ((Record)reminders.elementAt
                                                      (i)).toString());
                                        }
                                  }
                            }
                            else if ("All".equals(evt.arg))
                            {
                                  RecordList.delItems(0,RecordList.countItems()-1);

                                  // add All
                                  for (int i=0; i < reminders.size(); i++)
                                        RecordList.addItem(
                                           ((Record)reminders.elementAt
                                                (i)).toString());
                            }
                            break;
                     case Event.WINDOW_DESTROY:
                            System.exit(0);
                     default:
                            return false;
              }
              return false;
       }
}

class Record {
       private Date reminderDate;
       private String reminderInfo;

       public Record(Date inDate, String inInfo)
       {
              reminderDate = (Date) new Date(inDate.getTime());
              reminderInfo = (String) new String(inInfo);
       }

       public String toString()
       {
              return (reminderDate.toLocaleString() +
                     "-" + reminderInfo);
       }
```

```java
static Record getRecord()
{
    Date outDate = null;
    String outString = null;
    Record outRecord = null;
    try {
        DataInputStream dis = new DataInputStream(System.in);
        System.out.print("Enter Reminder Date as (MM/DD/YY HH:MM) : ");
        System.out.flush();
        String DateStr = dis.readLine();
        String timeStr=null, dateStr=null;
        int hours=0, mins=0, date=0, mon=0, year=0;

        // tokenize date
        StringTokenizer split = new StringTokenizer(DateStr);
        if (split != null && split.countTokens() == 2)
        {
                dateStr = split.nextToken();
                timeStr = split.nextToken();
        }
        else
        {
                System.out.println("Malformed date string <" +
                                        DateStr + ">");
                return null;
        }


        StringTokenizer theToks = new StringTokenizer(dateStr,"/");
        if (theToks != null && theToks.countTokens() == 3)
        {
                mon = Integer.parseInt(theToks.nextToken());
                mon--;   // enter from 0-11
                date = Integer.parseInt(theToks.nextToken());
                year = Integer.parseInt(theToks.nextToken());
        }
        else
        {
                System.out.println("Malformed Date string <" +
                                        dateStr + ">");
                return null;
```

```
        }

        theToks = new StringTokenizer(timeStr,":");
        if (theToks != null && theToks.countTokens() == 2)
        {
          hours = Integer.parseInt(theToks.nextToken());
          mins = Integer.parseInt(theToks.nextToken());
        }
        else
        {
                System.out.println("Malformed time string <" +
                                        timeStr + ">");
                return null;
        }

        outDate = new Date(year, mon, date, hours, mins);

        // Enter the info with this date
        System.out.print("Enter reminder: ");
        System.out.flush();
        outString = dis.readLine();

        // create the record
        outRecord = new Record(outDate, outString);

    } catch (Exception e)
      {
        e.printStackTrace();
        return null;
      }

    return outRecord;
}

static Record parseRecord(String inLine)
{
    Date outDate = null;
    String outString = null;
    Record outRecord = null;
    String DateString = null;

    try {
```

```
StringTokenizer split = new StringTokenizer(inLine,"-");
if (split != null && split.countTokens() == 2)
{
        DateString = split.nextToken();
        outString = split.nextToken();
}
else
{
        System.out.println("Malformed line: <" +
                                inLine + ">");
        return null;
}

String timeString=null;
String dateString=null;
int mn=0,dt=0,yr=0,hr=0,min=0,sc=0;
StringTokenizer dtg = new StringTokenizer(DateString," ");
if (split != null && dtg.countTokens() == 2)
{
        dateString = dtg.nextToken();
        StringTokenizer datePieces = new
                StringTokenizer(dateString,"/");
        if (datePieces != null && datePieces.countTokens() == 3)
        {
                String mnStr, dtStr, yrStr;
                mnStr = datePieces.nextToken();
                dtStr = datePieces.nextToken();
                yrStr = datePieces.nextToken();
                mn = Integer.parseInt(mnStr);
                dt = Integer.parseInt(dtStr);
                yr = Integer.parseInt(yrStr);
        }
        else
        {
                System.out.println("Malformed date: <" +
                                        dateString + ">");
                return null;
        }

        timeString = dtg.nextToken();
        StringTokenizer timePieces = new
```

```
                StringTokenizer(timeString,":");
        if (timePieces != null && timePieces.countTokens() == 3)
        {
                String hrStr, minStr, scStr;
                hrStr = timePieces.nextToken();
                minStr = timePieces.nextToken();
                scStr = timePieces.nextToken();

                hr = Integer.parseInt(hrStr);
                min = Integer.parseInt(minStr);
                sc = Integer.parseInt(scStr);
        }
        else
        {
                System.out.println("Malformed time: <" +
                                        timeString + ">");
                return null;
        }
    }
    else
    {
            System.out.println("Malformed date: <" +
                                    DateString + ">");
            return null;
    }

    mn--; // month must be between 0-11

    outDate = new Date(yr,mn,dt,hr,min,sc);

    // create the Record
    outRecord = new Record(outDate, outString);

} catch (Exception e)
  {
    e.printStackTrace();
    return null;
  }

return outRecord;
}
```

```
        public Date getDate() { return reminderDate; }
        public String getInfo() { return reminderInfo; }
}


class ReminderGUI {
        public static void main(String args[])
        {
                // create the main Window
                new ReminderWindow();
        }
}
```

A run of Source 6.11 produces Figure 6.16.

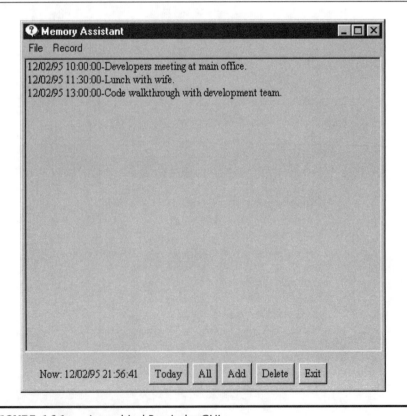

FIGURE 6.16   A graphical Reminder GUI.

The add Dialog for the ReminderGUI application is depicted in Figure 6.17:

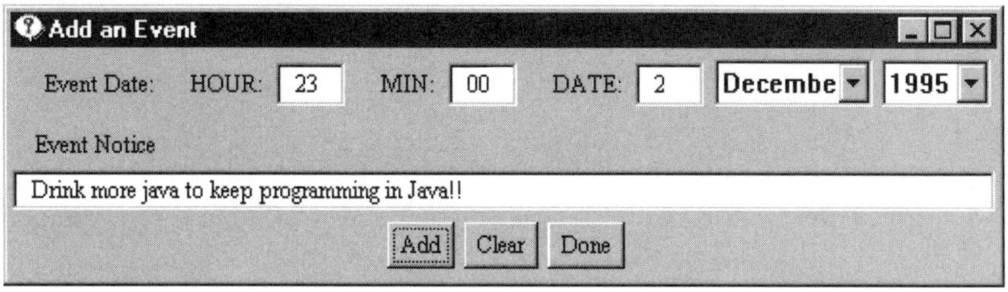

FIGURE 6.17   The Add Record dialog

There are six key points to note about Source 6.11:

1. The AddDialog uses Panels within Panels. Remember a Container is also a component.
2. I switched from using a Hashtable in the original application to using a Vector. The Vector was a better match to the AWT List class.
3. For the ReminderWindow, I used Toolkit.getScreenSize( ) to get the screen dimensions. I then used that to size the main window. This will allow this application to be moved to other hardware configurations and size itself to the monitor.
4. In the handleEvent( ) method of the ReminderWindow, I was able to use a single block of code for both the menu actions and the button actions. This was only possible because they both had identical names.
5. Using the list and Vector also made it simple to add a delete feature.
6. The "Today" filter is both used at startup and as a button (and menu choice). This lets the user "declutter" at any moment to just see today's events.

I hope you will agree with me that this is now a much better application. One enhancement I leave for you as an exercise: Allow the user to tab between fields in the AddDialog.

CHAPTER 7

Hot Java, Applets, and JavaScript

Sun's Java language could be the next killer web application.

> —Dave Tubbs, "Pop, Fizz, and Dance," *Internet World*

I have seen the future of the World Wide Web, and it is executable content.

> —Ray Valdes, "Net Gets a Java Buzz"

OBJECTIVE

This chapter will show you how to energize Web sites using Java and JavaScript. You learn how to program applets by examining the steps that transition a standalone java application into an applet. The chapter closes with an introduction to JavaScript programming.

In April 1993, NCSA Mosaic 1.0, the first graphical browser for the Internet, was released. This web browser became the Internet's "killer app" and fueled the Internet's explosive growth as well as its switch to primarily a commercial medium. Now Java and JavaScript promise to bring the "third wave" to the Internet by making it come alive with interactive web sites, 3D games, animation, and multimedia.

7.1   AN OVERVIEW OF HOTJAVA AND APPLETS

These are truly exciting times! The Java language and HotJava web browser are not just technological achievements. They are just as much social achievements, and I don't mean that in a futuristic predictive way. I am not talking about society at large. I am talking about the society of programmers (the craftsmen of the electronic age). In Java and HotJava we have tools that make programming fun again! That is truly exciting because there is nothing more powerful than a programmer having fun!

Figure 7.1 depicts the HotJava browser developed by Sun Microsystems to demonstrate the power of executable content accessed from World Wide Web pages. At its inception, the HotJava browser works just like any other Internet browser with one crucial difference: the HotJava browser can download and run small Java programs called applets. An applet is a compiled Java subclass of the Applet class that resides on the computer hosting the World Wide Web server. Applet

FIGURE 7.1   The HotJava browser.

programming involves learning a new programming paradigm, just as GUI programming involved learning event-driven programming.

The applet paradigm involves two key concepts: first, an applet is a non-stand-alone program. Put in other words, an applet is NOT an application. Second, an applet is a Component of the browser's GUI. That does not mean it has to be a visible Component, but that is surely the most common use for applets. We will explore these two concepts in great detail. The methodology we will use to explore applets will be to transition an idea from a stand-alone application to an applet. Let's get to work.

7.2   PROGRAMMING APPLETS

Many businesses promote their goods by advertising them on an electronic scrolling message board (also known as a marquee). With the World Wide Web being pitched as an electronic marketplace, a scrolling message board could come in handy for many businesses. Let's examine first how we would build a stand-alone application to do this, then we will transition the stand-alone application to an applet. The basic idea behind the application is simple: animate a single text line so that it moves across the screen. Instead of just writing an application without an awareness how it would transition to an applet, you will see how seamlessly a well written Component fits the applet model.

Source 7.1 implements the scrolling message board. The program simply consists of the invoking of a single class. This single class will later become our applet.

SOURCE 7.1

```
// a scrolling message
import java.awt.*;

class scrollMsg extends Panel implements Runnable {
        String theMessage;
        Font textFont;
        FontMetrics fontMetrics;
        int stepPixels;
        int oldX, oldY, newX, newY;
        int speed; // in milliseconds

        scrollMsg(String msg)
```

```
{
        setBackground(Color.lightGray);

        theMessage = msg;

        textFont = new Font("TimesRoman",Font.BOLD, 18);

        stepPixels = 6;
        speed = 15;
}

public void run()
{
        paint(this.getGraphics());
        while (true)
                repaint(speed);
}

public void paint(Graphics g)
{
        // initial background
        g.setColor(Color.black);
        g.drawRect(0,0, size().width,
                size().height);
        g.setColor(Color.white);
        g.fillRect(1,1, size().width - 1,
                size().height - 1);

        // set the font
        g.setFont(textFont);
        fontMetrics = g.getFontMetrics();

        // set initial X and Y to drawString
        oldX = newX = size().width -
                fontMetrics.charWidth(theMessage.charAt(0));
        oldY = newY = size().height/2 +
                (fontMetrics.getHeight()/2);
}

public void update(Graphics g)
{
        g.setFont(textFont);
```

```
               // Erase the old
               g.setColor(Color.white);
               g.drawString(theMessage, oldX, oldY);

               // draw the New
               g.setColor(Color.black);
               g.drawString(theMessage, newX, newY);

               // step
               oldX = newX;
               newX -= stepPixels;

               // restart?
               if (newX <= -(fontMetrics.stringWidth(theMessage)
                            - fontMetrics.charWidth(
                              theMessage.charAt(
                                theMessage.length() - 1))))
                       paint(g);  // start at the beginning
        }
}


class tstScrollMsg {
        public static void main(String args[])
        {
                Frame myFrame = new Frame("Scrolling Message");
                scrollMsg myScroll =
                      new scrollMsg("Big Sale!!! Internet terminals for $299!!!");
                myFrame.add("Center", myScroll);
                myFrame.move(100,100);
                myFrame.resize(400,100);
                myFrame.show();

                Thread animateThread = new Thread(myScroll);
                animateThread.start();
        }
}
```

A run of Source 7.1 produces Figure 7.2.

Let's now examine Source 7.1 in detail and then discuss how we transition it into an applet. The application is composed of two classes: the scrollMsg class and the tstMsg class. The tstMsg class has the

FIGURE 7.2   A scrolling message GUI.

main method. Let's begin with the scrollMsg class because that is the class that will become our applet. The declaration of the class is:

```
class scrollMsg extends Panel implements Runnable
```

The fact that this class extends Panel and implements Runnable is no accident. An applet also extends Panel. We know that a Panel is a Container, which is a GUI component. So it is easy to see the correlation between an Applet being a Panel in the browser and any Panel we create for a stand-alone application. They can almost be used interchangeably (with the exception that an applet has a few extra requirements, which we shall cover). The scrollMsg class also extends Runnable, which means that it can be the target of a thread (run in its own execution path). This is not a requirement for an applet but it is definitely recommend programming practice for EVERY applet you create. The benefit of making your applet runnable is that your applet will run in its own execution context and not hold the browser hostage to your applet. If your applet is in its own execution context, the user is free to still choose other options on the browser, for example, jump to another Web page or quit the application.

The implementation of scrollMsg class involves four methods. Each method is relevant to transforming the application into an applet. The four methods are:

- scrollMsg(String msg). This constructor serves two purposes. The first is to initialize the object's key data members. Secondly, the method accepts key parameters from its caller (which is the main method of the tstMsg class). In this case the scrollMsg class only receives one parameter—the string to scroll across our message board.

- public void run( ). This method makes the class Runnable. In our scrolling message board this method first calls paint and then enters an endless loop. Inside the endless loop it calls repaint( ). All the real work is done in the paint( ) and update( ) methods.
- public void paint(Graphics g). This program uses the dirty rectangle animation technique to scroll the message. To do this the paint( ) method merely creates our initial scene. The initial scene is simply a white background.
- public void update(Graphics g). The animation of our scrolling text is very simple. It only requires stepping the x coordinate to where we draw the String. Update first erases the old string, draws the new string, and then calculates the next x position.

The implementation of the tstMsg class is also relevant to the transition to an applet because the services that our tstMsg class performs in its main( ) method are similar to the functions that the browser is required to perform for our applet. There are primarily three key services the tstMsg class provides for the scrollMsg class:

- Providing a Frame. This is the top-level window that the subclass of Panel will inhabit. This is analogous to the a portion of the browser window that is provided to the applet.
- Instantiating and initializing the scrollMsg class. The Browser instantiates the applet without any arguments and then calls the applets init( ) method. When we examine the applet source code you will see how the applet is passed information from the browser.
- Starting the new thread with the scrollMsg class as its target. The browser calls the applet's start( ) method to begin running the applet.

Now that we have studied our stand-alone application, let's see how easy it is to convert it into an applet. The applet in Source 7.2 is named simpleMarquee, but it started with a copy of tstScollMsg.java. Before we discuss the differences, let's cover what is identical: the run( ), paint( ), and update( ) methods. Also, notice how similar the class declaration is:

```
public class simpleMarquee extends Applet implements Runnable
```

As we stated previously, the Applet class extends Panel. In fact, the only difference between an applet and a panel is that an applet has some additional methods that allow it to be initialized, started, and stopped from another application (a browser or the appletviewer).

Those applet methods are also the only difference between the simpleMarquee class and the scrollMsg class. Let's examine each of those methods:

- public void init( ). This method allows an applet to initialize its data members and access parameters passed to the applet from the HTML page.
- public void start( ). This method starts the applet's execution.
- public void stop( ). This method stops the applet's execution.
- public void destroy( ). This method allows your class to perform final cleanup before the class is unloaded. An example of when to use this class would be to close file pointers or connections. It is not necessary to try to free memory since Java programs are garbage collected; therefore, most applets will not need to override this method. The applets demonstrated in this chapter do NOT override this method.

Now that we know the difference between the scrollMsg class and the simpleMarquee Applet, you can examine Source 7.2 to see a working applet.

SOURCE 7.2

```java
// simple marquee applet
import java.applet.Applet;
import java.awt.*;

public class simpleMarquee extends Applet implements Runnable {
        String theMessage;
        Font textFont;
        FontMetrics fontMetrics;
        int stepPixels;
        int oldX, oldY, newX, newY;
        int speed; // in milliseconds
        Thread scroller=null;

        // standard applet methods
        public void init()
        {
                theMessage = getParameter("message");
                if (theMessage == null)
                        theMessage = new
```

```
                        String("A simple Marquee by Michael Daconta.");

        String speedStr = getParameter("speed");
        if (speedStr == null)
                speed = 15;
        else
                speed = Integer.parseInt(speedStr);

        textFont = new Font("TimesRoman",Font.BOLD, 18);
        stepPixels = 6;
}

public void start()
{
        if (scroller == null)
        {
                scroller = new Thread(this);
                scroller.start();
        }
}

public void stop()
{
        if (scroller != null)
        {
                scroller.stop();
                scroller = null;
        }
}

public void run()
{
        Thread.currentThread().setPriority(Thread.NORM_PRIORITY-1);
        paint(this.getGraphics());
        while (true)
                repaint(speed);
}

public void paint(Graphics g)
{
        // initial background
        g.setColor(Color.black);
```

```java
        g.drawRect(0,0, size().width,
                size().height);
        g.setColor(Color.white);
        g.fillRect(1,1, size().width - 1,
                size().height - 1);

        // set the font
        g.setFont(textFont);
        fontMetrics = g.getFontMetrics();

        // set initial X and Y to drawString
        oldX = newX = size().width -
                fontMetrics.charWidth(theMessage.charAt(0));
        oldY = newY = size().height/2 +
                (fontMetrics.getHeight()/2);
    }

public void update(Graphics g)
{
        g.setFont(textFont);

        // Erase the old
        g.setColor(Color.white);
        g.drawString(theMessage, oldX, oldY);

        // draw the New
        g.setColor(Color.black);
        g.drawString(theMessage, newX, newY);

        // step
        oldX = newX;
        newX -= stepPixels;

        // restart?
        if (newX <= -(fontMetrics.stringWidth(theMessage)
                    - fontMetrics.charWidth(
                      theMessage.charAt(
                        theMessage.length() - 1))))
                paint(g);   // start at the beginning
    }

}
```

The html page for the above applet is:

```
<title> A simple Scrolling Marquee </title>
<hr>
<applet code="simpleMarquee.class" width=400 height=80>
<param name=message value="Big Sale!!! Internet Terminals
$299!!!">
<param name=speed value="25">
</applet>
<hr>
<a href="simpleMarquee.java">The Source.</a>
```

When run in the applet viewer, Source 7.2 produces Figure 7.3.

This applet has also been tested under Netscape 2.0 and works great! Before we can feel confident about applets, though, we need to briefly examine the Hyper Text Markup Language (HTML) file and the applet HTML tag that the browser uses to load our Applet subclass.

An HTML file is a normal text file that has special tags in it that the browser treats as commands. HTML documents are divided into logical elements. Elements are marked by tags of the form

```
<TagName> ... some text  ... </TagName>
```

There are many different HTML tags and many fine books on the market about preparing HTML documents. We are only concerned with one new tag: the applet tag.

```
<applet  attributes>  </applet>  --this is the applet tag.
```

Non-Java enabled browsers will ignore this tag.

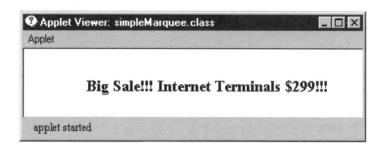

FIGURE 7.3   The simpleMarquee applet.

HTML tags can have attributes. The applet tag has four attributes and may contain any number of param elements. Here are the four applet attributes:

- codebase="path/classes". Specifies a path to search for the class
- code="classname.class". The class name
- width=#. The width of the Panel to contain the applet
- height=#. The height of the Panel to contain the applet

An applet tag can also contain a param element. A param element does not contain any text and is called an "empty element." Here is what the param element looks like:

```
<param attributes>
```

The param element can have two attributes:

- name=parameter_name. The name of the parameter
- value="value". The value of the parameter

That is all there is to the applet tag. The param elements are used to pass parameters into the applet. In the init( ) method you call the getParameter( ) method with the name of the parameter as the argument. The getParameter( ) method will return the string in the value attribute of the param element.

To cement all the topics we discussed about applets, we will examine one more example. Although not shown here, this applet was also developed first as a stand-alone program. To me it just makes more sense to do it that way. It is easier to experiment with concepts as well as test prototypes with an application than to use the appletviewer.

Source 7.3 implements a bouncing ball. This applet could be the start of a simple "breakout" type game. This applet also uses dirty rectangle animation to move the ball. I recommend switching this applet to double buffered animation as an exercise.

SOURCE 7.3

```
// simple bouncing ball applet
import java.applet.Applet;
import java.awt.*;
import java.util.Random;
```

```java
public class simpleBounce extends Applet implements Runnable {
        final int SOUTHWEST = 0;
        final int SOUTHEAST = 1;
        final int NORTHWEST = 2;
        final int NORTHEAST = 3;

        Point oldP, newP;
        int BresenhamError;
        int Rise, Run;
        int Direction;
        Point wallPoint;
        Color ballColor;
        int speed;
        int Increment;
        int ballSize;
        Thread bouncer=null;

        public void init()
        {
                setBackground(Color.white);
                speed = 1;
                Increment = 2;
                ballSize = 12;
                ballColor = Color.red;
        }
        public void start()
        {
                if (bouncer == null)
                {
                        bouncer = new Thread(this);
                        bouncer.start();
                }
        }

        public void stop()
        {
                if (bouncer != null)
                {
                        bouncer.stop();
                        bouncer = null;
                }
        }
```

```java
// implement Runnable
public void run()
{
        while (true)
                repaint();
}

public void paint(Graphics g)
{
        Random dice = new Random();

        // clears background
        // launch direction between 30-70
        int degrees = dice.nextInt() % 70;
        if (degrees < 0) degrees = -degrees;
        if (degrees < 30) degrees = 30;

        // convert to radians
        double radians = ((double)degrees/180.0) * Math.PI;

        // launch point is always the bottom center
        oldP = new Point(size().width/2, size().height -
                                ballSize);
        newP = new Point(size().width/2, size().height -
                                ballSize);

        // figure out wall intersection
        double oppositte = (double)(size().width/2) *
                                Math.tan(radians);

        if (degrees < 90)
                wallPoint = new Point(size().width, (int) oppositte);
        else
                wallPoint = new Point(0, (int) oppositte);

        Rise = (int) Math.round(oppositte);
        Run = Math.abs(oldP.x - wallPoint.x);

        // determine direction
        if (wallPoint.y < oldP.y)
        {
```

```
                if (wallPoint.x > oldP.x)
                        Direction = NORTHEAST;
                else
                        Direction = NORTHWEST;
        }
        else
        {
                if (wallPoint.x > oldP.x)
                        Direction = SOUTHEAST;
                else
                        Direction = SOUTHWEST;
        }

        if (Rise >= Run)
                BresenhamError = Rise;
        else
                BresenhamError = Run;
}

boolean BresenhamIncrement(int majorDimension,
                           int minorDimension)
{
        if (BresenhamError >= majorDimension)
        {
                BresenhamError = minorDimension;
                return true;
        }
        else
                BresenhamError += minorDimension;

        return false;
}

public void update(Graphics g)
{
        // clear old ball
        g.setColor(Color.white);
        g.fillOval(oldP.x, oldP.y, ballSize, ballSize);

        // draw new ball
        g.setColor(ballColor);
        g.fillOval(newP.x, newP.y, ballSize, ballSize);
```

```
// old now is new
oldP.x = newP.x;
oldP.y = newP.y;

// step, use Bresenham
if (Rise >= Run)
{
        switch (Direction) {
                case NORTHEAST:
                        newP.y -= Increment;

                        /* No function call here!!
                           if (BresenhamIncrement(Run, Rise))
                                   newP.y -= Increment; */
                        if (BresenhamError >= Rise)
                        {
                                BresenhamError = Run;
                                newP.x += Increment;
                        }
                        else
                                BresenhamError += Run;
                        break;
                case NORTHWEST:
                        newP.y -= Increment;
                        if (BresenhamError >= Rise)
                        {
                                BresenhamError = Run;
                                newP.x -= Increment;
                        }
                        else
                                BresenhamError += Run;
                        break;
                case SOUTHEAST:
                        newP.y += Increment;
                        if (BresenhamError >= Rise)
                        {
                                BresenhamError = Run;
                                newP.x += Increment;
                        }
                        else
                                BresenhamError += Run;
```

```
                                     break;
                          case SOUTHWEST:
                                     newP.y += Increment;
                                     if (BresenhamError >= Rise)
                                     {
                                            BresenhamError = Run;
                                            newP.x -= Increment;
                                     }
                                     else
                                            BresenhamError += Run;
                                     break;
                          default:
                                     System.out.println("Unknown Direction");
               }
     }
     else  // Run > Rise
     {
            switch (Direction) {
                  case NORTHEAST:
                             newP.x += Increment;
                             if (BresenhamError >= Run)
                             {
                                    BresenhamError = Rise;
                                    newP.y -= Increment;
                             }
                             else
                                    BresenhamError += Rise;
                             break;
                  case NORTHWEST:
                             newP.x -= Increment;
                             if (BresenhamError >= Run)
                             {
                                    BresenhamError = Rise;
                                    newP.y -= Increment;
                             }
                             else
                                    BresenhamError += Rise;
                             break;
                  case SOUTHEAST:
                             newP.x += Increment;
                             if (BresenhamError >= Run)
                             {
```

```
                                        BresenhamError = Rise;
                                        newP.y += Increment;
                                }
                                else
                                        BresenhamError += Rise;
                                break;
                        case SOUTHWEST:
                                newP.x -= Increment;
                                if (BresenhamError >= Run)
                                {
                                        BresenhamError = Rise;
                                        newP.y += Increment;
                                }
                                else
                                        BresenhamError += Rise;
                                break;
                        default:
                                System.out.println("Unknown Direction");
                }
}

// now check for a "bounce"
if ( (newP.x + ballSize) >= size().width )
{
        if (Direction == SOUTHEAST)
                Direction = SOUTHWEST;
        else
                Direction = NORTHWEST;
}
else if ( newP.x <= 0 )
{
        if (Direction == SOUTHWEST)
                Direction = SOUTHEAST;
        else
                Direction = NORTHEAST;
}
else if ( (newP.y + ballSize) >= size().height)
{
        if (Direction == SOUTHWEST)
                Direction = NORTHWEST;
        else
                Direction = NORTHEAST;
```

```
            }
            else if (newP.y <= 0)
            {
                    if (Direction == NORTHWEST)
                            Direction = SOUTHWEST;
                    else
                            Direction = SOUTHEAST;
            }
    }
}
```

Here is the HTML file for this applet.

```
<title> A simple Bouncing Ball </title>
<hr>
<applet code="simpleBounce.class" width=100 height=100>
</applet>
<hr>
<a href="simpleBounce.java">The Source.</a>
```

A run of Source 7.3 produces Figure 7.4.
There are four points to note about Source 7.3:

1. The applet uses Bresenham's line drawing algorithm to determine the path of the ball.
2. All bounces are reflections of the previous line.
3. The update( ) method erases the previous ball, draws the ball in its current location, and calculates the next point. After this, a colli-

FIGURE 7.4   The simpleBounce applet.

sion check is made to see if the ball should bounce off a wall. All bounces are done by simply changing the direction of movement. This algorithm will have problems with non-square Panels.

4. The algorithm is ripe for enhancements and improvements. Here are a few suggestions: launch and update multiple balls, switch to double-buffered animation, and optimize the code to speed up the animation.

That concludes our study of applets. Applets are actually just a repackaging of everything else you have learned to run within a browser. Now we are ready to examine the new scripting language based on Java called JavaScript.

7.3   NETSCAPE AND JAVASCRIPT

On December 4, 1995 Netscape Communications Corporation and Sun Microsystems, Inc. announced JavaScript an easy-to-use, cross-platform scripting language that complements Java. In actuality, Netscape Communications merely changed the name and the focus of LiveScript, a web-page scripting language based on Java that Netscape had announced several months prior. The move was good for both Sun MicroSystems and for Netscape Communications but for different reasons. JavaScript gives Sun a scripting language with ease-of-use comparable to Microsoft's Visual Basic. JavaScript allows Netscape to leverage off the success of the Java language as the defacto standard for Internet programming. Now that we understand what Netscape and Sun are doing and what their motivations were, we can examine the current state of JavaScript and how it compares to Java.

Figure 7.5 depicts the running of a simple script written in JavaScript. The script runs within the Netscape browser with the script source being part of the HTML file. The figure is a screen shot of the Macintosh version of Netscape Navigator. Figure 7.6 shows the same script running on Windows 95.

There are three distinct parts to learning JavaScript programming: the first is the basics of the HyperText Markup Language (HTML); the second is the JavaScript language, and the third is the JavaScript Object Hierarchy. In this section we will just highlight the key parts of Source 7.4 and in the next chapter we will delve into JavaScript in detail.

Source 7.2 is an HTML file. HTML started as a document-formatting language that allowed hypertext links but is steadily growing into GUI/multimedia description language. I say this because forms, buttons, and textfields existed prior to JavaScript. The difference is that

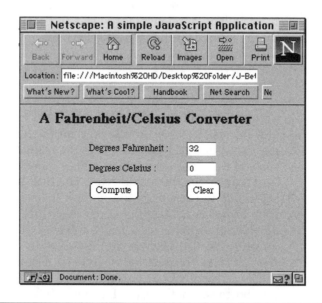

FIGURE 7.5   The Fahrenheit/Celsius converter in JavaScript.

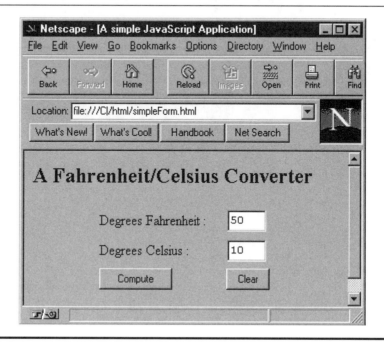

FIGURE 7.6   The Windows 95 version of the Fahrenheit/Celsius converter.

now the client browser can control the behavior of these HTML elements where previously there was no control at the client. We are primarily interested in one new HTML tag

```
<SCRIPT LANGUAGE="LiveScript">    ... the script ... </SCRIPT>
```

As you can see, the language name has not yet changed from "LiveScript" to "JavaScript." That is scheduled to change in the next release of Netscape; however, the LiveScript tag will be supported for a while after that while developers make the transition. As we discuss the features of LiveScript, we will highlight other changes due on the horizon as it transitions into JavaScript. The next line in the file is a comment (<!— hide the script ...) that allows the script's contents to be hidden from browsers that do not support scripting. This is followed by three JavaScript functions: checkNumber( ), computeForm( ), and clear-Form( ). We will discuss the language in detail in the next chapter. Last, we see the rest of the HTML document. In the HTML, some graphical elements are displayed, a form, a table, two textfields, and two buttons. In the tags for these fields you also see calls to our JavaScript function when some event occurs (i.e., onClick). When the functions are called, they execute right in the browser window. Figure 7.6 depicts the script executing in Windows.

SOURCE 7.4

```
<HTML>
<HEAD>
<TITLE> A simple JavaScript Application </TITLE>

<SCRIPT LANGUAGE="LiveScript">

<!-- hide the script tag's contents from old browsers

function checkNumber(numStr, fieldName)
{
    msg = fieldName + " field has invalid data: " + numStr.value;
    str = numStr.value;
    for (var i=0; i < str.length; i++)
    {
        var ch = str.substring(i,i+1);
        if ( (ch < "0" || ch > "9") && ch != '.')
        {
```

```
                alert(msg);
                return false;
            }
        }
        return true;
}

function computeForm(form)
{
    // if both forms empty - error
    if ( (form.fdegrees.value == null ||
            form.fdegrees.value.length == 0) &&
            (form.cdegrees.value == null ||
            form.cdegrees.value.length == 0) )
    {
        alert("Both fields empty.");
        return;
    }


    // if both forms filled error
    if ( (form.fdegrees.value != null &&
            form.fdegrees.value.length > 0) &&
            (form.cdegrees.value != null &&
            form.cdegrees.value.length > 0) )
    {
        alert("Error: both fields have data.");
        return;
    }


    // calculate fahrenheight
    if ( (form.fdegrees.value == null ||
            form.fdegrees.value.length == 0) &&
            (form.cdegrees.value != null &&
            form.cdegrees.value.length > 0) )
    {
        if (checkNumber(form.cdegrees,"Celsius"))
        {
            var degs = 0.0 + form.cdegrees.value;
            degs = (degs * 9.0/5.0) + 32;
            form.fdegrees.value = degs;
        }
    }
```

```
        }

        // calculate celsius
        if ( (form.fdegrees.value != null &&
              form.fdegrees.value.length > 0) &&
             (form.cdegrees.value == null ||
              form.cdegrees.value.length == 0) )
        {
            if (checkNumber(form.fdegrees,"Fahrenheit"))
            {
                var degs = 0.0 + form.fdegrees.value;
                degs = (degs - 32.0) * (5.0/9.0);
                form.cdegrees.value = degs;
            }
        }
}

function clearForm(form)
{
    form.fdegrees.value="";
    form.cdegrees.value="";
}

<!-- done hiding -->
</SCRIPT>

</HEAD>


<BODY>
<CENTER>
<H2> A Fahrenheit/Celsius Converter </H2>

<FORM method=post>
<TABLE>
<TR>
<TD> Degrees Fahrenheit : </TD>
<TD> <INPUT TYPE="text" NAME=fdegrees SIZE=5> </TD>
</TR>
<TR>
<TD> Degrees Celsius : </TD>
<TD> <INPUT TYPE="text" NAME=cdegrees SIZE=5> </TD>
```

```
</TR>
<TR>
<TD> <INPUT TYPE="button" VALUE="Compute"
onClick=computeForm(this.form)> </TD>
<TD> <INPUT TYPE="button" VALUE="Clear" onClick=clearForm(this.form)>
</TD>
</TR>
</TABLE>
</FORM>
</CENTER>
</BODY>
</HTML>
```

This integration of HTML and a simple scripting language is the power of JavaScript. As the domain of web browsers grow, so will the number of objects that can be manipulated by JavaScript. You may be thinking, "Where do Java applets fit in here?" and "If this is so great, why should I program in Java?"

Java applets are an element within an HTML document. As such, JavaScript will have the ability to manipulate them as objects. That will mean the ability to run them, pass data to them, receive data from them, and more. An applet will be another generic tool that the web page builder (the primary audience for JavaScript programming) has at his or her disposal; however, JavaScript scripting is much simpler than Java programming and also less powerful. JavaScript complements Java but does not come close to its power or capabilities in any area (GUI construction, data manipulation, object creation, text parsing, etc.). The differences between a scripting language and a programming language will be discussed in the next chapter.

CHAPTER 8

Comparing JavaScript to Java

I won't go so far as to call it a network operating system, but it's beginning to look like one.

—Jim Clark, Netscape Communications Corp. Chairman

OBJECTIVES

The reader will learn to understand the difference between a scripting language and a programming language, learn the key elements of JavaScript and how it compares to Java, and last, examine useful examples of JavaScript scripts.

JavaScript is not Java. It is important not to confuse the two. JavaScript is a scripting language and Java is a programming language. Both are interpreted languages; however, Java will also be a compiled language. In general, a scripting language controls high-level operating system functionality (of which running programs is just one aspect) and a programming language creates programs. JavaScript is currently focused on web scripting and not operating system (OS) scripting; however, Sun and Netscape have indicated that it could evolve towards a cross-platform OS scripting language.

Every major operating system (UNIX, MVS, VMS, Mac OS, and

DOS) has one or more scripting languages to assist in the automation of common operating system tasks. Scripting languages have evolved over the years. They started as simply a packaging of OS commands in a file with a few control flow constructs added to allow repetition (loops) and decision points (if statement). DOS batch files are the most common and simplest form of this type of scripting. In fact, the name "batch file" stands for a "batch" of commands to be executed sequentially.

Over the years, scripting languages have evolved in two directions: first, in expanding the capabilities of the scripting language, and second, in the number of "system objects" that the language can access and manipulate. The best examples of powerful scripting languages are on the UNIX operating system. Languages like Tcl and Perl have such extensive capabilities that they rival programming languages in everything except speed of execution. The Mac OS has meshed the scripting language concept with the event-driven programming paradigm by including OS events (called Apple Events) in the application event queue. This allows "scriptable applications" that permit scripting to be extended to an application's internal functions. This also allows Macintosh applications to be active participants in the scripting process by sending Apple Events to communicate with or control other applications. Now that we have a general idea of the purpose of a scripting language, let's examine the major characteristics of the JavaScript scripting language.

JavaScript is the first major Internet scripting language. It is important to understand that the Internet and World Wide Web are its initial and primary focus. There are currently five major characteristics of JavaScript:

- A script can be as simple as a sequence of commands. You do not have to use functions or methods. This goes back to scripting as a "batch" of commands. Of course, for longer scripts you should use functions and methods. Currently in JavaScript methods are just functions that are assigned to a property in a Object.
- There is no static typing of variables. A variable can hold any of the primitive types or a string.
- Only a small subset of Java keywords are supported, mostly consisting of the flow control keywords; however, all the Java keywords are reserved for future use.
- The JavaScript predefined objects are currently all browser-type objects (document, forms, form element, frames, window, etc.). This contrasts to OS scripting languages that deal with files, directories, pipes, and so on. The JavaScript predefined objects will

grow to accommodate these; however, this will happen only after security issues have been resolved.

- It is important to understand JavaScript is an unfinished product and is still evolving. Here is a quote from the Netscape Web Pages:

The Mother of all Disclaimers.
JavaScript and its documentation are currently under development. Some of the language is not yet implemented. That which is implemented is subject to change. Information provided at this time is incomplete and should not be considered a language specification. JavaScript is a work in progress whose potential we'd like to share with you, the beta users, in this development form.

That means that the contents of this chapter can be a guide but you should expect things to change. I will post the most current information on my web pages for this book, here's the URL: http://www.wiley.com/ So, even though JavaScript is a work in progress, there are still several benefits for the Java Programmer to learn JavaScript: you leverage existing knowledge of Java since JavaScript is based on Java, and JavaScript will evolve towards Java. You will notice that all of the Java keywords are reserved for future use. Of course, understand that even as JavaScript moves closer to Java, there is still the fundamental difference between a scripting language and a programming language. The two will never meld into one and that's a good thing. As an example of some of the future plans for JavaScript, the first changes will be making JavaScript case sensitive and adding UNICODE support.

- As the Internet becomes the focal point of all today's applications, the browser will become the central component of the client's software. Therefore, more and more operating system functions will be performed by the browser. This will make JavaScript evolve more towards a cross-platform OS scripting language.

Now that we understand the fundamental difference between Java and JavaScript and the major characteristics of JavaScript, we are ready to study the details.

You will see a fair amount of HTML in this next chapter. Unfortunately, I would be severely straying from the focus of this book if I detoured myself into HTML. Luckily, HTML is fairly easy. Source 8.1 is a skeleton HTML file that every one of the following examples begins with. I hope you find it useful.

SOURCE 8.1

```
<HTML>
<TITLE>  </TITLE>
<BODY>
<SCRIPT LANGUAGE="LiveScript">
<!-- hide from old browsers


<!-- done hiding -->
</SCRIPT>



</BODY>
</HTML>
```

8.1   JAVASCRIPT NAMES AND LITERALS

JavaScript variable names and literals are very similar to Java's. There are minor differences. However, these differences will be among the first things corrected in JavaScript as it evolves closer to Java. As an example, variable names will be changed to be case sensitive and JavaScript strings will support UNICODE characters. Figure 8.1 provides the details on JavaScript names and literals.

For the rest of this chapter, I will be using the screen shots of the web pages for a dual purpose. They will both present the key information for the chapter as well as simultaneously demonstrate those key points with code. The screen shots will be followed by the Source code. Source 8.2 both generates the above web page as well as tests its concepts. After presenting the source, I will highlight any points that are not intuitive or need to be stressed.

SOURCE 8.2

```
<HTML>
<TITLE> JavaScript Names and Literals </TITLE>
<BODY>
<H3> JavaScript Names and Literals </H3>

<H4> Names </H4>
<UL>
```

```
<LI> Must start with a letter or underscore ("_") </LI>
<LI> May include digits (0-9) </LI>
<LI> Letters include "A" through "Z" and "a" through "z" </LI>
<LI> names in Server-based JavaScript <STRONG>ARE</STRONG> case sensitive. </LI>
<LI> names in Client-based  JavaScript <STRONG>ARE NOT</STRONG> case sensitive. </LI>
</UL>

<SCRIPT LANGUAGE="LiveScript">
<!-- hide from old browsers
document.writeln("Name test <BR>");
var a_persons_name = "mike";
var _int32 = 65545;
var aNumber = 10;
var anumber = 20;
document.writeln("aNumber : " + aNumber + "<BR>");
document.writeln("anumber : " + anumber + "<BR>");

var this_is_a_very_long_javaScript_name_that_is_very_very_descriptive = true;
<!-- done hiding -->
</SCRIPT>

<H4> Literals </H4>
<UL>
<LI> Integer: expressed in base 10, 16 or 8.  leading 0 for octal, leading 0x for hex.
</LI>
<LI> Floating Point: can have an integer, decimal point, a fraction, <BR>
       an exponent and a type suffix. </LI>
<LI> Boolean: a true or a false. </LI>
<LI> String: characters delimited by double (") or single (') quotes.  <BR>
       Can also use \n,\t,\r,\a,\f.</LI>
</UL>

<SCRIPT LANGUAGE="LiveScript">
<!-- hide from old browsers
document.writeln("Literal Test <BR>");
var anInt = 252;
var PI = 3.14159;
var bigFloat = 3.2e10;
var done=false;
var name="Michael Daconta";
var lines="Mary had a little lamb \n whose fleece was white as snow";
```

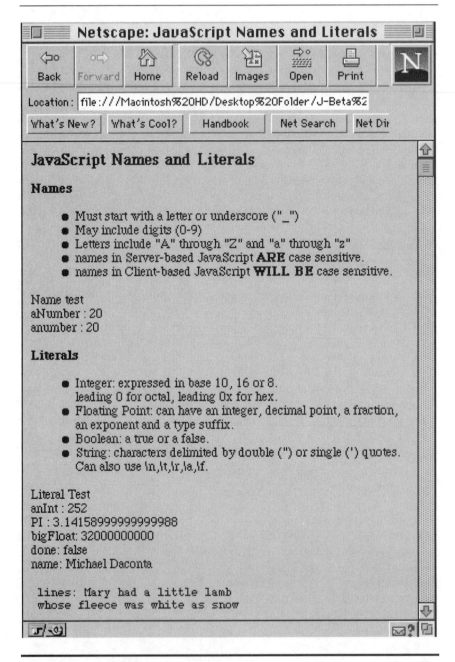

FIGURE 8.1   Web page on JavaScript Names and Literals.

```
document.writeln("anInt : " + anInt + "<BR>");
document.writeln("PI : " + PI + "<BR>");
document.writeln("bigFloat: " + bigFloat + "<BR>");
document.writeln("done: " + done + "<BR>");
document.writeln("name: " + name + "<BR>");
document.writeln("<PRE>lines: " + lines + "</PRE><BR>");
<!-- done hiding -->
</SCRIPT>

</BODY>
</HTML>
```

Source 8.2 is very intuitive. The only item to point out is the similarity to Java in allowing variable names of unlimited length. I encourage all programmers to make good use of that feature. It is always important to remember that the maintenance phase of an application's lifecycle is by far the longest phase.

8.2   JAVASCRIPT KEYWORDS AND OPERATORS

JavaScript only currently uses eleven of the fifty Java keywords. This is mostly due to JavaScript not performing any static typing of variables (eliminates all the types and type modifiers). JavaScript's object model is also much simpler, and there is currently no support for exceptions or inheritance. It is doubtful whether JavaScript will ever be object-oriented—there is just no need for it in a scripting language. More important are the four new keywords that JavaScript has added. These are:

- var. Declares a variable. You can also optionally assign the variable a value.
- function. Declares a JavaScript function. You can declare parameters to the function. All function arguments are passed by value. You can return a value from a function using the return keyword.
- in. Used within a for loop to allow you to iterate through the properties of an object. Here is an example that would print the properties of the car object:

```
for (i in car)
    document.writeln("car[" + i + "] = " + car[i] + " ");
```

- with. Similar to the with keyword in Ada, this keyword estab-lishes an object as the default object for the ensuing block of code. For example,

```
with car  {
        // car is the default object for these statements
    }
```

Figure 8.2 lists all the current JavaScript keywords and demon-strates their functionality.

Source 8.3 generates the web page in Figure 8.2 as well as demon-strates all of the JavaScript keywords.

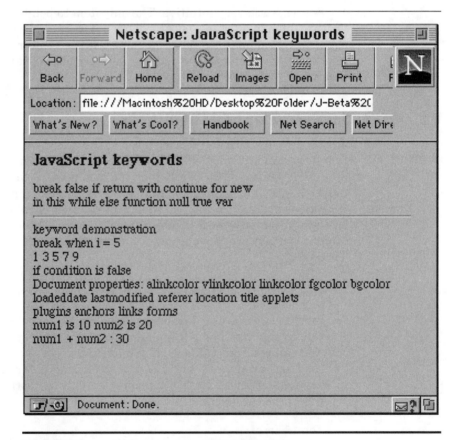

FIGURE 8.2   Web page on JavaScript keywords.

SOURCE 8.3

```
<HTML>
<HEAD>
<TITLE> JavaScript keywords </TITLE>
</HEAD>

<BODY>
<H3> JavaScript keywords </H3>

break    false    if    return    with    continue    for    new<BR>
in    this    while    else    function    null    true    var<BR>

<HR>
<SCRIPT LANGUAGE="LiveScript">
<!-- hide from non-netscape
document.writeln("keyword demonstration <BR>");
// break and while
var i = 10;
while (i-- > 0)
    if (i == 5)
        break;
document.writeln("break when i = " + i + "<BR>");

// continue and for
for (var j=0; j < 10; j++)
{
    if ((j % 2) == 0)
        continue;
    else
        document.write(" " + j + " ");
}
document.writeln("<BR>");

// else and false
if (false)
    document.writeln("if condition is true <BR>");
else
    document.writeln("if condition is false <BR>");

// function, in, null and var
```

```
function writeProps()
{
    var count=0;
    document.write("Document properties: ");
    if (document != null)
        for (props in document)
        {
            count++;
            if (count % 6 == 0)
                document.writeln("<BR>");
            document.write(" " + props + " ");
        }
    document.writeln("<BR>");
}

writeProps();

// return, this, true and with
function add(num1, num2, print)
{
    var result = 0;
    with document {
        if (print == true)
            writeln("num1 is " + num1 +
                    " num2 is " + num2 + "<BR>");
        result = num1 + num2;
    }
    return result;
}

tot = add(10,20, true);
document.writeln("num1 + num2 : " + tot + "<BR>");
<!-- done hiding -->
</SCRIPT>
</BODY>
</HTML>
```

There are two points of interest in Source 8.3:

- function writeProps( ) iterates through all the properties of the JavaScript document object. The document object is covered in detail in section 8.4.

- function add( ) uses document as its default object (via the with keyword). The function writeln( ) is a method of document. This allows us to just use writeln( ) instead of document.writeln( ).

JavaScript supports all of the Java operators. Figure 8.3 shows the Java operators and the results of examples using the operators is Source 8.4.

Source 8.4 should be familiar because it is similar to the Java program we wrote to test Java expressions (see Source 2.5).

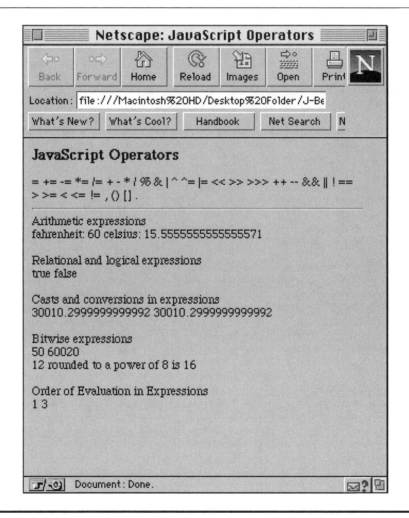

FIGURE 8.3   Web page on JavaScript operators.

SOURCE 8.4

```
<HTML>
<HEAD>
<TITLE> JavaScript Operators </TITLE>
</HEAD>

<BODY>
<H3> JavaScript Operators </H3>

=   +=  -=  *=  /=  +  -  *  /  %  &  |  ^  ^=
|=  <<  >>  >>>  ++  --  &&  ||  !  ==  >  >=
<  <=  !=  ,  ()  []  .

<HR>
<SCRIPT LANGUAGE="LiveScript">
<!-- hide for non-netscape
document.writeln("Arithmetic expressions <BR>");

var fahr=60.0, celsius=0;
celsius = (5.0/9.0) * (fahr-32.0);
document.writeln("fahrenheit: " + fahr + " celsius: " +
                 celsius + "<BR>");
document.writeln("<BR>");
document.writeln("Relational and logical expressions <BR>");
document.writeln(fahr > 20.0);
document.writeln(((fahr < 20.0) && (true)));
document.writeln("<BR>");

document.writeln("<BR>");
document.writeln("Casts and conversions in expressions<BR>");
var age=10;
var gpa = 0.0;
gpa = age;
var salary=30000.3;
age = gpa + salary;
document.writeln(gpa + salary);
document.writeln(age);
document.writeln("<BR> <BR>");

document.writeln("Bitwise expressions<BR>");
document.writeln(100 >> 1);  // division by 2
```

```
document.writeln(age << 1);  // multiplication by 2
document.writeln("<BR>");
var memoryBlock = (12 + 7) & ~7;
document.writeln("12 rounded to a power of 8 is " +
                    memoryBlock + "<BR>");
document.writeln("<BR>");

document.writeln("Order of Evaluation in Expressions<BR>");
var a = 5 & 1 + 2;
document.writeln(a);
a = (5 & 1) + 2;
document.writeln(a);
document.writeln("<BR>");
<!-- done hiding -->
</SCRIPT>
</BODY>
</HTML>
```

It is comforting to know that JavaScript implements all the powerful operators so well known from C, C++, Java, and now JavaScript. Also, like Java, JavaScript overloads the + operator for string concatenation.

8.3 STRINGS, OBJECTS, AND ARRAYS

Figure 8.4 lists the key properties and methods of the JavaScript String object and then demonstrates objects and arrays. The string object is very intuitive but objects and arrays will need further explanation.

Source 8.5 generates the web page in Figure 8.4 and demonstrates its key concepts. Pay careful attention to the code that demonstrates objects and arrays.

SOURCE 8.5

```
<HTML>
<TITLE> Strings, Objects, and Arrays </TITLE>
<BODY>

<SCRIPT LANGUAGE="LiveScript">
<!-- hide from old browsers
```

```
document.writeln("<H4> Strings </H4>");
var name = "Mike Daconta";
document.writeln("A String object is a sequence of characters.");
document.writeln("name : " + name + "<BR> <BR>");
document.writeln("Properties: ");
document.writeln("<UL>");
document.writeln("<LI> length - the length of the string.");
document.writeln("name.length : " + name.length + "</LI>");
document.writeln("</UL>");
document.writeln("Methods: ");
document.writeln("<UL>");
document.writeln("<LI> substring - returns a portion of the string.<BR>");
document.writeln("name.substring(0,4) : " + name.substring(0,4) + "</LI>");
document.writeln("<LI> toUpperCase - returns the upper case of all chars in the
string.<BR>");
document.writeln("name.toUpperCase() : " + name.toUpperCase() + "</LI>");
document.writeln("<LI> toLowerCase - returns the lower case of all chars in the
string.<BR>");
document.writeln("name.toLowerCase() : " + name.toLowerCase() + "</LI>");
document.writeln("</UL>");

document.writeln("<H4> Objects </H4>");
document.writeln("An object is a list of properties and values <BR>");

function makeObject()
{
    return this;
}

function addCoord(x2, y2)
{
    this.x += x2;
    this.y += y2;
}

function writeCoord()
{
    document.writeln(" x : " + this.x);
    document.writeln(" y : " + this.y + "<BR>");
}

var coord = new makeObject();
```

```
coord.x = 10;
coord.y = 20;
coord.addCoord = addCoord;
coord.writeCoord = writeCoord;

document.writeln("A coordinate Object: <BR>");
coord.writeCoord();
document.writeln("A call to coord.addCoord(10,10) <BR>");
coord.addCoord(10,10);
coord.writeCoord();

document.writeln("<H4> Arrays </H4>");
document.writeln("NOTE: arrays are just objects. <BR>");
var intArray = new makeObject();
for (i=0;  i < 3;  i++)
     intArray[i] = i + 10;
intArray.length = 3;
for (j in intArray)
     document.writeln("intArray[" + j + "] is " + intArray[j] + "<BR>");

<!-- done hiding -->
</SCRIPT>
</BODY>
</HTML>
```

Let me explain the JavaScript objects and arrays in more detail; however, you should be aware that these may change in future releases of JavaScript. The reason they will change is that they are fairly complex for a language that is competing in the ease-of-use category with Visual Basic. Second, the current implementation makes it fairly easy to crash the interpreter. Having said that, let's examine the current implementation in detail.

A JavaScript object is a dynamic associative array of property names and values. Lisp programmers will note the similarity of a JavaScript Object to a Lisp symbol (we see another similarity with the JavaScript eval function discussed in section 8.4). The object is dynamic in that you do not have to specify the number of properties it has at creation. You create an object with the new keyword and a constructor function. Since we can add properties dynamically, the constructor function can be as simple as the makeObject( ) function above.

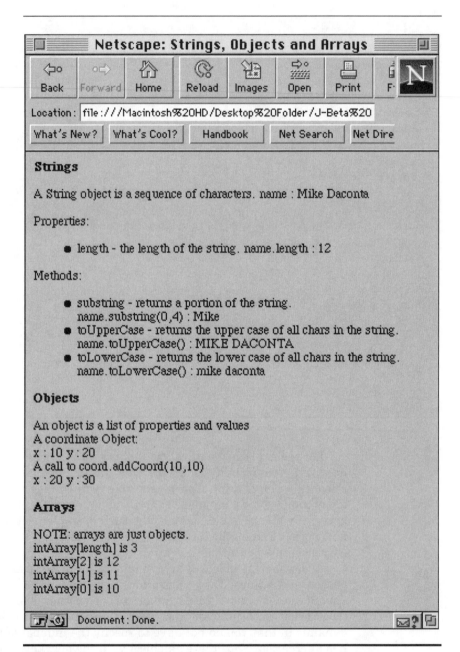

Netscape: Strings, Objects and Arrays

Back | Forward | Home | Reload | Images | Open | Print | F

Location: file:///Macintosh%20HD/Desktop%20Folder/J-Beta%20

What's New? | What's Cool? | Handbook | Net Search | Net Dire

Strings

A String object is a sequence of characters. name : Mike Daconta

Properties:

- length - the length of the string. name.length : 12

Methods:

- substring - returns a portion of the string.
  name.substring(0,4) : Mike
- toUpperCase - returns the upper case of all chars in the string.
  name.toUpperCase() : MIKE DACONTA
- toLowerCase - returns the lower case of all chars in the string.
  name.toLowerCase() : mike daconta

Objects

An object is a list of properties and values
A coordinate Object:
x : 10 y : 20
A call to coord.addCoord(10,10)
x : 20 y : 30

Arrays

NOTE: arrays are just objects.
intArray[length] is 3
intArray[2] is 12
intArray[1] is 11
intArray[0] is 10

Document: Done.

FIGURE 8.4   Web page on JavaScript strings, objects, and arrays.

Once the object has been created (probably implemented with a list, which means the interpreter created a single node in the list), we can add properties dynamically by specifying the property and assigning it a value. This is done using the dot operator like this:

```
coord.x = 10;
```

This created both a property name "x" and a value (10) attached to our object. It is important to note that a property could itself be another object. A property can also be a function. In fact, this is the way that object methods are "created." You assign the JavaScript function to one of the object's properties. The benefit this gives you is that the this keyword points to the current object, which you can use inside the function to make it behave like an object method. If you iterate through the properties of your object (using the for ... in expression) you will notice that the function property holds the actual text of the function. The last point to understand about objects is that you can optionally iterate through the properties using the index number of the property. However, you need to be careful when you do this in conjunction with assigning a new value to the property so that you don't accidentally assign an incorrect value to a property (like assigning a number to your method property).

Arrays in JavaScript are very different than arrays in Java, C, and C++. Again, this is another part of the language that will probably change. There are actually no arrays in Java script (not arrays in the sense of Java, C, or C++ arrays); however, an array can be emulated by using an object. As we have stated previously, a JavaScript object is an associative array of property names and property values. Therefore, creating an associative array is the same as creating an object. Second, you can even create a single dimensional array by creating an object and using numbers for the property fields (there is no requirement that a property must be a string, that is just the normal case). Source 8.5 demonstrates this. There is currently no way to do multidimensional arrays in JavaScript.

8.4   JAVASCRIPT PREDEFINED OBJECTS

JavaScript has predefined browser objects. Figure 8.5 depicts the current object hierarchy supported by JavaScript. These predefined JavaScript objects have properties and methods the JavaScript programmer can access and call to add client-side functionality to web pages. The window, location, history, and document objects always

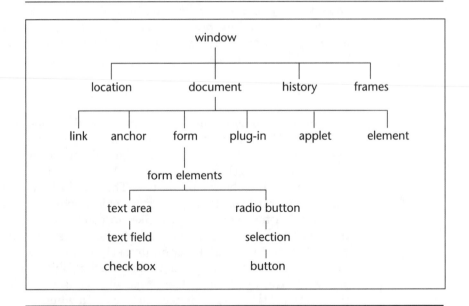

FIGURE 8.5   The JavaScript object hierarchy.

exist. The other objects (such as forms, text fields, anchors, etc.) only exist if they exist in the HTML document being displayed.

All of the above predefined objects should be familiar to HTML authors as well as being self explanatory. Not all of the objects are implemented in the current version (plug-ins, applets, and elements). It is not the focus of this book to demonstrate the use of every JavaScript object. We are examining the language in comparison to Java programming and its importance in complementing Java programming. As such, we will demonstrate two of the objects that always exist: the document and window class. Many of the other objects are demonstrated in the Form Validation example in section 8.6. Now let us examine the Window object.

The JavaScript window object refers to the browser window that displays the HTML document. Figure 8.6 explains all the properties and methods of the window object. It also demonstrates all of the window methods by attaching JavaScript functions to the button click event of the button object.

Figure 8.7 depicts the window that appears when the user clicks the alert button shown in Figure 8.6.

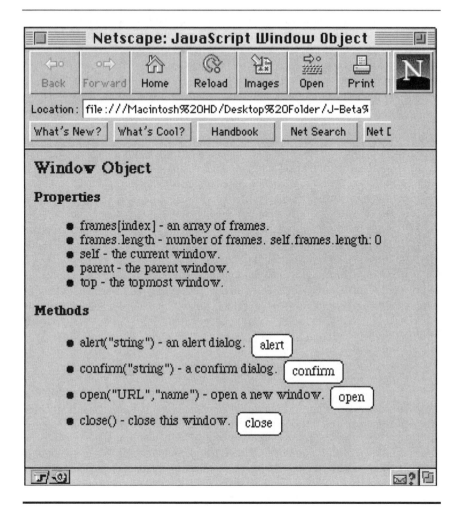

FIGURE 8.6   Web page on the JavaScript window object.

FIGURE 8.7   A JavaScript alert.

Source 8.6 generates Figure 8.6. The code is very straightforward and merely calls the window object methods.

SOURCE 8.6

```
<HTML>
<HEAD>
<TITLE>
JavaScript Window Object
</TITLE>
</HEAD>

<BODY>
<H3> Window Object </H3>
<H4>     Properties </H4>
<UL>
<LI>        frames[index] - an array of frames. </LI>
<LI>        frames.length - number of frames.
<SCRIPT LANGUAGE="LiveScript">
<!-- hide for non-netscape
        document.write("self.frames.length: " +
                        self.frames.length);
<!-- done hiding -->
</SCRIPT> </LI>
<LI> self - the current window. </LI>
<LI>      parent - the parent window. </LI>
<LI>      top - the topmost window. </LI>
</UL>

<H4>    Methods </H4>
<SCRIPT LANGUAGE="LiveScript">
<!-- hide for non-netscape
function showAlert()
{ alert("This is an alert"); }

function showConfirm()
{ confirm("This is a confirm"); }

function doOpen()
{
    open(document.location.toString(),
```

```
                "Another window");
}
<!-- done hiding -->
</SCRIPT>
<FORM>
<UL>
<LI>     alert("string") - an alert dialog.
<INPUT TYPE="button" VALUE="alert"
     onClick=showAlert()> </LI>
<LI>      confirm("string") - a confirm dialog.
<INPUT TYPE="button" VALUE="confirm"
     onClick=showConfirm()> </LI>
<LI>      open("URL","name") - open a new window.
<INPUT TYPE="button" VALUE="open"
     onClick=doOpen()> </LI>
<LI>      close() - close this window.
<INPUT TYPE="button" VALUE="close"
     onClick=close()> </LI>
</UL>
</FORM>
</BODY>

</HTML>
```

One thing that is important to notice about Source 8.6 is the fact that the calls to the window methods need not be preceded by an object. Since these objects create new windows, they are actually more like independent functions than methods. Now let's examine the document object.

The document object represents the current HTML document being displayed. Figures 8.8 and 8.9 list the document properties and object as well as display information about the current document loaded.

Sources 8.7 and 8.8 generate the above web pages. One of the very interesting things about the document object is the ability to write HTML right into the current document. This has been demonstrated in every Source code listing in this chapter. This "on-the-fly HTML" has many potential uses and is a very powerful capability of JavaScript. The primary method for doing this is the document.writeln( ) and document.write( ) methods. Sources 8.7 and 8.8 demonstrate these methods.

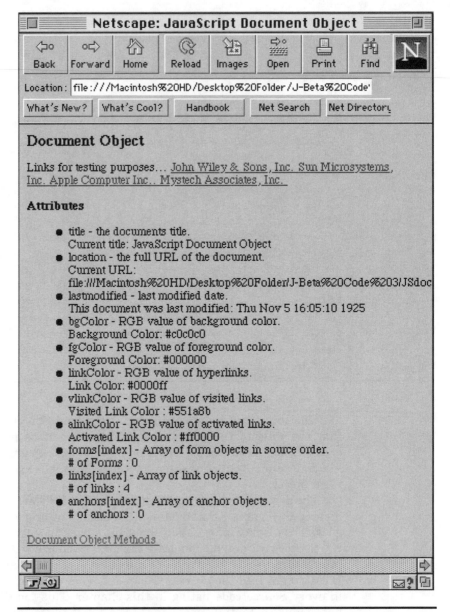

FIGURE 8.8   Web page on the JavaScript document object properties.

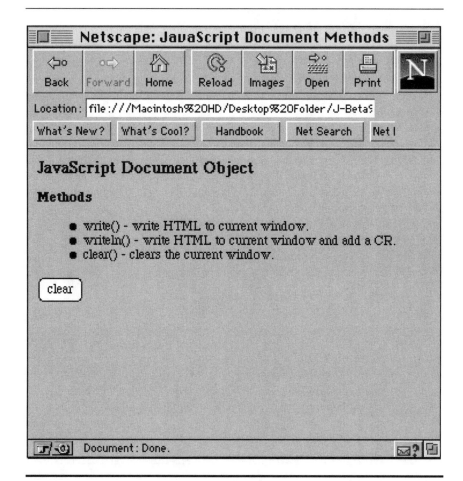

FIGURE 8.9   Web page on the JavaScript document object methods.

SOURCE 8.7

```
<HTML>
<TITLE> JavaScript Document Object </TITLE>
<BODY>
<SCRIPT LANGUAGE="LiveScript">
<!-- hide from old browsers

<!-- done hiding -->
</SCRIPT>
```

```
<H3> Document Object </H3>

Links for testing purposes...
<A HREF="http://www.wiley.com"> John Wiley & Sons, Inc. </A>
<A HREF="http://www.sun.com"> Sun Microsystems, Inc. </A>
<A HREF="http://www.apple.com"> Apple Computer Inc.. </A>
<A HREF="http://www.mystech.com"> Mystech Associates, Inc. </A> <BR>

<SCRIPT LANGUAGE="LiveScript">
<!-- Hide from old browsers
document.writeln("<H4> Attributes </H4>");
document.writeln("<UL>");
document.writeln("<LI>   title - the documents title.<BR>");
document.writeln("         Current title: " + document.title + "</LI>");
document.writeln("<LI>   location - the full URL of the document.<BR>");
document.writeln("         Current URL: " + document.location + "</LI>");
document.writeln("<LI>   lastmodified - last modified date.<BR>");
document.writeln("          This document was last modified: " + document.lastmodified +
"</LI>");
document.writeln("<LI>   bgColor - RGB value of background color.<BR>");
document.writeln("          Background Color: " + document.bgColor + "</LI>");
document.writeln("<LI>   fgColor - RGB value of foreground color. <BR>");
document.writeln("          Foreground Color: " + document.fgColor + "</LI>");
document.writeln("<LI>   linkColor - RGB value of hyperlinks. <BR>");
document.writeln("          Link Color: " + document.linkColor + "</LI>");
document.writeln("<LI>   vlinkColor - RGB value of visited links. <BR>");
document.writeln("          Visited Link Color : " + document.vlinkColor + "</LI>");
document.writeln("<LI>   alinkColor - RGB value of activated links.<BR>");
document.writeln("          Activated Link Color : " + document.alinkColor + "<LI>");
document.writeln("<LI>   forms[index] - Array of form objects in source order.<BR>");
document.writeln("          # of Forms : " + document.forms.length + "</LI>");
document.writeln("<LI>   links[index] - Array of link objects. <BR>");
document.writeln("          # of links : " + document.links.length + "</LI>");
document.writeln("<LI>   anchors[index] - Array of anchor objects.<BR>");
document.writeln("          # of anchors : " + document.anchors.length + "</LI>");

document.writeln("</UL>");
<!-- done hiding -->
</SCRIPT>
<A HREF="JSdoc2.html"> Document Object Methods </A>
</BODY>
</HTML>
```

Source 8.8 was necessary simply to present the information in a separate window as shown in Figure 8.9.

SOURCE 8.8

```
<HTML>
<TITLE> JavaScript Document Methods </TITLE>
<BODY>

<H3> JavaScript Document Object </H3>

<SCRIPT LANGUAGE="LiveScript">
<!-- hide from old browsers
document.writeln("<H4> Methods </H4>");
document.writeln("<UL>");
document.writeln("<LI>   write() - write HTML to current window. </LI>");
document.writeln("<LI>   writeln() - write HTML to current window and add a CR.
</LI>");
document.writeln("<LI>   clear() - clears the current window.</LI>");
document.writeln("</UL>");
<!-- done hiding -->
</SCRIPT>
<FORM>
<INPUT TYPE="button" VALUE="clear" onClick=document.clear()>
</FORM>
</BODY>
</HTML>
```

As we have demonstrated, the JavaScript predefined objects give you the ability to access information about the browser window, current document being displayed, and the HTML elements in that window. As the language evolves, the number of predefined objects will grow and so will the power and utility of the JavaScript language. The next section will discuss other features of the JavaScript language, such as scripting and the use of the built-in eval function.

8.5   OTHER JAVASCRIPT FEATURES

To round out our presentation of JavaScript, there are two other features that are key to the interactivity of the language. They are:

- JavaScript Events. We have seen examples of JavaScript events in the above sources. For example, in Source 8.8 you see the line:

```
<INPUT TYPE="button" VALUE="clear" onClick=document.clear()>
```

There are two points to understanding the above code: first, onClick is a method of the button object that is run when the button receives a mouse click in the browser. The events the browser will pass on are predefined for different HTML elements. Here is a list of the JavaScript event handler methods:

onFocus—Method run when the form element is input focused. Similar to the Java AWT gotFocus event.

onBlur—Method run on the loss of input focus. Similar to the Java AWT lostFocus event.

onSelect—Method to run when text in a field is selected.

onChange—Method to run when the text field's value is changed.

onSubmit—Method to run when the form is submitted.

onClick—Method to run when a button is clicked.

Now that we know the predefined event methods, we understand that the code

```
<INPUT TYPE="button" VALUE="clear" onClick=document.clear()>
```

is assigning the document.clear( ) function to the onClick method of the button in our form. It is important to note that you can assign any valid JavaScript commands to the onClick method as long as you enclose them within quotes (i.e., a string of commands). You will understand this better after we discuss the eval function below.

- eval Function—This function gives the JavaScript programmer access to the JavaScript interpreter. The eval function will evaluate any valid JavaScript expression, to include JavaScript functions. This is a powerful tool that is well-known to Lisp programmers. One of the exciting things this lets you do is generate code on the fly (i.e., in response to form input or selections by the user) and execute on the fly. Of course, since you are generating that code on the fly, it is infinitely flexible. Source 8.9 demonstrates a simple use of the eval function.

SOURCE 8.9

```
<HTML>
<HEAD>
<TITLE> JavaScript Expression Evaluator </TITLE>
```

```
<SCRIPT LANGUAGE="LiveScript">

<!-- hide the script tag's contents from old browsers

function computeForm(form)
{
    // if expression field empty - error
    if ( (form.expression.value == null ||
        form.expression.value.length == 0) )
    {
        alert("Expression field empty.");
        return;
    }

  // else evaluate and put result in result
  var theresult = eval(form.expression.value);
  form.result.value = theresult;
}

function clearForm(form)
{
    form.expression.value="";
    form.result.value="";
}

<!-- done hiding -->
</SCRIPT>

</HEAD>

<BODY>
<CENTER>
<H2> An Expression Evaluator </H2>

<FORM method=post>
<TABLE>
<TR>
<TD> Expression : </TD>
<TD> <INPUT TYPE="text" NAME=expression SIZE=30> </TD>
</TR>
<TR>
```

```
<TD> Result : </TD>
<TD> <INPUT TYPE="text" NAME=result SIZE=10> </TD>
</TR>
<TR>
<TD> <INPUT TYPE="button" VALUE="Compute" onClick=computeForm(this.form)> </TD>
<TD> <INPUT TYPE="button" VALUE="Clear" onClick=clearForm(this.form)> </TD>
</TR>
</TABLE>
</FORM>
</CENTER>
</BODY>
</HTML>
```

Source 8.9 generates the web page in Figure 8.10.

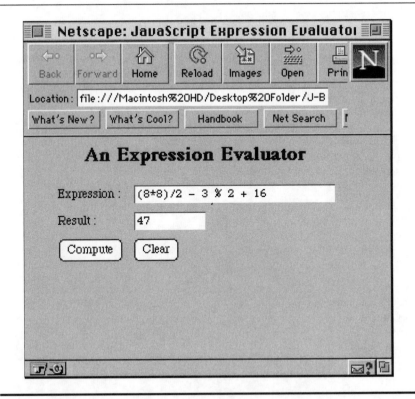

FIGURE 8.10   A JavaScript expression evaluator.

Now that we have covered all the major elements of JavaScript, we are ready to see a demonstration of how we would use this language to enhance our World Wide Web sites.

8.6   A FORM VALIDATION SCRIPT

Currently, JavaScript will have an immediate effect in three areas of Web authoring: performing mathematical calculations on web pages, writing HTML on the fly, and validating fields and forms before sending data to the web server. In the examples above, we have examined performing mathematical calculations and on-the-fly HTML. Now we complete this chapter with a simple example of field and form validation.

Source 8.10 demonstrates field and form validation using Java-Script. The idea is simple: We have a JavaScript function tied to every form element we want validated and a JavaScript function invoked before the data is submitted. Since the majority of input that needs to be validated is text input, the functions consist mostly of traversing and validating characters in the string. As the JavaScript String methods grow in number, this process will get easier.

SOURCE 8.10

```
<HTML>
<TITLE> JavaScript Form Object </TITLE>
<BODY>
<SCRIPT LANGUAGE="LiveScript">
<!-- hide from old browsers

function checkName(form)
{
    if (form.fullname.value.length == 0)
        return;

    // check for all alpha
    for (var i=0; i < form.fullname.value.length; i++)
    {
        var ch = form.fullname.value.substring(i, i+1);
        if ((ch >= "A" && ch <= "Z") ||
            (ch >= "a" && ch <= "z") ||
            (ch == " ") )
        {
```

```
                continue;
            }
        else
            {
                alert("Invalid name.  Please re-enter");
                form.fullname.value="";
                return;
            }
        }
    }
}

function checkAge(form)
{
    if (form.age.value.length == 0)
        return;

    // check for all numbers
    for (var i=0; i < form.age.value.length; i++)
    {
        var ch = form.age.value.substring(i, i+1);
        if (ch < "0" || ch > "9")
        {
            alert("Invalid age.  Please re-enter");
            form.age.value="";
            return;
        }
    }

    var num = 0 + form.age.value;
    if (num < 0 || num > 120)
    {
        alert("Invalid age.  Please re-enter");
        form.age.value="";
        return;
    }
}

function checkPhone(form)
{
    if (form.phone.value.length == 0)
        return;
```

```
    if (form.phone.value.length > 13)
    {
        alert("Invalid phone num. Please re-enter in this format:
            (###)###-####");
        form.phone.value="";
        return;
    }

    // check for all numbers
    for (var i=0; i < form.phone.value.length; i++)
    {
        var ch = form.phone.value.substring(i, i+1);
        if ( (ch < "0" || ch > "9") && ( ch != "(" && ch != ")" && ch != "-"))
        {
            alert("Invalid phone number.  Please re-enter");
            form.phone.value="";
            return;
        }
    }
}

function checkSex(form)
{
    // insure both are not checked
    if (form.msex.status == true &&
        form.fsex.status == true)
    {
        alert("Cannot be both sexes.");
        return false;
    }
    return true;
}

function checkForm(form)
{
    if (!checkSex(form))
    {
        alert("Cannot be both sexes. Form NOT submitted.");
        return;
    }

    if ( (form.fullname.value.length == 0) &&
```

```
              (form.age.value.length == 0) &&
              (form.phone.value.length == 0) &&
              (form.msex.status == false &&
               form.fsex.status == false)  )
      {
            alert("All fields must be filled in. Form NOT submitted.");
            return;
      }


      // if we got here - submit it!

}

function clearForm(form)
{
      form.fullname.value="";
      form.age.value="";
      form.phone.value="";
}

<!-- done hiding -->
</SCRIPT>

<CENTER>
<H3> JavaScript Form Validation </H3>
</CENTER>

<FORM>
<p> Full Name: <INPUT TYPE="text" NAME=fullname SIZE=30
onChange=checkName(this.form)> <BR>

<p> Age: <INPUT TYPE="text" NAME=age SIZE=3 onChange=checkAge(this.form)> </BR>

<p> Sex: <INPUT TYPE="checkbox" NAME=msex VALUE="Male" onClick=checkSex
      (this.form)> Male
                <INPUT TYPE="checkbox" NAME=fsex VALUE="Female"
                     onClick=checkSex(this.form)> Female

<p> Telephone: <INPUT TYPE="text" NAME=phone SIZE=15 onChange=checkPhone
      (this.form)> <BR>

<p> Press <INPUT TYPE="button" VALUE="Reset" onClick=clearForm(this.form)>
```

```
    clear this form.
<p> <STRONG> Press <INPUT TYPE="button" VALUE="send" onClick=checkForm(this.form)>
    when done.
</STRONG>


</FORM>
</BODY>
</HTML>
```

Source 8.10 generates the web pages depicted in Figure 8.11.
This concludes our discussion of JavaScript. As the language

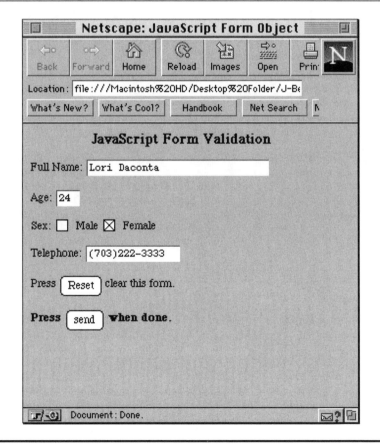

FIGURE 8.11   JavaScript field and form validation

evolves, I will post regular updates to my Web pages. Now you should feel confident in understanding the fundamental difference between JavaScript and Java as well as how they will complement each other.

APPENDIXES

Java/JavaScript References

APPENDIX A

The Java Language

KEYWORD LIST

abstract	continue	for	new	switch
boolean	default	goto	null	synchronized
break	do	if	package	this
byte	double	implements	private	threadsafe
byvalue	else	import	protected	throw
case	extends	instanceof	public	transient
catch	false	int	return	true
char	final	interface	short	try
class	finally	long	static	void
const	float	native	super	while

KEYWORD DEFINITIONS

break A control flow keyword used to exit from a do, for, or while loop that bypasses the normal loop condition. It can also be used to exit from a switch statement. In nested loops, the break always terminates the innermost loop.

char A basic data type used to declare character variables. A Java character is different than an ascii character. Java uses the UNICODE character set, which is a 16-bit unsigned value. Java is very explicit about the size of all types. Since Java uses a "virtual machine" representation in the interpreter, the Java language specifies the exact size in bits for all basic types. This aids portability as there are no differences between sizes of the basic types on different platforms. This also makes the sizeof( ) macro obsolete.

case A control flow keyword that is part of the "switch" expression. The case keyword is used to designate a single value (or "case") out of many in the entire switch expression. Also see the switch keyword.

continue A control flow keyword used to bypass the body of a loop and return to the loop's test condition.

const Reserved for future use.

default A control flow keyword that is part of the "switch" expression. See the case keyword above. The default keyword is used to designate the "default case" to execute if no other "case" is appropriate. Also see the switch keyword.

do A control flow keyword used in a loop expression. The do is specifically used when you want the loop executed once before the loop condition is tested.

double A basic data type used to declare double variables. A Java double is 64 bits and conforms to IEEE 754.

else A control flow keyword that is part of the "if" expression. See the if keyword. The else keyword designates a block of code to be executed when the if condition is evaluated as false.

float A basic data type used to declare float variables. A Java float is 32 bits and conforms to IEEE 754.

for A control flow keyword that is used in a loop expression. The for loop is the most common type of loop and is most often used when the exact number of iterations desired is either a constant or a simple expression. The for loop allows automatic initialization and incrementation of a counter variable.

if A control flow keyword used to perform create a branch or a decision point. The else keyword may be used as part of the if expression.

int A basic data type used to declare integer variables. A Java integer is a 32-bit signed value.

long A basic data type used to declare long integer variables. A Java long is a 64-bit signed value.

return A control flow expression used to pass program execution from a called function back to the calling function. The return keyword can also be used to return a value back to the calling function.

short A basic data type used to declare short integer variables. A Java short is a 16-bit signed value.

static Since Java is a pure object-oriented language, the static keyword has a restricted meaning in Java. The static keyword can be applied to either class data variables or class methods. In both cases, it means that those methods or variables apply to the entire class and are not instantiated with each object.

switch A control flow keyword used to implement a multi-way decision that tests whether an expression matches one of the following cases. See the case keyword. Each case is a constant integer value.

void A basic data type used to designate that a function (or method) returns no value.

while A control flow keyword used to implement a loop that continues "while" an expression is true. When the expression evaluates to false, the loop is terminated.

The above nineteen keywords, common to both Java and C, are also the ones most commonly used. These are the keywords that make up the bulk of your programs and the reason why Java retains the look and feel of C. Now let's move on to where the languages' keywords diverge and briefly examine why. Of course, most of the differences are purposeful omissions and object-oriented additions. The unique C keywords will be examined only to explain why they were omitted from Java.

Java Unique Type Keywords

byte A basic data type that represents a single byte as an 8-bit signed value.

boolean A basic data type that represents only two values: true or false. Both true and false are also keywords. The boolean data type only uses 1 bit of storage. The boolean type in Java eliminates the need for the common C and C++ practice of using #define to allow true and false to stand for 1 and 0 respectively.

Java Unique Statement Keywords

catch A control flow keyword that is part of the Java exception model. Exceptions are a mechanism for error-handling and when used properly can significantly increase an application's robustness. The model is based on the idea that error conditions can be recognized by both the application and the system and an appropriate exception is thrown. The application has the ability to handle such "exception conditions" by using the catch keyword and providing an error handler. The catch keyword is always followed by the exception to catch and a body of code that is the exception handler. The catch keyword and error handlers are often strung together in a series to handle multiple types of exception conditions.

finally A control flow keyword that is part of the Java exception model. The finally keyword ensures that a block of code is run whether or not an exception occurs. In fact, the finally code is executed even if there is a return in the try block.

throw A control flow keyword that is part of the Java exception model. The throw keyword is used to throw an exception.

throws This keyword was added in the beta version of the Java run time and did not exist in the alpha version. The throws keyword is added to the function prototype if that function (method) throws any exceptions. Just as strict type checking extended the function prototype, the throws keyword extends the function prototype to the Java exception model.

try A control flow keyword that is part of the Java exception model. The try keyword wraps or surrounds a block of code that we want to "try" and that may throw an exception. The throws keyword above lets us know what the function (method) will throw by examining its prototype.

Java Unique Modifier Keywords

abstract This is a type modifier keyword that is only used with classes and interfaces. It is used to mark a class or interface as a generic model with the sole purpose to be extended by a subclass. C programmers have no similar construct. This is another object-oriented technique.

final A method and type modifier keyword that is similar to the const keyword but much broader in scope. The final keyword can be applied to classes, methods, and variables. It marks a class as never having subclasses (never being extended), a method as never being overridden, or a variable as having a constant value.

native A method modifier keyword that signifies that the method is implemented in a platform-dependent language (like C) and not Java. This capability is important for several reasons:

1. Performance. You have the ability to code performance-sensitive areas of your Java application in platform-dependent code that is both compiled and optimized for your specific processor.

2. Reuse. The ability to reuse existing platform-dependent utilities. This is especially useful for the large volume of C and C++ utility programs available.

private An access modifier keyword for both types and methods. A key component of classes with the purpose of allowing class data to be protected. The private keyword limits access to a variable or method that follows it to only methods within the class.

public An access modifier keyword for both types and methods. The public keyword makes classes identical to structures (essentially, no protection on the data from methods external to the class).

protected An access modifier keyword for both types and methods. The protected keyword is similar to the private keyword except that it allows access to data and methods from subclasses. The package concept changes the meaning of this keyword. See section 5.1.

synchronized A method modifier keyword that insures use of a method (function) will be synchronized between multiple threads (if multiple threads exist). In essence, it means that this function can only be run by one thread at a time. The Java language has built-in support for threads. Threads are similar to processes. A process is a running program. The difference between a process and a thread is that each process is provided its own memory space and processor state (like registers and stack space) whereby threads share the memory and processor state of the spawning process. The benefit of threads is a measure of asynchronicity and simultaneous execution. A good example of the utility of threads would be a file server (or any server). A server is a program consisting of many procedures that are activated by client programs. There are usually many clients making requests of a single server. In a non-threaded server, the client requests are queued up and processed sequentially. In a threaded server, the server spawns a new thread for each request, which provides a quicker response time to most users. Second, the threaded server is always ready to perform a new action and is therefore never stuck in the middle of a low-priority job when a high-priority job comes along. Threading is also ideal for graphical user interfaces where you spawn threads for key functionality and therefore keep the application always responsive to the user.

threadsafe A type modifier that indicates that a variable will not be changed by some other thread while one thread is using it. This allows the compiler to perform some optimizations like the caching of instance variables in registers.

transient A type modifier used with persistent objects.

Java Unique Declaration Keywords

class A declaration keyword that declares a new user-defined type. Implements the central concept of object-oriented programming—encapsulation.

extends A declaration keyword that declares that a class is derived from a superclass and thereby "extends" the superclass.

implements A declaration keyword that declares that a class will implement the interface or interfaces that follow.

import A keyword that imports a package.

interface A declaration keyword that creates an abstract class that defines a high-level behavior via a set of methods that multiple classes can implement.

package A declaration keyword that creates a new namespace for all classes within the package. The package also permits the default access specifier to be friendly sharing of class data members among all classes within the package.

Java Unique Expression Keywords

byvalue Reserved for future use.

false A boolean value that represents "not true."

instanceof An operator that returns true if the class is an instance of a specified class type.

null A value that denotes "no instantiated object" or "no object."

super An uninstantiated object (equivalent to a pointer) to the parent class or superclass.

true A boolean value that represents true.

this An uninstantiated object (pointer) to the current object.

The JavaScript Language

JAVASCRIPT UNIQUE KEYWORDS

function	in	with	var

KEYWORDS INHERITED FROM JAVA

break	false	new	this
continue	for	null	while
else	if	return	

KEYWORDS RESERVED FOR FUTURE USE

abstract	default	goto	package	synchronized
boolean	do	implements	private	threadsafe
byte	double	import	protected	throw
byvalue	extends	instanceof	public	transient
case	false	int	short	true
catch	final	interface	static	try
char	finally	long	super	void
class	float	native	switch	
const				

APPENDIX C

The Java Class Hierarchy

C.1 JAVA APPLICATION PROGRAMMERS INTERFACE (API)

Shortly after I began programming with the alpha version of Java language, I quickly realized I needed a better way to find the API information for all the Java classes and methods available. So I wrote a quick and dirty program to zip through all the source directories and extract the API information. Source C.1 is that program. I have run this program for every new Java release since its inception and printed out the resulting file. It has served me well during the development of many non-trivial Java programs. I provide it for you here so that as the Java class hierarchy grows, you will still be able to print out a current copy of the API and have it instantly accessible. Of course, this program works well because of the good programming standards of the Java team. If they ever get sloppy, I'll be forced to write a parser (which I may do anyway).

SOURCE C.1

```
// printAPI.java
// NOTE: this does NOT do lexical analysis and only works correctly
//        due to knowledge of coding practices in the beta API.
import java.io.File;
import java.io.FileOutputStream;
import java.io.PrintStream;
```

```java
import java.io.DataInputStream;
import java.util.Stack;
import java.lang.Integer;
import java.io.FileInputStream;

class printAPI {
   public static void main(String args[])
   {
     try {
         String OSname = System.getProperty("os.name");
         System.out.println("Operating System is : " + OSname);

         // enter top-level path
         System.out.print("Enter top-level path: ");
         System.out.flush();

         DataInputStream dstream =
                 new DataInputStream(System.in);
         String topPath = dstream.readLine();

         File start = new File(topPath);

         if (!start.exists())
         {
                 System.out.println(topPath + " does not exist.");
                 System.exit(1);
         }

         if (!start.isDirectory())
         {
                 System.out.println(topPath + " is NOT a directory.");
                 System.exit(1);
         }

         System.out.print("Enter output file: ");
         System.out.flush();
         String ofilename = dstream.readLine();

         FileOutputStream outfile = new FileOutputStream(ofilename);
         PrintStream outPrint = new PrintStream(outfile);

         // read the directory, dump list into file
```

```
File curDir = new File(topPath);

int level=0;
String flist[] = curDir.list();
Stack fstack = new Stack();
int filesToDo = flist.length;
int fCnt=0;

String curPath = new String(topPath);

int curCnt=0;
int curMax = flist.length;

outPrint.println("");
outPrint.println("PATH: " + curPath);
while (filesToDo > 0)
{
        while (curCnt < curMax)
        {
                File curFile = new File(curPath, flist[curCnt]);
                System.out.println("Processing: " + flist[curCnt]);
                filesToDo--;
                if (curFile.isDirectory())
                {
                        level++;
                        System.out.println("***" + flist[curCnt]
                                + " is a directory.");
                        // Directory separator will differ for Unix,
                        if (OSname.startsWith("Win"))
                                curPath = new String(curPath + "\\" +
                                                        flist[curCnt]);
                        else if (OSname.equals("Solaris"))
                                        curPath = new String(curPath + "/" +
                                                        flist[curCnt]);

                        int m=0;
                        outPrint.println("");
                        for (m=0; m < level; m++)
                                outPrint.print("   ");
                        outPrint.println("PATH: " + flist[curCnt]);
                        File newDir = new File(curPath);
                        String dirfiles[];
```

```
                     dirfiles = newDir.list();

                     if (dirfiles.length > 0)
                     {
                             Integer theInt = new Integer(curCnt + 1);
                             fstack.push(theInt);
                             flist = dirfiles;
                             curCnt = 0;
                             curMax = flist.length;
                             filesToDo += flist.length;
                             continue; // go back up
                     }
                     else
                     {
                             // revert path
                             curPath = curPath.substring(0, curPath.
                                 lastIndexOf("\\"));
                             System.out.println("Current Path: " + curPath);
                     }
             }
             else
             {
                     // process the file.
                     int m=0;
                     outPrint.println("");
                     for (m=0; m < level + 1; m++)
                             outPrint.print("   ");
                     outPrint.println("FILE: " + flist[curCnt]);

                     // read entire file
                     // print out packages, classes and methods
                     FileInputStream fis =
                             new FileInputStream(curFile);
                     DataInputStream tis = new DataInputStream(fis);
                     while (tis.available() > 0)
                     {
                             String line = tis.readLine();

                             line.trim();

                             int classPos = line.indexOf("class");
                             int interfacePos = line.indexOf("interface");
```

```
                                int bracePos = line.indexOf('{');
                                int publicPos = line.indexOf("public");
                                int parenPos = line.indexOf('(');
                                int closeParenPos = line.indexOf(')');
                                int asteriskPos = line.indexOf('*');

                                if ( /* class and interface test */
                                    (((classPos >= 0) || (interfacePos >= 0)) &&
                                     (bracePos >= 0) && (asteriskPos == -1)) ||
                                    /* method test */
                                    ((publicPos >= 0) && (parenPos >=0) &&
                                     (closeParenPos >= 0) &&
                                         (asteriskPos == -1)) )


                                {
                                        for (m=0; m < level + 1; m++)
                                                outPrint.print("   ");
                                        outPrint.println(line);
                                }
                        }

                fCnt++;
        }

    curCnt++;
} // while curCnt < curMax

if (!fstack.empty())
{
        // pop the stack
        Integer anInt = (Integer) fstack.pop();
        curCnt = anInt.intValue();

        // change path
        curPath = curPath.substring(0, curPath.lastIndexOf("\\"));
        System.out.println("Current Path: " + curPath);

        // reload file list
        File aFile = new File(curPath);
        flist = aFile.list();
        curMax = flist.length;
        level--;
```

```
                }
        }

        // close the files
        outfile.close();
        System.out.println("Processed " + fCnt + " files.");
    } catch (Exception e)
    {
            e.printStackTrace();
            System.exit(1);
    }
  }
}
```

A run of Source C.1 is contained on the accompanying disk.

Index

CATCH THE
Technology Wave